Provocative Mothers

and Their

Precocious Daughters

*19th Century
Women's Rights Leaders*

Suzanne Gehring Schnittman

Suzanne Gehring Schnittman

Provocative Mothers and Their Precocious Daughters: 19th Century Women's Rights Leaders

Copyright © 2020 Suzanne Gehring Schnittman

1405 SW 6th Avenue • Ocala, Florida 34471 • Phone 352-622-1825 • Fax 352-622-1875
Website: www.atlantic-pub.com • Email: sales@atlantic-pub.com
SAN Number: 268-1250

Cover Photos:
Abby Kelley Foster ("From the Collection of Worcester Historical Museum, Worcester, Mass.")
Alla Foster ("From the Collection of Worcester Historical Museum, Worcester, Mass.")
Lucy Stone and Alice Stone Blackwell (Library of Congress)
Elizabeth Cady Stanton and Harriot Stanton (Library of Congress)
Martha Coffin Wright and Ellen Wright (Sophia Smith Collection, Smith College)

Library of Congress Cataloging-in-Publication Data

Names: Schnittman, Suzanne, author.
Title: Provocative mothers and their precocious daughters : 19th century women's rights leaders / by Suzanne Schnittman.
Description: Ocala, Florida : Atlantic Publishing Group, Inc., [2019] | Includes bibliographical references and index. | Summary: "The centrality of the mother-daughter relationship to women's reform movements is revealed through the collected journals, letters, and diaries of four women's rights pioneers and their respective daughters"— Provided by publisher.
Identifiers: LCCN 2019047641 (print) | LCCN 2019047642 (ebook) | ISBN 9781620236963 (paperback) | ISBN 9781620236970 (ebook)
Subjects: LCSH: Mothers and daughters—United States—History—19th century. | Women social reformers—United States—History—19th century.
Classification: LCC HQ755.85 .S3748 2019 (print) | LCC HQ755.85 (ebook) | DDC 306.874/3—dc23
LC record available at https://lccn.loc.gov/2019047641
LC ebook record available at https://lccn.loc.gov/2019047642

Printed in the United States

PROJECT MANAGER AND EDITOR: Katie Cline
INTERIOR LAYOUT AND JACKET DESIGN: Nicole Sturk and Aaron Schnittman

Table of Contents

Introduction 1

From Conflict to Resolution: Martha Coffin Wright and
Ellen Wright Garrison 11

Martha Coffin Wright: Mothering Ellen Wright with Advice, 1840–
1861 11

Ellen Wright Garrison: Maturing Through the Civil War, 1861–1865. 29

Ellen Wright Garrison: Marriage and Motherhood, 1864–1875 36

A Long-Distance Bond: Abby Kelley Foster and Alla Foster .51

Abby Kelley Foster: Mothering Alla Foster from the Road, 1847–1858 ...
51

Abby Kelley Foster: Mothering Alla Foster at Home, 1858-1868 63

Alla Foster: Finding Herself at Vassar, 1868-1872 70

Alla Foster: Teaching the Young How to Learn and Abby How to Live,
1873–1887 78

A Dependence Denied: Elizabeth Cady Stanton and
Harriot Stanton Blatch 93

Elizabeth Cady Stanton: Mothering Harriot Stanton with
Ambivalence, 1856–1874 93

Harriot Stanton: Becoming Her True Self at Vassar and in Europe,
1874–1883 104

Harriot Stanton Blatch: Finding Peace with Elizabeth and
Motherhood, 1883-1902 115

Partners for the Cause: Lucy Stone and Alice Stone Blackwell ......
133

Lucy Stone: Mothering Alice Stone Blackwell Joyfully, 1857–1870 ... 133

Alice Stone Blackwell: Experiencing Adolescence, 1870–1881 145

Alice Stone Blackwell: Writing Her Public Life, 1881–1893 156

Conclusion 171

Bibliography 179

Abbreviations 183

Endnotes 185

Index 205

Acknowledgments 211

Introduction

In the fall of 1883, Elizabeth Cady Stanton closed the top of her trunk, exhausted from packing. While they waited for the driver, she and her daughter, Harriot Stanton Blatch, tiptoed into the nursery, where "the blessed baby was sleeping, one little arm over her head." They "stood mute, without a tear, hand in hand, gazing into each other's eyes." When they finally separated, Elizabeth recalled, "My legs trembled so that I could scarcely walk to the carriage." It would be nearly three years before she would see her daughter and granddaughter again.[1]

Stories like this, which fill the lives of women's rights leaders, compelled me to write a book about mothers and daughters. Such accounts are new to us because most historians concentrate on women's roles as friends, sisters, wives, church members, charity workers, and activists. I chose to peer through a lens that focused on a group of women I call reform mothers and their reform daughters. Four pioneer women's rights leaders—Martha Coffin Wright, Abby Kelley Foster, Elizabeth Cady Stanton, and Lucy Stone—and four of their daughters—Ellen Wright Garrison, Alla Foster, Harriot Stanton Blatch, and Alice Stone Blackwell—comprise the subjects. These women's letters, diaries, and journals reveal the centrality of motherhood and daughterhood to reform movements. Mothers' and daughters' behavior over the decades and the generations give us the personal story of women's rights from the mid-1800s, when the first of these four reform daughters was born, until the early 1900s, when the last reform mother died. In 2020, the year that we celebrate the centennial of woman suffrage, this examination is most appropriate. A brief introduction to each player follows.[2]

∗ ∗ ∗

From Conflict to Resolution: Martha Coffin Wright and Ellen Wright Garrison

Martha Coffin Wright's impressive height, stark, gray Quaker dress, and brown hair that was severely parted down the middle and combed into a tight bun at the nape of her neck conveyed a stern demeanor to the casual observer. But her steely eyes revealed humor more often than disapproval, a tool she relied on to navigate the complexity of both her private and public life. Wife to David Wright and mother to seven children, Martha played a prominent role in the abolitionist and women's rights movements. I chose to highlight her interactions with her middle child, Ellen, because they had a complicated relationship of tumultuous beginnings and delayed reconciliations, experiencing many ups and downs along the way. Ellen, who married William Lloyd Garrison's son and played a small role in the women's rights movement herself, bore five children, including a daughter, Eleanor, who went on to fight for the vote in New York State.[3]

Martha kindled her zeal through extended visits at the Philadelphia home of her more-famous sister, Lucretia Mott. A devout Quaker who kept the Quaker Ways alive in Martha, Lucretia also introduced her to William Lloyd Garrison long before the other reform mothers had embraced his ideas. The sisters attended the first meeting of Garrison's American Anti-slavery Society in 1833, which led Martha to endorse radical Garrisonian abolitionism to her family, friends, and associates, advocating the immediate emancipation of enslaved people. She began to harbor runaway slaves and sponsored controversial speakers, winning the status of a "dangerous woman" in her community of Auburn, New York.

Martha combined her considerable domestic responsibilities with public actions and let her provocative opinions about slavery be well known through scathing letters to local newspapers and national magazines, such as *The Nation* and *The Auburn Advertiser*. The Seneca Falls Women's Rights Convention, of which she was an architect, awakened a passion in Martha against the injustices women had endured over the ages and further persuaded her to speak out for her sex as well as for enslaved people. She added a defense of women to her many published articles, arguing for their right to speak publicly, to own property, and to vote. After colleagues convinced Martha to serve as the secretary of the Third National Women's Rights Convention at Syracuse in 1852, she began to develop a network of other reform women and grew confident at the lectern, assuming the role as presider at conventions for two decades following.

Having earned the respect of women's rights leaders, Martha might have been the woman who shortened the schism that developed in the movement after 1869. No story about women's rights leaders in the mid-19th century can be told without an explanation of the rift that divided them for 20 years. The break between two factions, fully explored in these pages, personally affected all the players in this book—but so did the reconciliation that finally occurred in 1890, long after Martha's death in 1875 and 30 years before her dream of woman suffrage was realized.

A Long-Distance Bond: Abby Kelley Foster and Alla Foster

Abby Kelley Foster's pleasant facial features, simple Quaker garb, and attractive auburn hair tied loosely above a scarf at her neck belied her heated persona as a passionate, uncompromising reformer. The most enigmatic among our four reform mothers, Abby was inspired in her twenties by Sarah and Angelina Grimke, whose Charleston family owned enslaved people, but who moved north to pursue new lives. The sisters eventually embraced abolitionism and began preaching their new beliefs to outraged "promiscuous" audiences composed of both women and men. Abby followed in their wake, enduring taunts and brickbats. She married abolitionist Stephen Foster in 1845 after resisting his marriage proposals for four years, fearing marriage would interrupt her work. Abby gave birth to a daughter, Alla Foster, in 1847 but spent the next decade on the road pursuing radical abolitionism. Much of the time she yearned to be home with her only child. When Alla graduated from college, she devoted her single life to teaching, mentoring young people, and promoting woman suffrage in the mountains of New Hampshire, where she bought a home specifically for these purposes.[4]

Abby began her speaking career in 1836, a few years after Martha Wright became an active antislavery advocate but well before Lucy Stone or Elizabeth Cady Stanton entered the reform arena. Not only was she one of the earliest antislavery pioneers, but Abby was also a participant in organized abolitionist groups, which raised ire within the ranks of male reformers. When she was appointed a member of the American Antislavery Society's business committee in 1840, it drove many men away and triggered a division in the group that was felt internationally. When the World Antislavery Convention met in London in June 1840, it banned the participation of all women. A few American male abolitionists objected but failed to change the rules that positioned women in a separate gallery during the meeting.

Abby, like Martha Wright, followed William Lloyd Garrison, drawing inspiration from his radical beliefs for her speeches and her writings. She founded a network of regional newspapers, including the *National Antislavery Standard* in New York and the *Anti-Slavery Bugle* in Ohio. Besides guiding their content, she raised money to keep the papers afloat, pleaded for funds at antislavery meetings, and conducted tireless door-to-door campaigns.

Like other reform mothers, Abby determined how to fight her causes from a domestic venue when circumstances kept her out of the public eye. In the years leading up to the Civil War and throughout its hostilities, serious illnesses—both Abby's and Alla's—confined her to home, from where she exercised every opportunity to pursue her causes. After the war, Abby and Stephen continued their strident campaigns, championing full racial equality for African Americans, a battle that the American Antislavery Society was not ready to embrace. They joined Martha Wright, Lucy Stone, and Elizabeth Cady Stanton, among others, to form the American Equal Rights Association (AERA) in 1866, which broadened their work by advocating for universal suffrage. Illnesses in their old age made the parents look to Alla to care for them, effectively switching their roles.

A Dependence Both Denied: Elizabeth Cady Stanton and Harriot Stanton Blatch

Elizabeth Cady Stanton's vast intellectual contributions, spirited behavior as the mother of seven, and regal posture crowned with curly white hair and direct, challenging eyes helped to establish her timeless reputation as a pioneer of the women's rights movement. Her second daughter, Harriot Stanton Blatch, resembled her mother in temperament and calling, championed woman suffrage, and had an equally dedicated daughter, Nora Stanton Barney. Unlike her stalwart mother, Harriot had the advantage of a college education at Vassar; she enjoyed a satisfying life as a mother and activist in England, her adopted country for 20 years. Grandmother, mother, and granddaughter all committed their public lives to righting injustices and their private lives to family concerns.[5]

Elizabeth learned the complicated politics of abolitionism through the 1840 London antislavery meeting she attended on her honeymoon with delegate Henry Stanton, where she was relegated to obscured seating with other women. During the first eight years of their marriage, while Henry worked for Elizabeth's father, Judge Daniel Cady and then practiced law in Boston, Elizabeth gave birth to three sons. Throughout this time, she also took advantage of access to the Boston antislavery social scene, attending meetings more for the purpose of creating new social ties than to passionately pursue abolition, though she was by no means against the cause. The Stantons' move to Seneca Falls presented Elizabeth with a chance to pursue the calling closest to her heart: championing women. Her authorship of *The Declaration of Sentiments* and her leadership of the 1848 Seneca Falls Women's Rights Convention stamped her indelibly in history.

While she acted as an indulgent mother and the principal overseer of a sizable household, Elizabeth rarely attended conventions after the one she first organized, but used her pen to defend her causes, most initial of which were toward temperance and education reform. As her seven children matured, she joined forces with Susan B. Anthony, and the two led a campaign for women's rights from the Stantons' kitchen. The power awarded to Elizabeth through this undertaking propelled her to keep her name and cause alive through every available outlet. She occasionally left her toddlers at home to speak at the New York State legislature, but it was not until 1860 that she once more attended women's rights conventions. Bolstered by her success and newfound kinship, Elizabeth gradually amended her texts, written and spoken, with radical points of view on marriage and divorce, religion, and free love.

In 1869, Elizabeth Cady Stanton and Susan B. Anthony broke ranks with the proponents of universal suffrage in the AERA and formed a new organization called the National Woman Suffrage Association (NWSA). They attempted to launch a journal that presented their views, *The Revolution*, but it lasted for only a few years. However, this newspaper, plus many articles and books, act as a written legacy to Elizabeth's many causes. Three major publications further served her purpose: *The History of Woman Suffrage*, co-authored with Susan B. Anthony and Matilda Joslyn Gage; *Eighty Years and More*, her autobiography; and *The Woman's Bible*, her controversial take on scripture.

Elizabeth spent her last decade practically confined to home by blindness, excessive weight, and a failing heart. Her role of Stanton family matriarch, however, was not handicapped by her infirmities, ensuring that her daughters and granddaughters would memorialize her private and public life after her death in 1902.

Partners for the Cause: Lucy Stone and Alice Stone Blackwell

Lucy Stone's visage above a modest stiff white collar, short pageboy hair skimming her cheeks, and a mole just above the left corner of her lip presented a countenance that was softer than her aggressive personality. Shortly after graduating from Oberlin Collegiate Institute, she emulated Abby Kelley, becoming a pioneering lecturer brave enough to face jeers and projectiles of rocks and rotten fruit, similar to those her predecessor had been subjected to. Speaking to "promiscuous" audiences like Abby and the Grimke sisters, Lucy presented highly regarded talks that placed her among the most esteemed male speakers of her era. They also triggered tears from the mesmerized women who identified with her passion for female rights.[6]

Lucy learned early on how to use her domestic position advantageously. Though Henry Blackwell finally persuaded her to marry him after four years, she astutely retained her maiden name and kept control of the money she had earned from her lecture career and properties, which she sold at a profit. This enabled her to comfortably support the life of her daughter, Alice Stone Blackwell.

Beneficiary of her mother's wealth, Alice graduated from Boston University and devoted her single, independent life to editing the paper Lucy and Henry had founded in 1870. She ran the *Woman's Journal*, which owed its enduring success to Lucy's dedication and financial support, for years after her and Henry's deaths. Alice also became an officer of the united National American Woman Suffrage Association, was a skilled opponent to the "antis" (a group of men and women who were opposed to woman suffrage), and later championed various causes for international human rights, such as those for Armenians.

Lucy expertly maintained balance between her private and public worlds. Motherhood briefly suspended her active participation in women's rights and antislavery endeavors. She spent the Civil War caring for her young daughter, nursing her elderly parents, and running the farm she and Henry owned.

Lucy rose to fame through her lecturing, but she also demonstrated great aptitude for organizing active movements. She collaborated with other pioneers to form the First National Women's Rights Convention in Worcester, Massachusetts in 1850 and oversaw subsequent conventions throughout the next decade. In the late 1860s, Lucy returned from domestic duties to promote the AERA, campaigning alongside Henry in Kansas. However, disagreement over the Fifteenth Amendment, which granted the vote to black men but not women, drove the group apart. Six months after Elizabeth left to found the NWSA, Lucy and Henry organized the American Woman Suffrage Association (AWSA). Though she had been going strong, to say the least, by the late 1880s, Lucy was beginning to accept the limits of her failing health. Lucy's last public appearance was in Chicago at the 1893 World's Columbia Expedition, a few months before she died, urging Alice to carry on her work.

* * *

Reform mothers and daughters strongly affected each other within their domestic and public realms. Daughters remained in their mother's orbit for a long time, each becoming their mother's assistant and pupil, as well as her child. Theirs was often a relationship characterized by egalitarian friendship. Mothers and daughters each gained from the association. Mothers advised their daughters as fathers instructed sons, but the mothers received something in return—companionship and support. Throughout their lives, they shared joys, as well as anguish. Reform daughters participated in the family's life cycle, attending births, caring for young siblings, and nursing sick or dying relations, usually under the close guidance and tutelage of their inspiring mothers. They tied generations together, establishing positions that endured for their entire lives.

During my research into these fascinating women, I found that whatever the nature of the association—close or tumultuous—reform mothers' groundwork prepared their reform daughters for any areas they pursued as adults. Demonstrating how these mothers passed their wisdom and convictions on to their daughters in ways the daughters accepted, especially as women gained more rights, is the thesis of this book.

Family Trees

Martha Coffin Wright (1806-1875) m. David Wright (1806-1897)

- Marianna Pelham Mott (1825-1872)
- Eliza Wright Osborne (1830-1911)
- Matthew Tallman Wright (1832-1854)
- Ellen Wright Garrison (1840-1931) m. William Lloyd Garrison, Jr. (1838-1900)
  - Agnes, Charles, Frank, William Lloyd III, Eleanor
- William Pelham Wright (1842-1902)
- Frank Wright (1844-1903)
- Charles Edward Wright (1848-1849)

Abby Kelley Foster (1811-1887) m. Seven Symonds Foster (1809-1881)

- Paulina (Alla) Wright Foster (1847-1923)

Elizabeth Cady Stanton (1815–1902) m. Henry Brewster Stanton (1805–1887)

Daniel "Neil" Cady Stanton (1842–1891)
Henry "Kit" Brewster Stanton, Jr. (1844–1903)
Gerrit "Gat" Smith Stanton (1845–1929)
Theodore "Theo" Weld Stanton (1851–1925)
Margaret "Maggie" Livingston Stanton Lawrence (1852–1930)
Harriot "Hattie" Eaton Stanton Blatch (1856–1940) m. William Henry Blatch (1852–1915)

Nora, Helen

Robert "Bob" Livingston Stanton (1859–1920)

Lucy Stone (1818–1893) m. Henry Brown Blackwell (1827–1909)

Alice Stone Blackwell (1857–1950)

From Conflict to Resolution

Martha Coffin Wright and Ellen Wright Garrison

Martha Coffin Wright: Mothering Ellen Wright with Advice, 1840–1861

When Martha Wright felt the first twinges of labor with Ellen on the hot morning of August 19, 1840, she probably sent one of her other children down the street to her husband David's law office, asking him to fetch the midwife and come home. In 1840, middle-class women, rural and urban alike, gave birth in their own beds. Occasionally, they would call upon doctors, especially if problems were anticipated, but most often they relied on the expertise of midwives. With her mother, Anna, at her side and three successful births behind her, 34-year-old Martha had no reason to doubt that all would go well with this delivery. By nightfall, Ellen had arrived.

Martha later wrote to her sister and confidante, Lucretia Mott, that Ellen's three siblings, Marianna, 14, Eliza, 10, and Tallman, 8, saw themselves perfectly competent to care for a new baby sister. The girls, especially, treated healthy, rosy-faced Ellen as their "own special doll." They learned a few tricks from their mother, who was well known in her family for being skillful at calming upset infants. When Ellen fretted, Martha would undress her completely and hold her in her arms, alternately perching her on her knee and "cooing softly." Then "the creature would drop off to sleep almost immediately." Bedtime sessions were not always so successful. Martha's letters to Lucretia are replete with stories of having to walk Ellen to sleep or hold her all day. Martha depended on 10-year-old Eliza to leave school to help care for Ellen until she could find adequate help.[7]

Martha also expected her children to learn other housekeeping skills they'd need to know for later life. They knew how "to put the parlor in order," sweep their own bedrooms, and lay a fire and keep it going with the best wood available. The kitchen's huge fireplace, equipped with cranes and pot-hooks for cooking, invited the family to its side on Auburn, New York's frequent cold days. Martha taught her daughters how to appropriately hire and retain household help, a skill they would make use of in any future domestic situation. The Wright family relied on cooks to help prepare the meals and special foods with aromas Ellen could recall years later: molasses candy, Nantucket corn pudding, pan-broiled steaks, and cottage cheese, as well as Martha's famous gingerbread.[8]

Occasionally, the pressures of the household spoiled Martha's baking. After one unusually busy morning when Ellen was 15 months old, it was noon and Martha still had the dining room to sweep, her bedroom to straighten, and many more chores to complete before she could rest. She wrote to Lucretia, "I left the baby in Eliza's care and gathered the ingredients for gingerbread, rushing before 'the snipe' began to cry. Upon completion, I popped the cake in the oven and collapsed in a chair before I tended to the baby."

In an hour, Martha rose to tidy the kitchen, noting as she did so that the smell wafting from the oven was somewhat less-than aromatic. It was then that she saw the ginger, resting high on the shelf untouched for the delicacy that bore its name. Of course, for Martha, nothing but the perfect ginger-bread was acceptable, so she removed the spiceless bread from the oven and discarded it. "I went to work and made another batch, remembering the vital ingredient."[9] Though she was markedly tired, Martha's perseverance with the gingerbread recalled her personality accurately: good-naturedly determined, with high expectations from herself. What's more, she assumed the same from her family members.

As she grew older, Ellen did not always conform to her mother's guidelines. When she was at home alone with Martha, Ellen would sometimes sneak out the door—a habit Martha cured by tying the toddler to a tree with a long tether. She was a tomboy, the troublemaker in their teeming family, rejoicing when three more boys joined the family within eight years, making the entire crew sound like a herd of "boys who rhymed with noise." At such times, Martha wished there was not a child in the world under 20. But she always bounded back in good humor after an evening to herself, admitting to Lucretia, "Home is the place for people who have unruly children."[10]

It seemed that Ellen's tongue got her in trouble as often as her restlessness. When her older sister Marianna failed to give her molasses, Ellen, at 2 ½ called her "Fool." That same year, her cousin Sarah threw a soft ball too soon and hit Ellen, who said, "Yo [you] don't do that again, old lady." When she was 5, Ellen asked her mother, "Ma, you ain't a Quaker, are you?" Martha answered that she was and inquired about who had asked. Ellen's playmates had provoked the question.

When Ellen was old enough to understand, Martha would explain that, though raised Quaker, she only practiced "Quaker Ways" and rarely attended meeting. Martha taught her children that being a Christian meant acting in a manner that followed the example and teaching of Jesus and did not, in fact, depend on any "formality of worship" or declared beliefs in "barren theories." She subscribed to the statement from William Penn that Lucretia liked to quote: "Men are to be judged by their likeness to Christ, rather than their notions of Christ."[11]

Martha turned her attention away from the clamoring children from time to time, leaving them to their chores or play, to participate in community activities. She attended meetings and wrote letters to local and national publications, many of which led shocked readers of conservative Auburn to label her an infidel. Antislavery and women's rights issues claimed the highest priority of Martha's pen, but she also expressed an opposition to capital punishment and a support for temperance. Whenever Martha entertained an overnight guest who was less enthusiastic about women's rights than their hostess, she would leave her copy of Mary Wollstonecraft's *Rights of Women* "displayed on the table in place of the gilded fashionable [figurines], such as animals and the like."[12]

Martha insisted that "one's life is in the right" only if he or she openly opposed slavery. In January 1843, when 2 ½-year-old Ellen was too young to remember, the family hosted its first runaway slave. Martha housed him in their kitchen, locking him away from the rest of the household. Nevertheless, the slave stole Tallman's scarf, a crime that David and Martha tried to hide from their son so it did not "shock his philanthropy." After this incident, David allowed the family to keep harboring slaves, but told Martha, "You must no longer detail our illegal activities in family letters that are so widely circulated."[13] As Ellen matured, she understood more about what her family was willing to do for slaves.

When Martha was 39 and content with six children, she told Lucretia, "I have no prospects [read 'pregnancies'] but pleasant ones just at this present time." The spring of 1846 was the first time in six years that she did not have an infant or "worse," and she could only pity other people's "prospects." But pregnancy often catches a mother by surprise. Two years after Martha's confident declaration of freedom, at 41, she found herself again "with prospects."[14]

The same summer, Martha also found herself at a parlor in Waterloo, New York, where in July 1848, she and her sister Lucretia joined Elizabeth Cady Stanton, Mary Ann McClintock, and Mary Ellen Hunt in launching the world's first Woman's Rights Convention. Martha, expecting her seventh child and fully aware of the additional work a new baby would add to her busy days, accepted the invitation to plan a convention with keen awareness of the complaints the women shared. She well knew motherhood's demands, which came at a cross purpose with her independence. Longing to contribute to the cause, Martha had already written about women's rights and welcomed a formal venue to continue this effort.

Today, a bronze statue in the Seneca Falls Women's Rights Park depicts six-month pregnant Martha Wright standing proudly with Elizabeth Cady

Martha Coffin Wright, c. 1845
(Sophia Smith Collection, Smith College)

Stanton, Frederick Douglass, and five unidentified women. The Convention was the first of its kind along with its *Declaration of Sentiments*, which endorsed women's right to vote. Less frequently noted is the opportunity the Convention provided mothers, who inspired the gathering and attended in large number, often with their daughters. Accounts of the meeting note the surprising attendance, though the Convention was planned on short notice, of some 300 people from miles around. Women in Seneca Falls extended hospitality to anyone who wanted to come, welcoming friends and strangers alike. Martha Wright and Lucretia Mott "accepted with pleasure" Elizabeth Cady Stanton's invitation to stay at her house if she "should not be too much crowded with company."[15]

On the first morning of the Convention, July 19, 1848, families arrived with picnic baskets, leaving their horses to graze on church lawns. For two nights, people located lodging in town, slept at friends' homes, or camped out in their wagons. Attendees drifted in and out of the meeting, probably uncomfortable sitting on the hard pews, but nevertheless excited by the event and its importance. Custom dictated that pregnant women should not appear in a major public role, but decorum deterred Martha only slightly. She took a seat in the back of the Seneca Falls Wesleyan Chapel. The meeting changed her life.

Congeniality of women towards one another set the tone. They warmed to Elizabeth Cady Stanton's *Declaration*, which accused men of "making women, if married, in the eye of the law, civilly dead." For the women present, most of them wives, this was a sobering confirmation of their daily reality. The laws of marriage made them dependent on their husbands, giving them little social and civil liberty with limited access to divorce. The *Declaration* catalogued women's complaints but placed no blame on the economic system and the benefits that middle-class women gained from it.[16] Being mothers likely strengthened their resolve and unity, as they perhaps looked to their daughters, hopeful for a freer future for them.

A seventh baby was in Martha's future. In the fall of 1848, she gave birth to Charley. Though she was mildly worried before he arrived that she would be less than enthusiastic about an addition to her brood, Martha fell in love with him immediately. She warned Lucretia, "I advise you not to tire of this subject, for it is the only one destined for the next 500 pages, save an occasional digression to notice the receipt of your letters."[17]

Unfortunately though, Martha's newborn joy lasted just over a year. On November 1, she awoke to find a terribly sick child. At 13 months, an unexplained illness had struck Charley. An otherwise healthy, good-natured 1-year-old, he had given Martha no previous reason for alarm. Now she watched him steadily lose strength, worsening terribly in a matter of days. On the evening of the second day, Charley stopped breathing. Before the night was over, Martha's baby boy had passed. She was devastated. Inconsolable and furious with God, she told Lucretia that "life protracted is protracted woe."[18]

Though she was miserable, Martha had to maintain her role of spiritual authority and act as a model for her children, so she "made the best of everything." Her 19-year-old daughter, Eliza, found herself alone with Martha every day for months after Charley's death and was witness to her mother's mourning. She told Ellen that she never saw Martha "other than cheerful," a lesson for both daughters. However angry she was with God, Martha sought spiritual solace, even attending occasional Quaker meetings. Little by little, her serenity returned.[19]

Martha, who had been invigorated by the Seneca Falls Convention the year before, recalled how much it had fed her. She began to attend subsequent conventions, gaining the notice of sister reformers. They honored her with an invitation to serve as convener at the 1852 Third National Women's Rights Convention, held in Syracuse, New York. Here she had the great pleasure of meeting other pioneers she had previously only heard of: Susan B. Anthony, Lucy Stone, and Antoinette (Nettie) Brown. The *Syracuse Standard* praised the 46-year-old woman as "the gray-haired matron presiding over a convention with an ease, dignity and grace that might be envied by the most experienced legislator in the country."[20]

Martha was establishing a network of women whom she could call on for support in the reform concerns they shared. But when life brought profound sorrows, she had to look deep within herself for resiliency and was afflicted often by deaths that might have felled a weaker woman. In 1854, five years after baby Charley died, Martha and David again mourned for a child. In June 1851, their 19-year-old son, Tallman, had traveled to California to try to win his fortune in the Gold Rush. After three years, he had made only enough for his voyage home, but he lost that and was stranded until he could earn more money. Tallman wrote his family that he would try to come home the next spring to oversee the farm the Wrights owned outside of Auburn, but he never had that chance. In the fall of 1854, crushing news reached Martha and David. Tallman, working on a schooner sailing from San Francisco to Sacramento, had been knocked overboard into the bay by a swinging boom. The 22-year-old's body was never found. Storms had twice tossed Martha ashore when she was married to Peter Pelham, who died when she was 21, and when they took the life of another lover by drowning. Once again, water brought huge loss.[21]

The death of Tallman coincided with Martha's separation from Ellen and Willy, when they left to attend a boarding school 300 miles away in Raritan Bay, New Jersey. Ellen, 13, and Willy, 10, had left for Eagleswood, a school opened by Sarah and Angelina Grimke, along with her husband, Theodore Weld, as part of a radical Quaker settlement and utopian community. The curriculum combined physical activities, such as gymnastics, calisthenics, rowing, and swimming, with academics; all underpinned with lessons on moral reform, which included antislavery sentiments.[22] Eagleswood's strong emphasis on character development reinforced Martha's attempts to instill social mindfulness in her children. She expected Ellen to assume care of Willy and "act as his guardian angel." This inspired letters between Martha and Ellen that hold invaluable clues about their relationship and the direction it would take in the coming years.

From the beginning, Martha placed daunting expectations on her adolescent daughter. It was her job to unpack Willy's trunk and put his things in order, store his winter clothes, and purchase any forgotten items. She also had to persuade him to write notes home that satisfied Martha. Ellen defended her brother's efforts. "Don't you think Will writes nice letters?" she asked her mother, responding to Martha's endless criticism.[23]

Martha tasked Ellen with managing her personal property as well. When Ellen lost a ring during the long journey to school, Martha insisted that the less jewelry people wore while traveling the better. Her practical mother advised Ellen that when she packed her skirts and waists, she should fold them neatly together, emptying her dress pockets to avoid wrinkles. "Use every part of the trunk for storage," she advised, and bury breakable items among her skirts. When Ellen was in need of a "flat hat" for fall, Martha insisted that Ellen could wait a season and rely on her sunbonnet instead.[24]

Ellen maintained a humorous, casual attitude toward her clothing and delighted in teasing her mother as she ignored the advice. Three weeks after she arrived at Eagleswood, Ellen was so tired of her muslin dress that she "jumped off of high limbs of trees to dirty it and was successful so it is in the wash!" Martha was at least partly to blame for the sorry state of her daughter's wardrobe, which had items that had become too tight, too thin, or too old, but she admonished Ellen to be patient until the family seamstress or Martha herself could make new ones.[25]

Ellen showed less humor about the friendships she unsuccessfully tried to establish. Sensing her discontent, Martha admonished her to "pursue an unselfish course and resolve not to magnify trifles into importance" in order to be happy at school. When Ellen told her mother that the older girls excluded her from their trips into the city, Martha suggested that she "cultivate an amiable and pleasant disposition, which would soon attract them to you again." Meanwhile, Martha advised Ellen that she should seek out someone younger who might also desire a companion. Making such efforts "would fit you for the future, so that you will never have to look back with regret."[26]

Martha continually instructed Ellen to write proper letters, use clear penmanship, correct her spelling, and read only non-fiction, even though she herself enjoyed novels. Ellen finally relayed her exasperation. "You write such lectury letters always," she told her mother in early November 1854. Martha was miffed. "So you think my letters too lectury," she replied, proceeding to offer even more suggestions. She reminded 13-year-old Ellen to take advantage of the school in every way, especially by making new

Martha Coffin Wright and Ellen Wright, c. 1850
(Sophia Smith Collection, Smith College)

friends, studying hard, and welcoming relatives as visitors or prospective students, thereby strengthening the family network. Ellen was upset. "I thought you were not to write me any more lectury letters," she reminded her mother. Martha never mentioned the term again, but she continued to lecture.[27]

Ellen and Martha shared one passion—playing the piano—,which eased the discord they sometimes experienced. When her parents noticed her talent when she was younger, they purchased a piano for Ellen. Her Eagleswood piano teacher, Mr. Neustadt, helped her improve her skill. Martha sent her printed sheet music and ruled paper on which to copy songs that Ellen liked. Her performances progressed, as did her self-assurance. "Wasn't my playing much better at Christmas in Philadelphia?" she asked Martha. For once, they agreed. As her mastery of music grew, she advanced other skills as well and discovered independence. Martha encouraged her to "resolve to be dependent on no one for the means of enjoyment." Martha implored Ellen to find out, if she could, "what occupation your genius best suits you for, and qualify yourself for that, by earnest study and effort."[28]

Ellen's burgeoning enthusiasm for school, however, was often hampered by intense headaches, an affliction from which she would suffer for most of her life. In the spring of 1855, her headaches intensified to such a degree that they almost drove her to hysterics. Theodore Weld, head of Eagleswood, came to quiet Ellen one night when friends alerted him to her condition. He called a nurse to tend her, and the next morning she "didn't feel quite so crazy," but her head continued to ache, and a fever soon followed. Martha inexplicably blamed her daughter's headaches on homesickness, writing, "Your good sense will tell you, that unless you are really too ill to study it would be a [bad choice] to give up all your lessons and incur the expense of a journey home and back." Ellen would remain in school and take advantage of the "opportunity for improvement" that Eagleswood promised.[29]

Though her response to Ellen's illness seemed heartless, Martha was more worried about her daughter than she revealed. That summer of 1855, she sent Ellen to a sanitarium at Clifton Springs, New York, accompanied by her older sister Eliza, to address her headaches. The holistic treatment of the resident doctors probably included water cures along with rest. Water treatments included "head baths," cold showers, and cold water therapy, or cold rubbings. Ellen felt better after a few weeks of therapy. In the wake of her recovery, she begged Martha to let her attend the Women's Rights Convention at Saratoga, New York that summer. Martha disapproved of this journey, but when Ellen's doctor gave his permission, she joined her mother at the August meeting. That decision refueled the tension between them that had diminished only slightly.[30]

By the age of 15, Ellen had become an attractive, mature-looking young woman aware of the charm her long skirts had as they skimmed along the floor. She arrived at Saratoga with a variety of intentions. She, of course, hoped to meet a few pioneers of the Women's Rights Movement: Susan B. Anthony, Lucy Stone, and Antoinette Brown. But she also intended to see a man named Reverend Thomas Wentworth Higginson, whose sermons she had been reading. Hearing her daughter's plan, Martha worried that the older man might be an inappropriate influence on Ellen, and questioned her daughter's objectives. When Ellen went on to meet Higginson at the Saratoga Convention, she was immediately captivated. Though he was a married man, he described his wife as "an invalid," and Higginson invited the 15-year-old to accompany him on evening walks that she described as "romantic." Martha cautioned her daughter to "remember [that she] was no longer a little girl" and that any admiration she might express for a man many years her senior could be "misconstrued." Martha feared that Higginson "might not be equally worthy of the homage" Ellen displayed.[31]

The month after the Saratoga Convention, the Wrights withdrew Ellen from Eagleswood School because they could only afford to send one child and chose Willy. Ellen transferred to Sharon Female Academy in Darby, Pennsylvania to continue her studies. Martha anticipated her daughter's disappointment but saw this as an opportunity for Ellen to meet people who distracted her from Reverend Higginson.[32]

Contrary to her mother's expectations, Ellen accepted the change in schools positively and reflected her thoughts in a new journal. Remembering the influence of the Women's Rights Convention, as well as her advance in piano playing, she wrote, "I can't think what is to become of me with my woman's rights mama and my music mania." She did not believe she could "attend to both," but thought "'twd be useless to try to exist without music." Separation from her music teacher, Mr. Neustadt, saddened Ellen deeply, but she was consoled by new friends, many of whom she treasured all of her life.[33]

While at Sharon, Ellen's pursuit of music wavered slightly as she was met with opportunities, lectures, and exciting new ideas. With recent stellar talks from the Saratoga Convention fresh in her mind, Ellen began to think about entering the reform movement, mimicking her "woman's rights mama." But she was uncertain, writing in her journal, "I know so well what I must do, but so little how I must do it." She imagined having a talk with "lovely" Antoinette Brown but wondered if Nettie would listen to "such a child." Ellen might feel more at ease with Lucy Stone, who had put her arm around her at Saratoga, or with Susan B. Anthony, to whom she had begun to write. Whatever developed, Ellen had begun to feel "more grown in thought." She told Martha that the next chance she had to talk about women's rights, Ellen would "embrace it as a godsend although it pain me never so much to do it."[34]

Ellen perhaps thought she could acquire public speaking skills if she were at liberal, coeducational Eagleswood, which she missed, but it was Sharon Academy that helped her gain confidence. Early on in her second term, school officials invited 15-year-old Ellen to speak at a forum called "What is Woman's Proper Sphere?" She agreed, hoping to prove to herself and to her mother that she could succeed. When the principal introduced Ellen as the niece of Lucretia Mott, whom the students recognized because she lived in nearby Philadelphia, her pride swelled. She took advantage of her "illustrious relative's" reputation. When the students told Ellen that she resembled her aunt, as well as Lucy Stone, she leapt forward to imagine a career in lecturing. She wrote to a friend, "See if I'm not a speaker someday. See if I don't rouse the people. Yes, John, I'm a real thorough Reformer and so glad of it. Opposition is nothing." She performed less than spectacularly but found comfort in writing to Reverend Higginson in search of inspiration.[35] She determined to go to the next women's rights convention.

Besides giving her confidence, Sharon Academy taught Ellen how to build a sisterhood among the young women who might join her to make those rights a reality. With only housemothers nearby and no biological mothers in their vicinity, the girls learned from and relied on each other. Sharing living space and domestic duties trained them for future housekeeping; it also taught them how to assign and manage chores equitably. They kept their rooms swept and tidy, nursed one another through illnesses or accidents, and built "emotional unity."[36]

Such institutions as Sharon and Eagleswood, which inculcated morals, academic discipline, and domestic skills in their curriculum, exposed Ellen to young women and men from a reform background like her own. Befriending a group who called her "Elfie," Ellen encountered people who became role models, helped shape her character, and taught her how to integrate her reform interests with a new social set. Many were related to her Philadelphia kin, but others exposed her to a broader world. She confided to her journal that despite Sharon's shortcomings, social opportunities provided a "splendid time."[37] Besides grooming its students to form networks of friends and associations, Sharon emphasized mental discipline and helped prepare young women for the next, perhaps more rigorous, steps in their educations.

The money her parents saved by having Ellen attend Sharon Academy for nearly a year combined with Eagleswood's lowered tuition made it possible for her to return to the liberal school she loved in October 1856, where she remained until graduation. She demonstrated more independence than during her first years there. Martha again expected Ellen to oversee Willy, but Ellen told her, "Please don't tell me what I come to school for, for I am studying and getting along nicely."[38]

Ellen was no less fascinated with Women's Right Conventions and Reverend Higginson, even after she returned to Eagleswood. She asked Martha if she could attend another Convention in the fall of 1856, where she might meet Higginson, as well as the other women's rights leaders who she saw as her new friends. Martha discouraged her, citing school obligations and suggesting that she learn about the Convention by reading the published

Reports. But when her daughter begged her permission, Martha reluctantly granted it. Ellen could come to New York, if she was chaperoned by a teacher from school, but only for one day.[39]

Mr. Weld did give Ellen authorization to attend the convention in late November 1856, which only served to peak her interest in Reverend Higginson. A month later, Ellen bragged to Martha that he had written to her. "Didn't [Reverend Higginson] write soon?" Her mother reminded her that the reverend was too busy to "keep up a very vigorous correspondence." Martha, remembering that a few years earlier Ellen had announced she would avoid marriage for a life of "perpetual celibacy," worried that Ellen had changed her mind regarding this "wise resolution." Martha suggested Ellen wait 10 or more years to see "if [she] should chance to meet someone worthy enough for [her]." She also tried to steer Ellen away from future conventions, at least for the time being. Ellen turned her interest to Lucy Stone after she heard that her new heroine had refused to speak at the Philadelphia Hall that excluded blacks. "I wouldn't [speak] either," she wrote in her journal early in 1857. "It's perfectly outrageous the way people act, and makes me as disgusted with this noble America as 'tis proper to feel."[40]

During the last few months of school, she broadened her interests, acting in plays, performing in musicals, and resuming piano lessons with Mr. Neustadt. When Ellen graduated from Eagleswood in October 1857, she did not see it as an end to her formal education. She wanted to attend college, but her father disapproved of any child receiving a college education, and Martha acquiesced to his decision.[41]

That fall of 1857, at home in Auburn from boarding school for the first time in three and a half years, Ellen informally continued developing her mind. She studied Latin and arithmetic, practiced the piano, and attended lectures, while still finding time to socialize with friends. As Ellen observed her family's home life, she grew to recognize Martha's major role in the domestic setting. Here, her mother made most of the important decisions, wielding power that Ellen did not previously recognize. "Pa does consider you the head of the family, don't he?" Ellen asked her mother—but she already knew the answer.[42]

In the spring of 1858, Ellen rekindled her interest in lecturing and wanted to attend the New York City conventions. She admitted that she "had few ideas and no words to express them," but she longed to see Mr. Higginson at another convention. If her mother forbade it, Ellen asked Martha to "give my dear love to him" if he enquired.[43]

Ellen guessed correctly. Martha kept Ellen away from conventions and, in turn, Higginson, suggesting instead that her daughter connect with the women's rights cause through Susan B. Anthony and other women leaders. Ellen wrote her first letter to "Dearest Susan" in October 1858, but it was a few years before Susan answered. Once she did, the two began a regular correspondence that continued for several decades. Ellen expressed "every much of affection" for her new friend who inspired her to "think more than usual about [her] future." She imagined that Susan and others saw her as a potential public speaker, but, like her mother, Ellen Wright never felt equal to lecturing.[44]

But Ellen's confidence demonstrates something all the reform daughters shared. Their parents had paved the way for them to express once outrageous ideas—antislavery or women's rights. One historian finds that Ellen's teenage letters, "infused with a wit and irreverence much like her mother's," showed both "awe and familiarity with famous reformers." They provide a "wholly un-self-conscious, if breathless, portrait of growing up in a community where the ultraism of her parents' generation remained vital."[45]

Over the course of the following year, Ellen entered a period of uncertainty. While pondering a career in public speaking and the issues she might encounter, she had the opportunity to test her philosophy about relationships between the races. In December 1858, when she was 18, Ellen entered into a liaison with a black man, one that startled her in its rapid intensity and the feelings that accompanied it.

As she had done many previous years, Ellen spent Christmas with her sister, Marianna Mott. During her visit, she and a cousin, Anna, accepted an invitation to the Robert Purvis's family in nearby Byberry, which required travel first by foot and then by boat from Philadelphia. Bear in mind, Robert was black and Ellen white, a combination not well tolerated even in the City of Brotherly Love. When Anna cancelled, Ellen decided to go along on her own. Roberts Sr. and Jr. met her at the wharf and took her by carriage to their house. She told Martha that she felt "kinda horrid" to be alone with two black men, even those whose acquaintance she had met previously. During the visit, she enjoyed socializing with the rest of the Byberry community, including Charlotte Forten, tutor to the Purvis children, a "lovely mulatto" abolitionist writer who was three years older and more educated than Ellen.[46]

While in their company, Ellen accepted an invitation from young Robert Purvis, Jr. to accompany him on a horseback ride. She borrowed his sister's riding outfit, a "beautiful blue velvet cap the border and ears made of handsome fur," then mounted her friend's horse and joined Robert. In the best of circumstances, this activity would have been questionable for an 18-year-old woman, but they were also unaccompanied by a chaperone or any other riders, which only added to the scandalous nature of the evening. Ellen had socialized with gentlemen through boarding school and beyond and even entertained romantic notions with a few of them, but they had been only harmless flirtations. This was different.

During their ride, it began to snow heavily. Ellen had "hoped to meet with some sort of romantic scene such as being snowed up but it soon stopped." She began to flirt with Robert and allowed him to reach over her saddle to calm a horse that she could have controlled on her own. After 10 miles, with no true storm developing, the two arrived back at the Purvis home. Exhausted, she slid off the horse and into his arms "like so much lead." When he invited her to his home for supper after the ride, she readily agreed. While there, she noted how much fun Robert had with his younger siblings, observing that the smaller two boys were darker than the others and that the "youngest little girl was quite dark and not at all pretty." Meanwhile, she saw Robert, a very light color, as "growing more and more handsome." She loved "talking about everything" with him.[47]

Christmas came and passed, with Ellen's feelings increasing. She discovered that evenings at her sister's were "less jolly" than she had hoped because her mind was on Robert. The two continued their relationship by joining the junior antislavery association. On their many walks from meetings, they "were sorry to get home even after having protracted the way some half dozen squares." Ellen "joyfully anticipated" future strolls. She was amused by the nicknames they assigned to each other—she was "little Dorrit" and he was "child," even though he was seven years older. She became more and more comfortable with Robert in one sense, but less so in another. She wrote in her journal, "Robert has African blood which in this country is considered a disgrace (God help us!), but his features [are] entirely European." Ellen knew she could "never be his wife," but allowed that "Robert hasn't asked me to marry him!" Over the next several months, her zeal for Robert seemed to weaken, but the fact she had entertained it at all in such a time is a statement to her liberal ideas and growing independence.[48]

Ellen spent the next few months in Philadelphia trying to determine her future occupation. She contemplated becoming a governess or setting up a primary school, but she "was not in the least enthusiastic" about either plan. As she had in Auburn, she enjoyed a close group of friends who attended lectures, the theatre, and the opera together. But her heart was tied to the Junior Antislavery Society, which inspired her to learn more about the threat that slavery was presenting to her country. She fretted about the Union's dissolving, the consciences of congressmen, and other weighty questions about which she "knew nothing and therefore had nothing to say." She took an optimistic stance, promising her mother, "Well, there's a good deal of thinking to keep me busy." For the next two years, she divided her time between Philadelphia and Auburn before beginning another educational adventure ... and facing the Civil War.[49]

During that time, Ellen had the opportunity to ponder further her thoughts about interracial relationships and her conflicted feelings about Robert Purvis. In December 1859, a year after her flirtation with him, Robert showed interest in Ellen's then-engaged cousin, Anna Davis. Ellen offered herself as a "professional" in such circumstances. She told Anna "that there is the utmost of wretchedness in store for Bob! He is susceptible, and very sensitive. Of course no white person would want to fall in love with him— and of course he wouldn't marry any other than white as his father did."

Ellen could not let this alone, underlining her concerns a few days later. Robert Purvis' attentions to Anna must be "very disagreeable," "unendurable," and "unwelcome" from a "handsome fellow of African tint!" Then Ellen mentioned the unfathomable, belying her own private disdain and hinting that she almost experienced a similar catastrophe: "Think of having an octagon baby—Horrors! I have been thro' the wars and have scars and experience."[50]

Ellen Wright Garrison: Maturing Through the Civil War, 1861–1865

Universally troubled by the possibility of civil war, reform mothers made a dramatic effort to advocate for antislavery in the months before conflict erupted. In January 1861, with their families at home worrying about them, these mothers launched an abolitionist tour across New York State, titled "No Compromise with Slaveholders." They began in Buffalo and closed in Albany one month later. Martha joined Susan B. Anthony, who presided at each event, Elizabeth Cady Stanton, and other antislavery speakers on a perilous mission. Embarking in the coldest days of winter, the women told Northerners to not only oppose slavery, but to also give escaped slaves their freedom. If war were waged, emancipation should be the reason.

The women used the occasion to strengthen their bond of sisterhood. Susan, wiry hair clasped in a firm bun above her stony face, wire-rimmed glasses perched on her nose, stood unwavering at each appearance, even in the face of irate audiences. Elizabeth, white curls brushing her forehead, neither cowered in fear nor retired in resignation but "kept scratching [out] free speech articles," which she published along the speaking route. However, she departed for home one-third of the way into the campaign, after the Port Byron talks, where mobs pitched cayenne pepper on the central pot-bellied stove that heated the hall. This was not the only disruption along their circuit, though. In Utica, protesters locked the hall and barred the abolitionists' entry, although Susan had paid $60 in advance for its use. In Syracuse, rioters threw rotten eggs, broke benches, and brandished knives and pistols. In Rome, Abby and Stephen Foster joined Susan on

Ellen Wright Garrison, 1864
(Sophia Smith Collection, Smith College)

the stage and praised Susan for appreciating so entirely the "genius of our enterprise."[51]

Next the speakers lectured in Auburn, Martha's hometown. The afternoon session went forward with no problems, but by evening, sounds of upheaval erupted. Rowdies took over and conducted their own meeting. Martha, taking authority from her height and seniority, invited abolitionists to reconvene at the Wright home, where the leaders spent the night, "gathering strength for their next confrontation." Though acting as a resolute proponent, Martha told Ellen that, when exercising her right to speak as a woman, she felt threatened by a physical danger she had rarely known. Nevertheless, she continued on to Albany with the entourage and served as the meeting's chair. There the mob was kept under control by the police, and the mayor sat on the stage with a loaded gun while Martha and the others spoke. Ellen, now 20 years old and wishing she could have witnessed her mother's daring display of fortitude, wrote in her journal: "I am a Reformer (there are none others?) and expect to be odious to many, but dammit!"[52]

Ellen chose a very different way from Martha's to occupy herself while she waited for what seemed to be an inevitable war—she enrolled at Miss Catherine Sedgwick's Music School in Lenox, Massachusetts. Having found her own solace and relief in music, she had encouraged her mother to return to an art that would take her mind off war: creative painting. But, consumed by politics, Martha selected an alternate route.

The Civil War and the years surrounding it more greatly affected Ellen Wright's life than it did for the other young women in this study. Ellen experienced the war as an adult, attending antislavery and women's rights meetings with her mother, while the other daughters were far younger and experienced war as small children or only through their parents' reports.

Perhaps wishing she were at home for such meetings as Martha described, Ellen found that her piano study did not distract her from the reality of war. After the April 17, 1861 firing on Fort Sumter launched hostilities, she traveled to Philadelphia for a school break. From there, she wrote to her brother Willy that she heard troops training in the streets. Her message reveals her ambivalence: "The martial sound of drums inspires me, the war-like tramp of many feet fills me with a desire to write and tell you about it…Everybody here is enlisting for the war and it seems very sad." She admitted that it "would be pretty severe to settle down again to studying in the midst of all this excitement, but Lenox will be so beautiful in the summer weather that perhaps we [she and the other piano students] can make it go down [sic]."[53] She was unable to rationalize the study of music during such a time, however, so she went home six months after she had begun.

Upon her arrival, Ellen found her mother facing the effects of war in the most personal way. Willy, Ellen's little brother for whom she had cared at Eagleswood, had been commissioned at the age of 18 as a second lieu-tenant and mustered into service with the Army of the Potomac. "He goes [to battle] dutifully, but I shall be full of anxiety," Martha wrote Lucretia. With heavy heart, she admitted to husband David that she was willing to sacrifice their son, but the daily cost of knowing he was in battle made it difficult to interest herself in anything else.[54]

Like Martha, Ellen also found it challenging to think about anything be-sides Willy. She confided to Mr. Higginson, who had enlisted for the Union long before war was declared, that with Willy in battle, watching the fight-ing was getting more "vital" every day, just as Higginson had thought it would once she had a brother in uniform. She confessed, "It is hard for us women to feel that however necessary we are as implements of domestic utility, we are absolutely of no account upon the battle ground, for some of us feel as much burning ardor and enthusiasm as the wildest of the men."[55]

During this time, Ellen grew closer to Martha, comforted her as they shared their worries about Willy, and helped her mother to roll bandages, sew uniforms, knit socks, and write letters to soldiers. Some women "saved souls" by teaching freed slave children in Union-occupied territories, but Ellen did not feel this calling. "You don't think the nation is going to rack and ruin, do you?" she asked Susan B. Anthony. "People hereaway have been doleful to the last degree; and our friends in Philadelphia half expect to be scalped in their beds." Ellen, finally, found herself able to practice the piano and considered presenting concerts but admitted: "I can't have any musicals or anything else, while the war is on."[56]

Ellen's male friends began to die in battle, leaving her devastated. She commiserated with her dearest friend and former classmate from Eagleswood School, Lucy McKim, after they lost a mutual male friend. "Oh, Luce," she wrote, "we never thought of this, did we?" It was like a "pang" when she heard it the first time, but "now comes the sadder part of the growing accustomed to it." When Lucy regretted that they were doing nothing, Ellen suggested that they "exult" that they had been able to endure the tragedy of war, even though "it tears our hearts." They had to believe that "the end will be justice, and that each battle may be the last." They had to live on, from one day to the next, and "accept what is given." Did Lucy "call that doing nothing?" Ellen wondered if it would be different if they were men. "Do you chafe at not being a man?" she asked Lucy. "It is the last thing I should sigh for. Since I was sixteen I've been contented with my lot, as far as sex is concerned."[57]

As the war continued, Ellen developed a relationship with William (Will) Lloyd Garrison, Jr., the son of her mother's hero and friend, the radical abolitionist William Lloyd Garrison, Sr. The two shared values that Ellen had long embraced but had never found in a man she could also love. As they deepened their discussion about the war, one issue posed a small worry for Ellen. Since Will's youth, he and his brother Wendell had followed their father's example in declaring themselves non-resisters who refused to fight.[58]

With her brother Willy now at war, Ellen rejected pacifism, but she listened to Will and Wendell, who paid the $300 fine for not fighting and argued their case for non-resistance so effectively, and she made an exception for them. In fact, she told Willy that she would find it "unnatural for a Garrison to wield a sword." Martha agreed. Since the Garrison boys had been raised to uphold the strictest principles of non-resistance, working at their father's antislavery paper, the *Liberator*, was perhaps as effective as anything they could do in the Army. "Where would the nation have been but for Mr. Garrison's persistent antislavery teaching for thirty years?" Martha asked.[59]

In July 1863, the tragedy of war struck the Wright family. At the Battle of Gettysburg that month, Willy had been among its nearly 8,000 casualties, wounded but not dead, on the third and final day. Ellen told Lucy, "I find it impossible to realize a sense of the dreadful danger [Willy] has passed through." When she looked back to a few weeks earlier, she wrote, "I think what we suffered for him, it all seems a miserable dream. Are we who are alive, spared for some purpose, and why should we pray—'From sudden death, Good Lord deliver us?'"[60]

Ellen and Will looked to each other for comfort and for a future in the face of such horror. Their courtship brought joy to the war-weary Wrights and Garrisons, reconnected two abolitionist families whose leaders had met 30 years before, and transformed a relationship based on reform to one cemented in family. When Will proposed to Ellen on Valentine's Day 1864, all the parents were delighted. Martha welcomed the union, "not only on account of [Will's] own moral worth, but because he is the son of one whom we have so long regarded with reverence." Will assured his future in-laws that he could support 24-year-old Ellen. At 26 years old himself, he was comfortably employed as a clerk for Richard Halloway's Wool Firm at a salary of $1,200 per year (the equivalent of $24,000 in 2019). He promised, "I shall try never [sic] so hard to be a good son to and make Ellie the happiest little wife possible."[61]

Ellen was delighted with Will and the prospects of marriage but worried that her persistent headaches would spoil her plans. Through her adolescence and early 20s, she had tried many treatments—a water cure and sitz baths, in which one sits up to soak the perineal area; refraining from eating certain foods, jumping, or performing gymnastics; and attending two stints at a sanatorium. Ellen was seeking treatment in an era when formalized medicine delivered by trained doctors was competing with homeopaths who preferred "natural remedies." Homeopathy opposed harming the patient by any invasive procedure, like cutting or bleeding; it advocated using "less rather than more," greatly diluting whatever medicine was suggested. Perhaps because Martha had "dreaded a wavering from homeopathy," Ellen declined pills proffered by a Dr. Hall who visited the Wrights often in the summer of 1862. Will Garrison initially made light of her pain. "I hear that those horrid headaches still assail you," he wrote in July 1863. "Why don't you come and let our Boston magician recreate you with his rings and sticks and beanbags?" Ellen knew that he was joking, so she tried to submerge her headaches and focus on her courtship.[62]

Turning to a last resort, in the spring of 1864, Ellen agreed to enroll in a month-long treatment in New York City, where she rested, ignored the war, and tried to concentrate on her happy future. While there, she had time to face an additional challenge marriage would bring, the painful separation from her dear friend, Lucy McKim, to whom she had divulged her deepest secrets and fears. During her treatment, Ellen found it difficult not to "shake New York dust off my shoes" and "dash to Philadelphia" to see Lucy "for one huge night." But it seemed best to wait until she was released. "We will sleep together again," Ellen vowed. "Of all the feminine kingdoms, I love you best and should dread most to give you up."[63]

Intimacy like that shared by Ellen and Lucy was common among 19th century women, who shared beds and outward affection as naturally as they shared walks in a park. Will knew how attached his fiancée was to her friend and hoped that eventually she "would feel as happy and easy with me as you are with Lucy." Ellen had assured him that she would, but promised Lucy, "Your whole soul and body are mine until after September 14th [the wedding date]." She then reminded her, "Don't say that I must be divorced from you in order to marry William." A month before the wedding, Ellen was ecstatic to hear splendid news, which eased her dread of losing Lucy. Wendell Garrison, Will's brother, had proposed to Lucy, making the two friends future sisters-in-law and clinching their bond. "I cannot sleep o' nights, for thinking so and planning and laughing to myself," Ellen wrote Lucy. "I will embrace you and kiss your little ring for you and say how you make me more than happy," she mooned.[64]

Ellen returned to Auburn somewhat relieved from her headaches and determined to concentrate on her relationship with Will. After he spent two weeks at the Wright home, she missed him when he left. She told Lucy, "I found much to admire in him that I had never known before." Not only was Will gentle, he "suffered to do what is right." Central to Ellen's love for

Will was his belief in his father's causes of antislavery and women's rights, which meshed with priorities that Martha had instilled in her throughout her life.[65]

Ellen was a pretty bride, shorter than her tall mother, with her light hair swept up in the style of the day and her dress the epitome of modesty, perhaps in deference to the war. Her black unwavering eyes demonstrated a determination to make this work. Ellen's generous wedding greeted far more guests than that of Martha to Peter Pelham or David Wright, or of the other reform mothers or daughters. Because both families were large and had many friends and acquaintances to invite, the number of guests soon grew to 125. Martha told Lucretia that "the Lord and Matthews are to provide sending dishes and waiters and loaves and fishes" for the crowd gathered for the ceremony at her home, but "it will all get through somehow." There were too many for Martha to make a wedding cake, but she knew "the world would not come to an end for want of it." Reverend Samuel J. May, who had married Will's parents 30 years earlier and whom was friends with many abolitionists, performed the ceremony. Susan B. Anthony served as one of the witnesses. "How can I say but yes I don't see," she had told Ellen when she asked, "so expect me as per your orders." A joyous celebration, Ellen and Will made their wedding day, September 14, 1864, a welcomed break from the war.[66]

Ellen Wright Garrison: Marriage and Motherhood, 1864–1875

For the first few years of their marriage, before their children were born, Ellen and Will settled in the home of the senior Garrisons in Roxbury, outside of Boston, near to Will's wool business. The couple had planned to live in a modest cottage, which Ellen insisted she would love, remarking earlier, "Give me a humble cottage, a dinner of herbs where love is!" Now she had to adapt to a different situation, to which she adjusted resignedly. "I shall be quite busy for several days arranging my things," she revealed to Martha, "I shall have no time to remember that Ellen Wright is no more." She told Lucy she doubted "we would ever get a closet of our own," but admitted that "that's neither here nor there." Despite the change in housing plans, Ellen told her parents that she was "wildly happy."[67]

The Garrison family soon recognized Ellen's domestic management skills, well-honed by Martha, and asked her to take charge of the house in lieu of Helen Garrison, who had suffered a debilitating stroke the previous year and welcomed her help. "I had scarcely been into the kitchen and was much too ignorant to be married," Ellen later told Lucy, but she accepted the challenge. Martha had spent her early domestic days occupied with home production and keeping flames alive in her fires. Ellen could shop for candles, soap, and clothing and enjoyed the Garrisons' central heating, which made fireplaces obsolete. With Will working away from the house all day, she resembled other middle-class wives whose influence in the family reached an all-time high.[68]

In homes like the Garrisons', husbands left their wives in firm control of all things domestic, including the household servants. Ellen became an expert at hiring and supervising help, a daunting chore for the Garrison women. Their girl Winnie left them "in a pet," and Will's sister Fanny could not get a substitute. Ellen solved the problem, hiring a tall, pale new girl called Mary, who was "as active in her movements as a cat" but resembled "a corpse who has escaped from some neighboring cemetery and forgotten to take off her shroud."[69]

A woman's place was supposedly at home, but Ellen found a world larger than those four walls. Martha had exposed her daughter to a variety of intellectuals and reformers as a young woman, both in their home and at public gatherings. She had attended talks by radical thinkers, gone to women's rights conventions, debated publicly at boarding school, and served as an officer of the Junior Antislavery Society in Philadelphia. Now, as a young wife living near Boston, still unencumbered by children, Ellen had access to streetcars and trains that could take her even further into the world. She used her freedom to join clubs, which acted not only as "agents of personal growth and transformation," but a way for her to acquire culture and meet friends.[70]

Ellen married for compatibility as much as for love. Her background in reform and interest in intellectual ideas reinforced her desire for "real intimacy and companionship" in a husband, rather than solely looking for the potential of economic security. Will had entered wool merchandising as a young man and remained in this occupation throughout his life, although it never led to more than an adequate income for the household. Ellen filled a domestic role that preserved her independence and "strong sense of self," just as Martha had taught her was important. She reiterated Martha's advice to her brother Willy when he married, using a quote from Lucretia Mott: "We can only pray that you may both be happy—'your dependence mutual, your independence equal, your duties reciprocal.'"[71]

"The more intimately I know my dear boy," she told Lucy McKim, "the more cordially I can say amen, to the vows we have taken." Ellen urged her not to wait too long before marrying Wendell Garrison, not that there was "any danger in waiting, that the salt will lose its savor," but Lucy might as well be happy as soon as possible. Ellen, living in harmony with a man she loved, wondered, "What good angel has spread her shining wings over me to guard me from the destruction my waywardness has richly merited?" Two months later, she did not waver in her sentiment. "Marriage is happiness," she wrote Lucy. "Try it."[72]

Will similarly recognized his good fortune in marrying Ellen. "Ellie is a delight to the household," he told Martha a week after their wedding. And the next month, he wrote: "My little wife passed the order of introduction and of being scanned so winningly that I'm sure her husband must be envied." Even when Ellen suffered headaches, Will claimed that she was able to maintain their daily household routine. In short, "sick or well, she's the dearest little wife one could wish. Bless her." After four months of marriage, his feelings hadn't wavered. "How the dear girl appears so well after her exhausting tortures is wonderful," he told Martha, "yet I think she never looked better than she has today."[73] Her ability to rebound after a headache, Will noticed, was impressive. One evening, after an attack had subsided, Ellen sat under the great lamp knitting a shirt for a friend's baby, showing Will that "marriage had not abated one jot of habit and this seems her normal condition when well."[74]

Will also loved Ellen's wit, which was quite reminiscent of her mother's. He recalled their joint amusement when he read from the essayist Charles Lamb. "Isn't it nice to have an auditor who knows where the laugh comes in?" he asked Martha. Then "you don't have to stop and say, 'There's a joke, do you see?'" Will perceived Ellen as so clever that he imagined that some of her letters could be printed alongside those of Charles Lamb.

Her good nature and desire for normality overflowed into an improved understanding with Martha. Though it had once been riddled with conflict, their relationship improved during the war. The long miles between Roxbury and Auburn stretched between them, sharpening their separation. Will recognized the loneliness felt by the mother and daughter, as well as the resilience they demonstrated in the face of the situation. He made sure they enjoyed regular visits in both homes. He accompanied his wife to Auburn when he could, if only for a few days. However, most of Will's time was occupied by the store, traveling to supply customers, and tending to his own parents' needs.[75]

The growing strength of Ellen and Martha's relationship affected all four parents and their children. Near-daily letters passed amongst the group. William Lloyd Garrison, Sr. wrote Ellen, "I rejoice that you are my daughter-in-law and that William is so happily mated." Helen Garrison frequently consulted Ellen about the doctors each relied on. And, of course, Will confided in Martha from the start, writing her letters that revealed his politics, his love for Ellen, and his business failures and successes, signing each letter, "Your loving son." Her father, David Wright, even felt confident in lending the couple money.[76]

Wherever they lived, Ellen and Will built an independent life filled with cultural and reform interests. They favored the opera and never missed a lecture if it addressed issues of their concern. Antislavery meetings found the young couple in the first row, supportive of the plight of the formerly enslaved people whom their parents had secreted in family attics during the years of the Underground Railroad. A neighbor and dear friend of Martha's, Harriet Tubman, supplied them with copies of her book to sell when they visited the Freedmen's rooms and Ladies' club. Ellen and Will chose to improve their minds in the evenings, a "blessed time," when they could enjoy "solid rest and cheerful recreation." They were so occupied with lectures, reading, and German instruction "that [hours] vanished like a dream." Will now belonged to a French club, which took him out on evenings, and gave Ellen a chance to "improve my time much more to my satisfaction."[77]

Ellen and Will had hoped—and had even heard doctors suggest—that marriage might improve her migraines. It did not take long, however, for the doctors to be proven wrong. Two weeks after their wedding, "Ellen had a symptom of headache" that Will thought would pass, but it drove her to bed for eight days. The following week, "a raging headache seized upon Ellie" and sent them home early from the opera.[78]

Before marriage, neither could have guessed how heavy the burden of Ellen's headaches would prove to be. From the beginning, however, Will's solicitousness made Ellen believe that the headaches were a shared challenge instead of one she'd have to face alone. He diligently tracked his wife's headaches, looking for any potential cause or explanation. When marriage itself did not seem to improve her health, he hoped instead that once they attained "the right living," the headaches "need never come." Through their hopes, Will and Ellen also sought other remedies, not unlike many Ellen had already tried, to control the headaches: diet, exercise, and loose clothing. Will also encouraged Ellen to take long morning walks with him, refrain from writing letters, and limit her exposure to extreme cold. He told Martha that, although "Ellen didn't promise obedience to her husband in the wedding night," he was pleased that she makes choices gracefully and "stops short when danger threatens" her health.[79]

Ideas to cure her headaches abounded, but none worked for long, and ultimately, Ellen was driven to seek the aid of drugs. This understandably frustrated her, as she had so long sought to rely only on homeopathic remedies. After another headache cancelled their morning stroll and sent Ellen to bed for three days and nights, they visited Will's doctor. The powders he gave her were less of a cure than a new, somewhat effectual treatment.

Ellen's headaches never disappeared; in fact, they persisted for most of her life. Indeed, except in rare cases, they occurred just as frequently. However, a drug that likely resembled today's analgesics and was probably slightly addictive helped to quickly ease the headaches. Will told Martha not to be "disheartened about Ellie's getting well" because they were hopeful she would. Though she suffered serious setbacks (she entirely missed her first Christmas with Will due to a headache), she was now willing to give Dr. Wesselhoept's daily powders "the 'due' that is theirs."[80]

The couple determinedly maintained that Ellen's headaches would not dominate their life together. Ellen had seen her mother bear a different kind of pain—the loss of multiple children—with aplomb by keeping busy and distracting herself. She also looked to the sufferings of Will's parents. Helen endured the effects of a stroke with dignity and William, Sr. patiently tolerated the agony of battered knees. When they learned about Ellen's "prospects," they welcomed the happiness a new baby would bring. In December 1865, she revealed her good news to Lucy McKim. "Do you believe that I expect a summer gift, such as is coming to me with the new leaves and blossoming trees?" she wrote.[81]

In the spring of 1866, Ellen and Will welcomed a baby girl, Agnes, and two years later, a boy, Charley. Soon circumstances made it possible for the couple to finally purchase their own house, after having lived at the Garrisons' for nearly five years. With a loan from Ellen's father for the down payment and with the assurance that Will's modest but regular salary from the wool business could manage the mortgage, their dream became a reality. Martha was no doubt proud that they put the deed in Ellen's name, since it had finally become legal for married women in Massachusetts to possess property in their own right. In addition to its proximity to Boston, the house in Roxbury was close enough to her in-laws to signal them by "waving a flag," as Will noted.[82]

Ellen found a great satisfaction in being a mother, owner, and mistress of their new "pleasantly settled" home. She told a friend, "You can't put on girlish airs when you have charge of two babies and two maids and a husband and a house." Every window afforded a different sight—of the town, of the countryside, of the hills, or of the sea. Second-story views made it possible for them to see the tides come and go and for Ellen to sit at her sewing and count sails in the harbor. It "was like being in the country for fine air and birds and trees!" In short, "life is not a burden, except when both children get tired and exacting at the same time."[83]

Ellen welcomed her role of mother with the courage and joy Martha had inspired. Close at hand for the first birth, her mother stood ready to assist the midwife physician who would become the Garrison family's doctor for all of their births. Ellen had feared the "horrors" of labor, but was reassured when her baby arrived, "precisely according to calculations." When Agnes was born on June 3, 1866, Ellen found herself "alive to the joy of seeing two tiny red fists striking about in the air, and hearing a funny little wail, which was like sweet music."[84]

When Ellen placed Agnes in the arms of William Lloyd Garrison, Sr., who had been depressed by his poor physical condition, discord within the anti-slavery community, and faltering finances, he forgot it all. Helen Garrison, as frail as an invalid, also delighted in her first grandchild. Frank Garrison told his sister Fannie, "I have never seen Father and Mother look so grati-fied as they did when they gazed upon their first grandchild, and said how it looked as all of us did at that tender age…and how it seemed like living their life over again."[85]

Ellen diplomatically divided Agnes' time between the two sets of grand-parents. The Garrisons sorely missed Agnes when, within a few weeks of the birth, Martha took Ellen and the baby to Auburn for one of their most congenial times, reaping the warmth of the summer and rejoicing in the birth of a daughter. One biographer suggests, "Now a mother herself, [El-len] seemed more tolerant of Martha's didactic manner." Martha offered Ellen her customary instructions and sent the new mother back home with reams of advice about feeding, preparing a warm bed, and eating a diet that produced healthy breast milk.[86]

In September, Ellen returned to her in-laws' home in Roxbury, bringing her sister Eliza to help shore up her mothering confidence for a few weeks.

Agnes fought sleep "like a roused Garrison struggling against a moral enormity," but clung to her adoring Grandfather Garrison for special bedtime comfort. Ellen loved counting Agnes's "little yellow hairs, which may curl, by devoted attention." The baby's blue eyes and head "look like her dear papa [David Wright]," while her "real cunning little mouth and chin" perhaps came from her Grandma Helen Garrison. When Agnes was 11 months old, 61-year-old Grandpa Garrison "felt well enough to march around with the little one perched on his shoulder and declare that he felt thirty years younger."[87]

Ellen and Will welcomed Martha's lessons about the "good habits which you taught us." Agnes at 11 months showed no signs of walking, but dragged her legs after her when she crawled on the floor. Martha suggested that if her ankles seemed weak, Ellen might strengthen them by rubbing them daily with a towel wrung out of saltwater and dried. Martha also reminded her to watch for consequences after Agnes's smallpox vaccination, to tend the baby's development, and to secure a skilled doctor in whom she could trust.[88]

Before too long, Martha slipped back into her old habit of criticizing Ellen, this time focusing on her mothering. After a long visit in Auburn, Martha sent Ellen a letter that resembled one of her "lectury" boarding school missives. "It was only by chance that I found your keys," Martha began. Ellen had broken apart the keys to the Wrights' workroom door that had been "safely tied together this forty years." She had left one key on the table, a second key inside the worktable drawer, and a third key mysteriously on the floor. Martha admonished her 27-year-old daughter: "What does that go to, Miss Careless? Are you missing a third key? I hope you will take better care of them in the future." It was unclear whether the worse crime was separating the keys or dropping them, but the final error was "giving keys to a baby to be made as rusty as Blue Beard's." Martha promised to send Ellen the keys by her son Willy "if he goes that way," but she did not offer to mail them.[89]

Martha demonstrated similar impatience when she heard about Ellen's second pregnancy—one that occurred two years after Agnes and at an incon-

Martha Coffin Wright, c. 1870
(Sophia Smith Collection, Smith College)

venient time for Martha. "Ma is sure I must have 'calculated' wrong," Ellen told Lucy McKim, "since appearances were 'so deceitful.'" Martha, who preferred to spend June in Auburn with Agnes instead of Roxbury with a new baby, told a cousin, "It was a pity to mortal vision that Ellen could not have waited till October [to have a baby] and spent June here with Agnes to enjoy the roses and strawberries." Even so, Martha adjusted her summer schedule for she wouldn't "turn my back on [Ellen and Will]." On June 20, 1868, Ellen gave birth to a second baby whom she named Charley after the one-year-old son the Wrights had lost in 1849. Agnes carried on jealously for the first few months after her brother's birth, but then became "very fond of her little bruder."[90]

With two children, Ellen lost the sheen of motherly perfection she had maintained for two years and found life far more challenging than before. Helen Garrison occasionally accused her of lax parenting. Charley, a precious "angel who slept through the night," had a muscular little body, was "agile as a fly," and never sat still. At 2, he ventured out onto the flat roof during a falling rain unbeknownst to Ellen, consequently proving Helen's point. Agnes was the noisy child. A tall girl with lovely blue eyes and fair curls like her mother and Grandma Martha, she took a fancy to music and singing. She called herself Agnes Harrison Garrison after her namesake, a close friend of Ellen's, and seemed to "relish the jingle."[91]

Ellen and Will's third child arrived in a household overshadowed by tragedy. The family had moved out from under the Garrison, Sr. roof and into their own home and were experiencing their first taste of independence. They still lived close to Will's parents in Roxbury and his business provided a sufficient income. But all of this was interrupted when a catastrophic accident in Boston one summer morning changed their lives. In late August 1871, Will was returning home on a local train from his wool shop in Boston when an express train following close behind slammed directly into the rear of the car he was aboard. Many deaths and severe injuries resulted. Will luckily survived, but he suffered debilitating burns to both hands, the worst of which was on his right.[92]

In the accident's aftermath, Ellen, who was seven months pregnant at the time, matured into a woman who bore her mother's courage and confidence. She sent the children to Will's parents and took total charge of her husband's long, difficult recovery. When he came home from the hospital, Ellen's sister Eliza arrived from Auburn to help nurse him. Together, they dressed his burns for a month. During the first few weeks, Ellen tried to distract Will from his pain and discomfort by rubbing his feet, singing to him, or playing the music box, so that he might sleep. By early September, Will's wounds were improving, and he was getting along "remarkably well," with his left hand somewhat better than the right, but the daily caustic salve was a "sad pox upon his nerves." Ellen did not see how it would be possible for him to use his stiff right fingers again, saying that "they look so like sticks," but the improvement of the left hand "gave them hope." By the late fall, he was going to the store nearly every day. He persevered in learning to write with his left hand, and Ellen was sure he'd be "very smart at it soon."[93]

Still, Ellen felt as if she "never could settle down to regular" life again. But, as babies always did for the Wright family, Frank arrived in October 1871, "an angel to us all." Ellen thought that, like Charley, he resembled her father and that his eyes were "coming out moderately dark but not blue," as Helen Garrison had claimed. Temporarily rattled by caring for Will, Ellen felt too nervous to even bathe her new baby alone, but Martha helped to restore her confidence and routine. With her mother present, Ellen didn't "feel very blue." The two women settled into a complementary relationship that served them well over the next year. Then, in July 1872, another misfortune struck. While traveling in Europe, Martha's oldest daughter by her first husband, Marianna Pelham Mott, fell and died from her injuries. Martha drew upon her inner reserves, as she had done previously, but deeply mourned her 43-year-old daughter.[94]

Life continued, Martha participated in conventions, and Ellen and Will's family grew. In 1874, they expected a fourth baby. When a third son arrived, the female members offered a few regretful comments. Martha described her grandson as "another irrepressible voter, instead of the little girl I had hoped for." Agnes, who at 8 "wished she was a boy and could sit on a fence and put her hands in her pockets and whistle," had wanted a baby sister. Even Ellen jokingly declared, "Another horrid boy had been born." When Will said, "But he can vote," Ellen suggested they name him William Lloyd Garrison III, in honor of his grandfather who had been a strong proponent for women's rights. Will was hesitant to bequeath the number III on a son, fearing that "he may not bear up the standard," but he finally consented.[95]

However, within a few weeks, the family faced a far greater trauma than naming young William. Martha, who had come from Auburn to help with the baby's birth, worried when she left her husband David at home because he was suffering from an undiagnosed illness. She fretted over his condition but hoped that a Florida visit to their son Willy would restore him. William Lloyd Garrison recalled that Martha was "apparently in good health," illustrated by her joyful participation in Christmas Eve festivities. "She made a stately and commanding presence with rare modesty, her features intelligent and striking," he said. "When we gave the parting hand to each other that night little did either of us imagine [the future]."[96]

On Christmas Day, Martha celebrated her 68th birthday with no outward appearance of illness, but a wagon filled with poor symptoms soon collided into her. In an otherwise cheerful letter, she told a cousin that she had been having "a slight indisposition for a day or two," and hoped it might be possible "for me to see you all again in the spring but I seldom plan far ahead." She gave no indication of anything more worrisome, writing in her diary on December 25, "It's Christmas. I'm 68 years old, and it's a beautiful bright day." Later that evening, Martha told Ellen that she had taken cold and felt "threatened with rheumatism." Ellen sent for Dr. Jackson, who prescribed a medicine that Martha bought for $3, resenting the purchase when "my own [pill] box would have done just as well."[97]

Within a few days, Martha knew something serious was ailing her. Her rheumatism symptoms had evolved into a "sick stomach" that might prevent her from leaving Boston to care for her husband. "How can I ever get there—poor David!" she bemoaned. When David heard about Martha's illness, he cautioned his wife to remain in Boston. Dr. Jackson paid subsequent visits, but Martha's condition continued to steadily decline. Ellen advised her sister Eliza to bring their father to Boston. Martha was delirious by the time they arrived. "What will become of me?" Martha shuddered feverishly. Then, calmer, she invoked her God: "He giveth his beloved sleep." In the past, Martha had indicated that she would feel peace at the end of her life. She did not dread death, but "trusted in the life beyond and [felt] that being ready to die is to be prepared to live as well as die."[98]

The family watched Martha, helpless against stemming her decline but offering whatever comfort they could. Ellen, David, and Eliza took turns sitting at her bedside while she moved in and out of a coma. "She seemed to want her hand held all the time," Ellen recalled. "Even at the very last, when it was almost cold, she raised it and laid it across my lap." The next day, she uttered her last words: "It's almost time for Marianna [her oldest daughter, who had died three years before] to come for me." On January 4, 1875, Martha Wright died from what doctors then called typhoid pneumonia.[99]

Ellen, stunned with grief, arranged to bury her mother at Fort Hill Cemetery in Auburn and marked her tomb with an engraving that was rather unusual for that era. The first line identifies her as "Martha Coffin [her maiden name]," the second line as "Wife of David." Ellen also contacted Martha's friends and colleagues in the women's rights movement, including officers of the National Woman Suffrage Association, whose annual meeting she had planned to open that month. At the event, Elizabeth Cady Stanton took the podium in Martha's place and paid her a final tribute filled with accolades. Susan B. Anthony wrote Ellen, "I was struck dumb, and ever since it has seemed as if all the rest of us older workers were doomed to pass over the dark river ere we reach the goal of freedom here." Susan told Ellen that she thought of her "almost constantly," and enclosed "Martha's two last letters," knowing "how precious they will be to you."[100]

Because there was no one else "to fill her place" unless it was one of her daughters, Susan suggested that Ellen continue Martha's work. She pushed this no further in her letter, however, closing with condolences and inviting

Ellen to visit her in Rochester because "I would so love to see you once more."[101]

Ellen did follow in Martha's footsteps, but not as Susan B. Anthony might have imagined. Instead of becoming a public speaker, she took up Martha's manual for life: how to thrive amidst adversity, how to parent, and how to find contentment in home, family, and friends. Ellen could not help but absorb Martha's passion for freed men and women, as well as her quest for woman suffrage, but not until later life did she act upon these causes. When her family had grown and she was in her 50s, Ellen rejoined the women she had met during her adolescence at their suffrage meetings. In 1890, she and her sister Eliza attended Susan B. Anthony's 75th birthday party and the seminal meeting that united the American and National Woman suffrage associations into one—the National American Woman Suffrage Association. Ten years later, Ellen became a life-long member of the NAWSA.[102] She had inspired both of her daughters, Agnes, born in 1866, and Eleanor, born in 1880, to be independent women; neither ever married or had children.

Eleanor picked up the gauntlet of her grandmother, Martha. She moved to New York City in 1912 to work as an assistant to suffrage leader Carrie Chapman Catt. Eleanor accompanied her aunt, Fanny Garrison, and her father, Will Garrison, to woman suffrage parades, the most famous one in Washington in 1916, where women were berated. By then, Eleanor was attending Pratt Business School in New York, where she remained until the New York State Legislature passed woman suffrage in November 1917. When Ellen died in 1931, she had birthed five children and had many grandchildren. Dozens of pictures show her as she liked to be seen—balancing a baby on her knee or chatting with a friend.

$$* * *$$

For the first 20 years of their relationship, Martha and Ellen bumped heads in conflict more often than they rubbed shoulders in companionship. Mother and daughter disagreed about Ellen's scholarly endeavors, her inappropriate behavior with men and boys, and her premature participation in Women's Rights

Conventions. They slowly mended their rifts through the piano music they both loved, Martha's introduction to Ellen of Susan B. Anthony and Lucy Stone as inspirations and mentors, and the Civil War horrors they shared. Gradually, Ellen understood her mother's advice: obtain a good education that did not end in the classroom, become an excellent caretaker of any home she inhabited, and be a true friend to everyone she encountered. Martha was determined that if her daughter chose to marry, she would be something before marriage and something after marriage.

Ellen could choose what that "something" was. Martha had prepared her with many technical skills. Her penmanship was excellent, her mind keen, and her intellect engaged in passions she shared in common with her mother. Ellen sewed admirably, managed meal preparation with the aid of a servant, cared for babies and children, and emulated her mother by facing life's crises with wit and humor. An attractive, witty, and educated daughter of a good reform family, Ellen could have pursued whatever the world offered women of her background. Once she grew to appreciate Martha's wisdom, she learned the best lesson her mother offered: how to be a good woman.

A Long-Distance Bond
Abby Kelley Foster and Alla Foster

Abby Kelley Foster: Mothering Alla Foster from the Road, 1847–1858

When she arrived on May 17, 1847, Alla Foster uprooted the lives of Abby and Stephen Foster shortly after they had moved into a rambling and neglected farmhouse outside of Worcester, Massachusetts. Born in her parents' sparsely furnished bedroom, as was the trend of the day, Alla was welcomed by a midwife to provide expertise and Paulina Wright Davis, a dear friend and women's rights advocate, to calm the new mother's 36-year-old nerves. Abby and Stephen thanked Paulina by naming their daughter for her, then shortening it to Alla.

Stephen and Abby, who had met at antislavery meetings in 1841 and fallen in love, struggled during a four-year courtship to divide their passion for each other with their passion for enslaved people.[103] They were equally enamored of Alla, but both of them identified so strongly with the antislavery movement that they never considered abandoning it entirely to remain home and care for their only child. After three months with Alla, Stephen tore himself away to resume his position as an agent for the American Antislavery Society, which sent him to Ohio. Abby, who understood and shared her husband's fervency, was accustomed to separations from Stephen. Life with Alla sharpened the impact of his absence. "How my heart yearns to help you," she wrote him. "But my pleasure with our little one at home is much greater."[104]

As Abby immersed herself in motherhood, her biggest challenge was living on a primitive farm. Stephen had left her in a home much larger and in far worse repair than Abby would have chosen. The farmhouse they had purchased a few months before Alla's birth fulfilled Stephen's dream of owning property and land that required restoration. A passerby's quick glance at 116 Mower Street would reveal an attractive, sturdy red-brick structure built in Georgian style that sported two chimneys and a fanlight over the front door. However, Abby, a life-long inhabitant of Worcester, knew the reputation of this 1797 house, which they could afford only because of its deteriorated state.

Located in what Abby called the "repulsive" hamlet of Tatnuck, the 39 acres of inferior land were dotted with a half dozen shabby-looking outbuildings but lacked a functional barn. The house, a historic landmark, today bears the name Liberty Farm, which was given to it by later owners, but the Fosters called it the Cook Place for the original inhabitants. When they moved in, repair was possible, but Abby detested living so far away— four miles—from the prosperous town of Worcester, which boasted a daily newspaper, post office, many rail lines, stores, and a strong abolitionist community. The lack of childcare and easy transportation from the farm deprived her of any opportunity to immerse herself in the culture she so craved. [105]

During the first summer, in Stephen's absence, Abby coped with the distractions of renovation, planting, and caring for a new baby. In addition, the house was filled with relatives. To bring the farm to a modicum of productivity, Stephen had invited his younger brothers, Gaven, who was single, and Newell, who came with his wife Eliza and several children, and two hired men to reside with them and continue the project. Abby depended on her sister-in-law, Eliza, and Eliza's oldest daughter Helen, who did the laundry and cooking while the men handled the farm. But their styles of keeping house differed significantly. Abby tended to be organized, fastidious, and careful of her belongings. She cringed to see the damage that Eliza and her family inflicted on her furniture. Eliza's kitchen clutter also drove Abby mad, as did the disorder that reigned throughout the rest of the rooms. Abby set up a refuge for Alla and herself in the parlor, the only room that was shaded from the intense summer sun by dark drapes and the only one free from the flies that overran every corner. [106]

Yet, it was still hard to escape the teeming household. She longed for the day when she would "go to housekeeping" independently instead of sharing it with Eliza, but it would not be possible for her to experience this benchmark in her marriage for some time. "I never want to keep house again till I live less mixed up," she wrote Stephen. Throngs of visitors, including Abby's sisters and their families, contributed to the summer congestion; then Stephen's elderly parents came for an extended stay. Only a few months earlier, Abby had claimed that she was "too much of a philosopher to take any such disappointment [as the purchase of a house] to heart."[107] By the end of the summer, life on the farm exasperated her.

Alla provided Abby's only solace. What she saw as the 3-month-old baby's signs of intelligence, plus her smile and her babble, proved to Abby that she loved her mother. Abby delighted in managing Alla's sleeping, eating, and developing, and reported every detail to Stephen in frequent letters. The new papa learned long distance about his daughter's nap schedules, increasing weight, and regular outdoor activities.[108]

Perhaps the knowledge that she would soon leave her baby to the care of others motivated Abby to establish a close bond with her daughter and express her expectations early. When, in the spirit of water cures and hydrotherapy, Abby plunged her tiny baby into daily cold baths at six weeks, Alla acted surprised but tolerated it. Riding in the wagon was uncomfortable and crowded, but they lived in the country—this was the only available means of transportation. Taking a regular nap was routine. Going to sleep at sundown and waking at "June light" was preferred.[109]

That first summer, Abby included Alla in her domestic routines. She carried her snugly in a pouch around her neck as she performed farm chores. Abby was sure that Alla watched knowingly as she tiptoed into the barn

Abby Kelley Foster, 1851
(From the Collection of Worcester Historical Museum, Worcester, Mass.)

and milked their cows. In only a few months, Alla would drink their milk and eat finely diced apples her mother picked from a previously abandoned orchard. Daughter and mother also entered the henhouse cautiously, so as not to startle chickens with a new presence. Abby fed them and gathered the eggs they proffered, cooing to Alla about their "good chicks." Abby was convinced this delighted her child, as did a new lamb. Alla learned well, for throughout her childhood, she performed similar tasks and appreciated healthy crops.[110] When Alla began to babble, Abby wrote Stephen, "She is a great talker and your brother says she will be a great lecturer. I think she will only preach the truth, but that powerfully."[111]

Abby envied Stephen his work on the road, but she was not quite ready to part with Alla, who had "so thoroughly entwined herself" about her mother that she feared it would "render [me] in pieces" if they separated. Abby regretted that Stephen was missing the opportunity to develop a similar engagement with their baby whose intelligence her mother claimed was "dawning and expanding every hour."[112]

Yet Abby knew her time at home with Alla would soon end. By early fall 1847, she was feeling an irresistible tug toward the antislavery cause. She had a mission, an obligation, to return to work and free enslaved families that were less fortunate than hers. Abby admitted her conflict to Stephen: "Yes, to me, there must always be a vacuum where our little one is not." For the rest of their lives, Abby faced this emptiness whenever she was without Alla. It would be a sacrifice she imposed on herself. For more than a decade, Abby had felt such strong empathy for enslaved women that she herself sometimes felt enslaved, or even tortured, like they were. When Abby had told her own mother that she was called to give her life to the antislavery cause, her mother wished she would resist this role because she believed that it would result in a difficult future. Abby now was suffering the conflict her mother had predicted. [113]

Abby worried that Stephen would think she was discontent, and she tried to assure him that her "peace of mind is not put on the rack." She remained at home for the fall, but as winter approached, she drifted toward gloominess, even exhibiting signs of what is today called postpartum depression.

Alla's "frolic, laugh, smiling eyes, and face lit up with growing intelligence" pleased her mother, but they did not "keep off the clouds which hovered." From the time they had married two years ago, Abby and Stephen's anti-slavery work had separated them for weeks at a time, a reality to which she had grown accustomed. Now, at home with a baby, she missed her husband terribly and knew that it was time to resume work on the road, preferably at Stephen's side. She began to persuade herself that since she had never loved the farm, leaving it would not hurt much.[114]

By the New Year, Abby was ready to venture from a home whose only attraction was Alla. Convinced that her daughter was thriving, especially compared to enslaved babies, and having consulted physiologists who said that 9 months was the perfect time to wean, Abby defied advice from friends and stopped nursing Alla. A close abolitionist friend openly scolded her. Abby's effect on the course of human freedom would be "good, but your influence on home duties and home virtues will be bad." She believed that if Abby "waited until your child is old enough to wean it would be less reprehensible" to leave her. Pregnant herself, she would "not feel like leaving her little stranger" to lecture when she was only 10 months old. [115]

An older friend agreed. When she heard that Abby planned to rejoin the antislavery field, she told her she did not like the thought of "thy deserting [her] even for the slave's sake." Trying to dissuade Abby without insulting her, she explained how important the obligation to care for a baby was, a relation "not to be entered upon lightly without consideration and care." At least one woman sympathized with Abby in her maternal feelings. She felt sure that Alla would "grow in grace" and that regardless of her location, "the good that is done by a good mother never dies, but brings appointed fruit sooner or later." Abby, undaunted, informed Stephen that she intended to join him on the road that spring. When Stephen expressed his doubts that she would leave Alla, she replied, "We shall see whether I care so much for my baby as to forget the multitudes of broken-hearted [slave] mothers." [116]

In the spring of 1848, when Alla was not yet 1, Abby took a job on the road as agent and speaker for the American Antislavery Society for $12.50

a week and launched a routine the family followed for the next 10 years. Stephen took no salary; he split his time between working in the antislavery field, frequently at Abby's side, and living at the farm where he kept up the property and monitored Alla's care. Sometimes it worked well for them; other times it agonized both parents and even Alla. What helped them all survive was Stephen's younger sister, Caroline (Callie), a gentle schoolteacher who lived with her parents at home in Canterbury but agreed to come and care for Alla.

Knowing her daughter was in a familiar place with loving care eased Abby, who saw Alla only a few times while she was a toddler. Despite the separation, mother and daughter coped fairly well. When in the spring of 1849 Callie was called home to Canterbury to care for her ill parents, Abby took Alla there to live for a time. After she dropped her off in what was a strange new home for her daughter, she encountered her antislavery friend Lucy Stone. Abby looked "so ill and suffering" that Lucy asked if she were sick. "Oh, no," she said, "But I have left my little daughter with my husband's sister in New Hampshire, and I feel as though I should die. But I have done it for the sake of the mothers whose babies are sold away from them." In that spirit, no matter what it cost her, Abby persevered in her struggle.[117]

Callie sensitively connected Alla to her parents by writing letters as the child dictated, speaking her thoughts before she was able to write them herself. Abby quickly assumed the same style, always writing to Callie and Alla together. After reporting an afternoon of playing in the mud, the 2-year-old asked Abby to buy her "a new frock" after she had ruined hers. When she went in the sun without her bonnet or broke up her grandmother's flowers, "Aunt Caroline makes me come into the house." At church services she experienced more restraint than she could tolerate: "I have been to meeting but I won't [sic] good, so I can't go now." She told Abby that she was very careful of her books most of the time, "but when the bad spirit gets into me, they go out of my hands and sometimes onto the floor but I hope they won't any more."[118]

From her earliest dictated letters to those she later wrote on her own in proud, proper cursive, Alla expressed how much she missed Abby and Stephen. She closed with kisses and pleas to answer her promptly. She knew they were away doing important work, but she wished it were not so. "I have been very well and happy since I came from Worcester," she told her mother, "but I want you and my father to come and see me, when will you come?" After being at Canterbury for a year, in 1850 she still wanted to live with her parents at Worcester all the time, but felt she could not leave Callie, Grandmother, or Grandfather.[119]

Stephen, like Abby, relished Alla and found her "truly an interesting child," even at 4 years old. She was selfless, sympathetic, and generous. When Alla asked Stephen for something he could not afford, she "seldom asks me a second time." When she tearfully requested a harmonica just before she left for Canterbury, he went to town the next day and bought it, plus a wagon. When he presented them to her, she covered him with kisses, insisting she save the exact same number of kisses "for Mother." Stephen was "struck with the fact that she always insists on your right to an equal part of everything which I possess, if she attaches any value to it."[120]

Abby appreciated Stephen's fathering of Alla but was convinced that she was her natural guardian, the person who was "under the most sacred obligations to make her happy." It was "of momentous importance" that Alla be "under the proper influences." Children were like "daguerreotype plates," an early form of photography, which caught the images that were thrown to them. "It feels like a great sacrifice for me to be away from Alla at this interesting period of her intellectual, moral and social development," she told Stephen. She thought she could "do better than any other person in forming [Alla's] character." What is perplexing is why Abby believed it worth the sacrifice to stay away from Alla for such long stretches of time. She defended her absence, arguing that it was neither preaching nor teaching, but "the passing life that affects most."[121]

Mothering from afar challenged Abby, who loved Alla like any other mother, but nothing could replace her abolitionist work. Abby's network of reformers grew, but she remained a major pioneer. She shared podiums with William Lloyd Garrison and Lucy Stone, who had been colleagues since they met on the lecture circuit during the 1830s. Susan B.

Anthony, initially reluctant to speak publicly, took Abby as an example and role model on her journey toward activism. Abby mentored Susan in the antislavery movement, and Susan helped her new friend recognize women's rights, then arranged her acquaintance with reform mothers Martha Wright and Elizabeth Cady Stanton. They both invited her to speak in their hometowns.[122]

Abby was instrumental in the First National Woman's Rights Convention, which was held near her home in Worcester in 1850. It attracted more than 1,000 attendees, including Stephen and his 85-year-old father, Asa Foster, as well as three of Abby's sisters. Paulina Wright Davis, Alla's namesake, presided; Stephen delivered a major speech; and Sojourner Truth, a freed slave in New York, argued that "slave women were the most grossly wronged of all."[123] The meeting, although similar to the Seneca Falls Convention two years before, was much larger and more inclusive toward men. Like Seneca Falls, the Worcester meeting did not call for the creation of formal women's rights organizations but encouraged individual states to hold their own regional conventions that would be open to all. They built networks and expanded them to those unable to attend.

Abby stood out as the most radical among the network of provocative pioneers who led the movements for abolition and women's rights. At the Second National Woman's Rights Convention, also held at Worcester, in 1851, she delivered some of her strongest words about mothers and daughters. When she addressed the crowd of 3,500, she urged women in the assembly to take responsibility for achieving their own rights; they should not "go home to complain of the men, but go and make greater exertions than ever to discharge your everyday duties." She told a room filled with many mothers to teach their daughters the domestic skills they would need to become independent no matter what their marital status turned out to be. They "should not hang upon the skirts of a paternal home for support, but secure subsistence for themselves." Furthermore, women must not marry until they could "provide for the physical necessities of a family." Turning to the experience she'd gained over the previous 14 years, Abby told the assembly, "My life has been my speech. Bloody feet, sisters, have worn smooth the path by which you have come up thither."[124]

This lesson was not lost on Alla. In the winter of 1853, Abby expected her daughter to accomplish more mature tasks than many of her contemporaries. Alla rarely complained, inspiring family friend Sallie Holley to say that the 5-year-old was "the very incarnation of sweetness and simplicity...a child of decided character...and just what you would expect from her father and mother." A few years later, Susan B. Anthony denied being as "extravagant as Sallie," but said of Alla, "It is a good word only that I can speak for her." Once when Alla was visiting her Aunt and Uncle Ballou, a cousin asked, "Will your mother let you do this?" Surprised, 6-year-old Alla replied, "My mother lets me do just as I please. If she wishes me to do a thing I generally do it." [125]

Aunt Caroline began to teach Alla to print and express thoughts directly to her parents, writing separate letters they treasured. Stephen praised her excellent spelling, "which will be of great use to you through life." He agreed with Abby that Alla should continue to improve her writing every day. Whenever she had time, she should "acquire a greater familiarity with the use of your pen." [126] Just as Martha Wright had encouraged Ellen, Alla's parents argued that having beautiful penmanship was an asset for any person.

One winter evening, longing for Alla, Abby pictured her daughter sitting beside the fire with her grandparents and Callie having such a good time that it "makes me feel quite homesick." To console themselves over missing her, Abby and Stephen told the people they met about Alla: "the things you have done, how large you are, the color of your eyes, and how smooth you keep your hair and how clean you can keep yourself." The consolation they received for their absence from Alla was meeting folks who were open to their antislavery message. [127]

Delighting in his daughter's character and personality, Stephen had always worried about Alla's physical form. From the time she walked, he fretted about her posture, but assumed her back would grow straight in time. They later learned the curvature was caused by scoliosis but did not understand it at the time. They probably even denied it. When he returned to the farm in late February 1854 after five months away, 7-year-old Alla ran out to the road and greeted him "in an ecstasy of delight which only wanted for

[Abby's] presence to make it perfect." Stephen nevertheless worried when he saw Alla, who appeared changed to him. She had grown very tall and was "not quite as good looking as when we left home." Stephen told Abby that Alla's posture was "less stooping" than before and hoped that "with sufficient care, she might yet be the possessor of a tolerably well-developed chest, a matter in which I have felt much interest for some time."[128]

But Alla's physical stature was not the focus of her relationship with Stephen. That turned more to her father's action for slaves. Only a few months later, the Fugitive Slave Law would take her father to jail. Always willing to privately shelter slaves through the Underground Railroad, Stephen ensnared himself with a case that was far more public. In late October 1854, Asa Butman, the federal marshal who had escorted the slave Anthony Burns out of Boston the previous summer, raised the suspicions of Worcester when he checked into a local hotel. People wondered if he had come to watch for other fugitive activity. When the War Vigilance committee began to threaten Butman's life, Stephen escorted him to Boston. For this peaceful action, Stephen and five black men were arrested for kidnapping and even assaulting Butman. Home with Callie, an excited Alla followed the story. When the family friend Sallie Hollie came to visit, she met her with a smile. "Father's in jail!" she exclaimed. After preliminary hearings, a grand jury dismissed the charges against Stephen, but indicted his co-defendants for assault. Alla had a good story to tell her friends and did so proudly. She was too young to comprehend the total implications, but the passion Stephen demonstrated probably helped her understand her parents' desire to help slaves, even if it required leaving home to do so.[129]

Abby continued her own advocacy. She insisted that enslaved children needed her even more than Alla. Unlike Martha Wright, who almost discouraged Ellen from pursuing reform work, Abby began to indicate a desire for her daughter to become an antislavery advocate when she was old enough, if she chose to. She asked her 5-year-old, "Do you often think of the little slave girls who can never see their dear mothers again?" Abby hoped that Alla would "pity the poor slaves, and sometimes get your Aunt Callie or grandfather to read about them to you, that you may be able to help them when you get older." She bragged about Alla, and many people asked about her. When Alla was 8, Abby asked, "Do you think you will try to help the world to grow better? If you will, you must learn while young to be very, very good yourself."[130]

Alla accepted her mother's absences, but it is less clear if she accepted her mother's invitations to join her in her antislavery work, if we can trust her Reminiscences from later years. She quotes her mother as saying, "the most precious legacy I can leave my child is a free country," in which no enslaved children were taken from their mothers. "Had she been less noble, less brave, less tender of her child," Alla wrote, "she would have remained at home to enjoy her motherhood at the expense of other mothers." [131]

Before long, Abby was forced to spend time resting at home. Years of travel wore on the 44-year-old more harshly than they did Stephen. She began to show poor health at the May 1855 antislavery meetings, where friends remarked on her thinness and pallor. They contributed money to grant her a leave of absence, so that she might stay home and rest, dismissing all worries about the farm, antislavery activities, or Alla. Abby should remember, "There's one thing you owe that little girl which no one but you can pay her; it is to live and to live in health if possible. Be a good girl and do as you're bid."[132]

Abby agreed to spend the rest of the summer at home in relative ease. She accepted some of the money her friends raised for her and enjoyed the farm, ate well, and gained six pounds. Alla, age 7, shared three of the best months with her mother, who behaved so light-heartedly that she even began to wear bloomers, loose turban pants considered scandalous by many at that time, around the yard. So many visitors descended on the Foster farm that there were seldom fewer than eight around the dinner table, including the family of William and Helen Garrison. They came for the weekend and left two of their four children, William, Jr. (who married Ellen Wright) and Fanny, for a month. Alla met another friend of her mother's, Susan B. Anthony, who was taking a water cure nearby so visited several times. Abby, who had always thought Susan an exceedingly interesting woman, grew to admire her even more. [133]

Travel became a challenge for Abby, and by late fall, she could not tolerate even brief trips. She was driven home by what she self-diagnosed as a serious catarrh, an inflammation of a mucous membrane characterized by congestion that sometimes chronically affects air and nose passages. She did not seek treatment, hoping a change of surroundings and a break would ease her discomfort. She encouraged Stephen to stay on the road, managing the farm for him while he continued to assume her western lecture schedule. "You are a capital housekeeper and can make a very creditable antislavery speech," he wrote, "but I have little confidence in your ability to manage a farm."[134] She good-naturedly relied on his expertise to get her through the ordeal. She filled her letters with questions that asked permission to sell this or that crop and warned him to be careful in his travels.

Abby recuperated slowly, but before she could resume a full schedule of meetings and lectures, a new affliction struck—this time in her mouth. For years, particularly during her western trips, she had been plagued by toothaches. The dentists in Ohio where she was lecturing often combined barbering with dentistry and knew only one remedy for an infected tooth—pull it. By the time Abby saw a dentist in Massachusetts, where a dental school had recently opened and nitrous oxide was being successfully used for anesthesia, her teeth were beyond repair. After months of stressful surgery (she fainted during one operation) all her teeth were extracted and false ones were prepared. Full dentures were common enough among her older associates, but Abby was only 46 when her last tooth was pulled. She was embarrassed to attend meetings, and lecturing was out of the question. Her sunken cheeks and pain-etched face made her feel even further alienated from the anti-slavery movement and its players. Abby felt old; she was toothless, nearing menopause, and exhausted. On good days, she promised that once her "underteeth were installed," she would try to once again speak publicly, to "sally forth and try what I can do." [135]

Abby Kelley Foster: Mothering Alla Foster at Home, 1858-1868

While Abby was away in April 1857, Alla's health deteriorated. Almost 10 years old, she grew so weak from the pain in her back that had been

Alla Foster, c. 1860
(From the Collection of Worcester Historical Museum, Worcester, Mass.)

steadily growing for years that she could not attend school. The strict exercise regimen that she had followed for months failed to curtail her condition. In the fall, Abby knew she could no longer ignore the situation. She was convinced "that to leave my daughter at home…I should be violating a trust that God has committed to my care."[136] Abby, struggling over her daughter's condition, decided to come home and care for Alla full-time for the first time since her birth.

During the next year, Stephen attended meetings and delivered lectures in his wife's place. Only on the rare occasion when Abby left the farm to fulfill her role as the American Antislavery Society's finance agent did she part with Alla, whose treatment she placed under the care of a specialist in diseases of the spine, referred by a doctor at Harvard Medical School. He ordered bed rest until Alla could be fitted with surgical corsets for a spinal curvature that was likely caused by scoliosis.[137]

In January 1858, Abby accepted the hospitality of friends in Boston, where Alla began the decade-long journey required for spinal corsets to relieve the effects of scoliosis. The initial fitting was "very disagreeable," but Alla worked hard from the beginning to adapt her body. The corsets chafed under her arm, a nuisance Abby tried to lessen by adjusting the shoulder brace. What worried Abby almost as much as the physical affliction of the brace was Alla's fever, weakness, and nervousness. She gave her a spoonful of laudanum (10 percent tincture of opium powder) before each meal, and Stephen suggested that Abby keep Alla lying down, confine her to only gentle exercise, give her a tonic to improve her appetite, and use magnetic massages to ease her pain.[138] Abby told a friend, "Her cause is alarming but I am in good heart, never for a moment believing that she is to be cursed with a life-long sickness or deformity."[139]

After four grueling months in Boston, during which Alla adjusted to her braces, mother and daughter were relieved to return to the farm to continue recuperating. Abby was delighted that Stephen had hired a housekeeper "to put her more at ease." Abby remained at Alla's side for most of the summer and fall, often suffering from her own medical problems but concentrating on Alla. Abby's clear choice to care for a child in need sacrificed her antislavery work, but she never regretted it.

By the spring of 1859, Alla was able to return to school in a surgical corset, but some days, even weeks, she was too frail to go to classes, so Abby or Stephen tutored her at home. Over the following years, as the back brace slowly corrected her scoliosis, she became acclimated to the restrictive metal garment and was able to spend more and more time at school, except after readjustments, when it pinched or caused especial discomfort; then, Abby kept her home but insisted that Alla wear the brace at least for short intervals while she became accustomed to it. Together, mother and daughter designed a schedule that accommodated Alla's education as well as the demands of her body. Knowing that her mother longed to return to her advocacy for slaves, Alla assured her that she could manage in her absence. Aunt Callie would come again.[140]

Abby returned to Ohio in the fall of 1860 as the country edged toward sectional discord that could not be mended. People who once embraced her uncompromising opposition to slavery were now less welcoming. After Abby spent six months in a state that still resembled a wild frontier, she was disheartened and ill. The conditions of the farmhouses and cabins whose owners provided her hospitality were primitive, and the food was inadequate. Her fragile health deteriorated seriously, descending nearly to the depth it had during previous illnesses. Before she left Ohio, the huge tent where many gatherings had been held was cut up and sold as secondhand canvas. The Antislavery Society stopped holding meetings. *The Antislavery Bugle*, Ohio's antislavery newspaper, was forced to dispose of its press and type. Abby, who left just after the April 12th attack on Fort Sumter launched the Civil War, could not call her mission a success.[141]

Returning to Worcester and Alla initially comforted Abby, but at home she met stark realities that overshadowed her joy. The country was now at war. Abby and Stephen joined William Lloyd Garrison in a pledge to be non-resistants, those who neither fought nor supported fighting. Abby did not fold bandages, knit socks, or send relatives to fight. "When rogues fall out, honest men get their best dues," she claimed, "Out of the present strife will grow a new Union in which the rights of all will be respected."[142]

As the Civil War years continued, Abby had more intensive battles to fight against her own tortuous poor health. Her teeth had finally mended from her earlier surgery, but she suffered from dyspepsia, a catchall diagnosis that could encompass anything from indigestion to depression to stomach ulcers. She was "worn out" from a raw throat and impeded eyesight, which kept her off most podiums in the early 1860s. Stephen worried about a wife "exhausted by public labor," his inability to make a living from the farm, and conflict with the antislavery leadership.[143]

Eventually, the couple pulled themselves together for a reunion with anti-slavery friends. They gathered in Philadelphia in December 1863 to commemorate 30 years of William Lloyd Garrison's American Antislavery Society, which had hired Abby to be one of its first speakers. Lucy Stone, Martha Wright, Susan B. Anthony, and Elizabeth Cady Stanton joined them. It was the final time they would be together, as the schisms among them would deepen, rather than improve, over the next two decades. It was also Abby's last public appearance until after the war.

The same month, December 1863, at age 16, Alla completed her formal education at the local grammar school, delayed somewhat by her brace. Now, because Worcester's high school did not admit girls, Alla embarked on a course of self-directed—and extremely effective—study to prepare herself for college. Stephen suggested that as she "stepped from the platform of youth to womanhood," each month would permanently mark her "future character and destinies." Each year "would require more thoughtfulness and self-reflection than previous ones." She should "discipline her faculties" and "depend on her principles to guide her." What's more, she should move beyond reading stories, to which she was "much addicted." This casual reading had been suitable when her health was "feeble," but he was sure it was not the best thing for the future.[144]

Alla had a scant six months to dwell on her own self-improvement before her mother's failing health dominated the household. Abby withdrew from most of her antislavery and women's rights activities and left even simple household chores to Alla. Only 55, Abby entered a very dark period of her life. Something was dreadfully wrong; some monstrous growth was taking over her body. She told Wendell Phillips, "I hardly have a desire to live another six months under such suffering as I have endured for the last." Stephen and Alla begged Abby to see a physician. She finally consented, "so ill I can do nothing, not even have the oversight of my family."[145]

In the summer of 1866, Stephen took Abby to Dr. Gilman Kimball, a pioneer gynecologist, who diagnosed her illness as "dropsical affection," caused by a tumor on her ovaries. Most of these were benign and tended to shrink after menopause, but Abby's was pressing on neighboring organs, intensifying the pain. An ovariotomy, the recommended surgery, resulted in 40 percent of Dr. Kimball's patients contracting postoperative infections. Considering this grim statistic, Abby decided to postpone the operation and see if diet, light exercise, and a tonic would dispel the pain. "Stephen has exhausted all of his energies in trying to build me up," she wrote Wendell from her sister's Rhode Island farm. "I am getting better," she cheerfully insisted. "The main difficulty remains, but I am so much stronger and have so much less suffering I think I shall throw it all off." [146]

Abby limped along for two more years, reassuring her friends at meetings that she felt better. Her brief respite from physical agony gradually ended. In early 1867, the torture of her swollen body grew steadily worse, so that she was never free from pain. She finally agreed to have an operation. Surgery at home being the preferred option to prevent a hospital infection, Abby and a nurse converted her bedroom into a sterile space. [147]

On the morning of July 30, 1868, a team consisting of Dr. Kimball, his associate, Dr. Hudson, and a surgical nurse arrived at the farmhouse. Together they performed the ovariotomy, removing her ovary in a fairly dangerous procedure. Dr. Kimball was astounded to discover a diseased mass in Abby's abdomen that weighed 35 pounds. She had endured its presence inside her for months, perhaps even years. Abby woke from the ether in about an hour. When Alla and Stephen entered the room, they saw the

Abby Kelley Foster, 1855
(From the Collection of Worcester Historical Museum, Worcester, Mass.)

first peaceful look on the face of their wife and mother that they had seen in months.

While Abby recuperated and with determination that marked her character and echoed that of her mother, Alla resolved to remove her back brace before she began college. Her small body was slightly misshapen, but her pain was for the most part gone. Alla chose Vassar College in Poughkeepsie, New York because no Massachusetts college accepted women. She was eager to face the world. Abby dismissed her nurse and enlisted the help of her friend and fellow abolitionist, Sarah Wall, to do the housekeeping her daughter had performed all summer. Abby worked hard to restore her health, reporting to Alla in early letters that she was feeling better and preparing a Foster Family reunion, for which she had made a new dress.[148]

Alla Foster: Finding Herself at Vassar, 1868-1872

Like many mothers of her era, Abby Kelley Foster wanted Alla to attend college but was ambivalent about her leaving home. In copious letters, she kept her daughter up to date on the gossip of family and friends and other domestic details. Abby missed her daughter terribly, even though she had left Alla for many months during her youth. After two years, still not accustomed to her absence, she wrote, "The longer we can have you with us, so your present purpose of obtaining a thorough education is not hindered, the better pleased we shall be." [149]

In the fall of 1868, precocious Alla was better prepared to attend Vassar, which was considered the first official women's college in America, than most other students. When the school opened three years before, 350 young women joined the first class, but most of them failed to meet the school's expectations. Alla, having studied independently for years before she arrived, was among only 28 young women who matriculated and qualified to graduate in her class. By the time Alla enrolled, officials realized that the college had to provide preparatory classes for most of its new students, or they would not be able to manage college-level classes. This intellectual dependence fit well with the founders' primary goal of providing "inmates the safety, quiet, privacy, and purity of the family," in short controlling young women, promising parents to be a bridge between them and their home.[150]

When Alla arrived at Vassar in September 1868, she might have been intellectually superior to many other students, but her need for protection matched theirs. When she recounted her trip from the train station at 10 o'clock in the evening with "a strange brakeman," her independent and adventuresome mother Abby complained that her daughter could have been "carried to a brothel and imprisoned beyond the reach and knowledge of [her] friends." She wondered if Alla knew who had directed the order for the pickup. Abby thought it "unpardonable" and believed "the guilty person should be sent away or at best severely censored."[151]

Matthew Vassar, whose dream for a college included a very secluded, safe place, would have been equally dismayed by this error. Originally intending to only hire male professors, women advised him to include female teachers, and especially a lady principal, who might best substitute for the mothers whom the Vassar students had left behind. The board of trustees hired Lady Principal Hannah Lyman to help the male President Raymond fulfill the school's mission. She supervised the students closely, posting details on everything from the length of skirts to bed times. Alla obtained permission from Miss Lyman for absences from campus when she met her parents at a convention or extended her Christmas vacation a day or two, a system the family tolerated and even welcomed. Additional supervision came from the 21 women instructors, all young, single, and college-educated, who lived in the end rooms of the student corridors, headed tables they supervised at meals, and monitored their charges closely, even regulating baths. Subjected to similar purveyance as their students, they were expected to act as role models in the dorms.[152]

Besides providing a controlled home setting, Vassar adhered to a philosophy that kept students' minds and bodies healthy. The school encouraged plain, nutritious foods, similar to the Sylvester Graham diet that Abby had established on the farm; fixed hours for rising and retiring; warm and cold baths; regular morning and evening walks; and loose dress, free from confining corsets and long skirts, perhaps launching the first generation

that showed a peek of female boots or ankles. Each day, women were required to do "new gymnastics" during two to four half-hour periods. Alla
benefited from the Swedish exercises prescribed for those with physical
deficiencies but sometimes found long walks challenging.[153]

Other aspects of Vassar tested some of its students' beliefs, but Alla seldom
complained. It promoted a conservative social viewpoint that coincided
with its orthodox academic standards, including a huge religious compo-
nent, with daily chapel and twice-weekly sermons. From the beginning,
the school offered instruction in anatomy, physiology, hygiene, English
grammar and literature, fine arts, ancient and modern languages, natural
history, astronomy, physics, mathematics, design, music, and mental and
moral philosophy. Much to the dismay of many students, its curriculum
did not include modern history, economics, or political science, all offered
by coeducational institutions. [154]

When first-year students like Alla Foster entered Vassar's red-brick Main
Building, they were thinking less about the classes than the elegant surroundings. They mounted a stairway to an ornate four-story edifice also
called The College (or Main) and were supposed to feel at home. Fashioned
in the French Second Empire style that its founder loved, Main included
spacious halls and lecture rooms. Its sculpted ceilings and enormous lead-
ed-glass windows lent a gracious air. Here the students slept, took their
meals, went to chapel, used the library, learned their recitations, and attended classes. At college, a boiler provided them with central heating
and a gashouse supplied light. Running spring water came into each suite.
A sewage disposal facility managed refuse. For storage, students brought
trunks to supplement their individual bureaus and replace nonexistent
closets. Near each of the four beds sat water pitchers, washing bowls, and
chamber pots, which were emptied in outside privies.[155]

For many of Vassar's mostly middle-class students, its handsome quarters were far superior to home. Alla's Worcester farmhouse was warmed
by wood-burning fireplaces and lit by candles and small oil lamps. Each
time she visited home during the next four years, she found that Abby and
Stephen had taken another step to renovate their house. They scrubbed

the brick façade, repaired leaky windows, leveled floors, and made it more of a haven than it was when Alla was growing up. Stephen even installed a bathtub, planted shade trees that surrounded the house, and provided a lawn that rolled down to the magnificent stone wall he had started building 20 years earlier. Ironically, even though Alla had been raised in less than ideal physical surroundings, during her first month at school, when she mentioned her cold room, Stephen told her to "ask for a comfortable place and if you cannot have it, come home."[156]

Even though they characterized Alla's arrival at Vassar as filled with "bad luck," Abby and Stephen were pleased that once settled in, she was "well contented" with "good prospects." When she learned about her daughter's excellent results in preliminary testing, Abby implied that they expected nothing less. Abby assured her daughter that they had sufficient funds to pay for either two or four years, but her "own desire has always been that you should have as thorough an education as you can have strength to obtain." Alla should at least embark on a course that would support her for life, just in the event that something occurred to "make it necessary" for her to give up school earlier than the four years. [157]

If anything disappointed Abby, it was Alla's mediocre score in Latin, which compelled her concerned mother to remark, "I was surprised that you stood no higher." She suggested that a "person of your organization" should choose the scientific over the classical course because "you have not much facility for the acquisition of language in consequence of your poor memory." Alla should not let those who acquire language easily to ignore the difficulties of others, and use her "mature judgment" to decide. [158]

Alla was probably accustomed to her mother's intense scrutiny but felt successful in the early classes she took, so she forged ahead, choosing classical as well as science courses. Stephen shared his daughter's confidence, ignored the moderate score in Latin, and suggested Alla also try Greek. He confided to a friend, "What Alla will do in life, time alone can tell, but in the absence of genius we mean as far as practicable, to supply its place with education." Alla proved both parents wrong, as she soared academically at Vassar, proving herself the highest Latin scholar in her year.[159]

Having been disappointed during her youth when Abby and Stephen could not attend school events, Alla also regretted that they did not visit the campus during the four years she resided there. Founder's Day 1869, celebrated on Matthew Vassar's birthday, left such a lasting impression that she sent her parents a program. Never before exposed to performances like those presented, Alla's descriptions demonstrate a refreshing naiveté. To her, the elaborate preparations reflected a perfect combination of celebration and solemnity. The students' abilities to "deliver their orations without even a note" astounded Alla, who wrote home, "It was very fine and would put to shame many, even most of the graduates of the boys' college [Yale]." Founders Day concluded with exercises in the dining room, followed by students "entertaining their guests—those who were fortunate to have them—in the parlors and corridors." Alla closed in a softer tone, reassuring her mother, "Some of the girls were dressed beautifully. I felt very comfortable in my white alpaca." [160]

Alla shared many other activities with her mother in the weekly letters they exchanged. She knew Abby showed them to Stephen, who wrote less often. On the rare occasions that Alla was sick, she reported it to her parents. During her second winter, in 1870, she fretted to Abby, "I am not very well." To treat her cold, she followed the Graham diet and health regimen. "I have starved," she reported, "according to the most approved style, till I was hardly able to walk my half hour today." She had not got up until 9 that morning and then took a hot bath. "I presume I shall feel brighter tomorrow." Abby wrote back as soon as she learned about Alla's illness: "We had a little anxiety, lest the cold, which gave you the headache, might make you sick." She prayed that Alla would keep them informed about any sickness she had because "we are less anxious while hopefully posted than when left in doubt."[161]

Mother and daughter had not lived apart since Alla was an adolescent, so these were the first letters they exchanged since reaching this significant point. In them we see evidence of the unique relationship all moms and daughters in this study shared. They discussed topics that neither woman was comfortable discussing with other women. Simple gossip filled their letters: who was engaged, had a baby, lost a spouse, or became divorced.

Perhaps more surprising, but certainly practical, was the concentration on wardrobes. In an era when young women knew how to sew their own clothing but could often afford seamstresses to handle that chore, Abby and Alla reflected the contemporary conversation between mother and daughter. Abby, knowing that Alla needed a decent silk dress to get her through the season, offered to either cut down her own best dress for her daughter or bring Alla fabric and a pattern from the *Worcester Spy*, so she could make her frock during spring break. Abby, in need of a dress for the next series of conventions, planned to refresh an old frock with a new silk basque. Weather was a constant factor. In March, Abby planned to reconstitute a grenadine (a silk dress covered by a gauzy material) for May but worried that it would be too warm. She could rip up an old silk, which would cost "but little difference" from a new dress, and use it to wear under a shawl at home, or into the city or to other places where the waist would be covered. [162]

Alla also discussed school assignments, including a paper she wrote on Chaucer, delightful experiments on natural philosophy, and her German studies. She frankly admitted that she was not yet worldly prepared for many. In February of Alla's second year, a teacher gave her a composition subject titled "The Signs of the Times." Alla liked the topic, but thought it is "too comprehensive for me, with my little reading and meagre knowledge of the great outside world." [163]

Alla also kept abreast of the causes her mother supported. She shared Abby's elation when the Fifteenth Amendment was ratified in March 1870, giving black men (but not freed or native women) the vote. Alla understood that the victory was somewhat bittersweet, however, because it meant the organization to which Abby had devoted her life, the American Antislavery Society, would now dissolve after 35 years. At least one historian calls this period, begun when the Fifteenth Amendment passed, a "turning point in Abby's life." Her mother lost no time "in useless repining over the inevitable," according to Alla. She kept the fate of freed men and women as an objective, but transferred most of her energy to women's rights. Alla was more enthusiastic about woman suffrage than the plight of formerly enslaved peoples. At least once she asked if a prospective husband of a friend "was on the right side of woman suffrage, i.e. our side." [164]

When Alla was much younger, Abby had hinted about her becoming involved in reform, especially antislavery, work. She closely watched her at school to detect any participation in campus controversies. During the fall of Alla's third year, a cause erupted that Abby thought might fire her daughter up. The Vassar faculty abruptly canceled a spring vacation day it had included in its original calendar, inconveniencing many students. Alla told her parents that she believed the school should restore the vacation, keeping their promise for a break. "Do you think it is the best course for people to lie?" Alla asked Abby. "[The President] might have asked us if we were willing to give up the day but to take it from us was to take away all respect for the authorities. They might violate any other pledge in the catalogue after that procedure."[165]

When a few students withdrew over the incident, Alla found their actions extreme, but Abby supported them. "You thought very little would be gained for students' rights by a small number leaving the college because of its oppression," Abby wrote Alla. "We think you entirely mistaken." If even only one student had left for a worthy cause and then published the reasons in a "good respectable journal," Abby believed a "radical change" might result. Abby did not let the case rest, promising to discuss it the next time she was with Alla in the hope she could persuade her daughter to be more of an activist when it came to her future rights.[166]

Other issues incensed Alla far more than the missed vacation day. During that same winter of her third year, Hannah Lyman, the lady principal, whom Alla and her classmates knew but did not especially like, died after a four-week illness. When the president insisted the students wear a crepe badge for 30 days, Alla refused, although she "was glad to honor her memory by helping to purchase flowers with which to adorn her dust." Abby must have been proud of Alla when her daughter wrote, "I do not bow to the decision of the majority."[167]

Still, Alla preferred intellectual dissent to activist protest. As a classics major, she was exposed to a plethora of new ideas, many of which she eagerly shared with her parents. Just a week after the vacations incident, Alla reported how a historical novel about the Spanish Inquisition "haunted" her. "How thankful we ought to be that the world has become more enlightened," she wrote Abby, displaying a naïveté that her abolitionist mother forgave. "It does seem as if humanity were growing more like the divine author," Alla remarked, since slavery was not quite but "almost wiped away from the face of the earth." In the past, such "organized wickedness was sanctioned by the state and blessed by the church." It was enough to "make me a misanthrope to think of all the horrible crimes that have been committed under the cloak of the church and in the name of the 'Prince of Peace.'"[168]

Perhaps her optimism prevented Alla from deeply engaging in fights against injustice or explained why she avoided conflict. During her second year at Vassar, she wrote Abby, "I am so proud of you and father, that you are both so devoted, according to your strength, to all the reforms." Alla knew that she could not do the same and prayed that she "would never be tested" as they were. "I think I could not stand the trial," she wrote, "but should be found wanting." Abby might have encouraged Alla to work for freed peoples, but she recognized her daughter's warning not to suggest it when she wrote, "I am sure that I shall never do anything half so useful [as her parents].'" She excused herself, noting that "the children of good and great people are apt to [be] ugly or forceless, and I think you and I should be thankful that I am not any worse."[169]

College graduation gave Abby and Stephen myriad reasons to take pride in Alla, who graduated on a "misty, moisty morning" in June 1872, among "twenty-eight damsels" in Vassar's third commencement class. Now 25, she had faltered at the beginning but proved to be a superior student and claimed first place in the program as the "Oratorio Salutatorio." Besides delivering the Latin oration, Alla received a Phi Beta Kappa stole and key from the first female college to bestow this honor on its students. Abby and Stephen, on their only trip to her campus in four years, sat proudly in the audience that watched Alla receive her Bachelor of Arts diploma and take her esteemed place among only four other student speakers. [170]

Alla Foster: Teaching the Young How to Learn and Abby How to Live, 1873–1887

With a degree in hand, Abby was off to Cornell for yet more education. Her parents had kept very busy with reform work during Alla's time at Vassar but treasured her visits home. Now she seemed to be designing a life far different from that of her mother or father. She spent the summer in Worcester but was admitted to Cornell University's graduate school that fall, where she was enrolled in the Master of History department. Abby and Stephen continued to scrutinize her studies, as during her college years. That fall, shortly after she completed her first term at Cornell, Stephen, having read in the newspaper that Cornell women were lagging behind their male classmates, asked the college to send him Alla's grades. He was satisfied to learn that she had a 4.25 average (out of 5) for the first semester. Alla easily proved that she was equal to the work and concluded her courses in June. She could not afford to remain on campus to write her thesis or pay graduate fees, however, so she moved back home to finish her master's while she earned some money. [171]

In September 1873, Alla accepted a position at nearby Worcester High School, which had recently begun to admit girls, joining the large group of women who chose teaching as a profession during that time period. Women who graduated from college in the late 19th and early 20th centuries entered a new world of possibilities unknown to—but made possible by—their mothers. Historians categorize a certain portion of them as New Women, a term popularized by the novelist Henry James in the 1890s. New Women, born between the late 1850s and 1900, were unique, a cadre of typically white, middle- or upper-middle-class women who were almost all professionally trained. Progressive attitudes drew them to intellectual or service sectors, where they primarily chose careers in the public and caregiving segments of the economy; education being a popular choice.

Alla Foster, c. 1870
(From the Collection of Worcester Historical Museum, Worcester, Mass.)

Like other New Women, Alla inherited what one historian calls "a consciousness of women's new role possibilities almost as their birthright." In order to live the socially autonomous lives that their mothers had hoped they would pursue through college education, young women left their mothers' hearth to create their own households. Like her New Women contemporaries, throughout her adult life, Alla maintained contact with former college peers and remained involved with her alma mater. In an article praising notable Vassar graduates, the Association of Collegiate Alumnae described Alla as "a child of stern reformers who was saved from a like fate by her vivid common sense and pungent wit." [172]

Living with Abby and Stephen, Alla was thus thrown into the "fate" of her activist parents and challenged to practice that "pungent wit." Alla, who thrived on stability, should have remembered what it was like to live with her radical parents. She must not have been surprised when they launched a war with the city of Worcester over their property taxes the fall Alla began to teach in Worcester. The battle resembled one that Lucy Stone fought a few years later. Alla endorsed the first steps of her parents' unwavering position, even acting as secretary to the association they formed, but she backed off when they persisted. Perhaps she feared losing her job as a teacher, but her earlier letters imply a different reason—she did not possess, nor did she want to possess, her parents' audacity.[173]

Alla eventually managed to fulfill her dream of teaching and living independently from her parents, maintaining her own home and practicing the domestic skills Abby had taught her, giving her hope for advancement as well as independence. In 1875, at age 28, she moved to Cincinnati, where she accepted a teaching position at what Abby called a Young Ladies' School. Abby, who had left Alla for most of her childhood, now found her daughter's departure unbearable: "It was like plucking out right eyes for us to let her go."[174] However, Abby and other reform mothers knew that their efforts had contributed to the advantages of their reform daughters, while still fighting for more of their rights, especially that of suffrage.

Abby resembled other contemporary mothers of college graduates, who respected their daughters' academic achievements and did "not impede their aspirations." They rarely worried about marriage, but strongly encouraged them to expand their horizons. Mothers "regarded professional or graduate training in the same light as they had undergraduate study—as a substantial investment and a significant choice." Reform mothers probably recognized paid work as a vehicle through which young women could assert their influence, emotionally and practically, in ways the mothers never experienced. Such work "became a further step in validating the desire to hold a job after college." It also kept graduates like Alla in the workforce and "testing themselves," for education had opened up their world to a variety of opportunities. Eventually, Abby and Stephen not only accepted Alla's independence, but they also welcomed her financial help.[175] One historian counted Alla among the women "whose mothers' achievements only spurred the daughters' determination to create radically different roles for themselves." [176]

Like other New Women, Alla joined women's clubs, educational and industrial unions, and cultural groups. She spent her leisure time attending concerts and lectures, visiting museums, and enjoying the occasional women's suffrage parlor gathering. She forged strong friendships that nourished and inspired her for decades. Besides having access to a superb education, Alla worked and traveled and lived wherever she could afford, independent of her parents, except for the two years she was forced to return home.[177]

Resigned to Alla's move and career, her parents tried not to interfere in their daughter's life, but tragic circumstances intervened. In 1876, at the age of 67, Stephen suffered a paralytic stroke that left him nearly helpless. Alla's parents begged her to come home and help. They also ended their four-year struggle with the city of Worcester over unpaid taxes because it was "too heavy a drain on [Abby's] strength and sympathies." With Alla's help they paid a $2,400 settlement in order to keep their house. Now, Abby directed all her attention to Stephen, whom she described as "more to her than her own soul." [178]

The year 1876 began a new phase for Alla, who was now 29. Having completed her Masters Thesis and earned her degree from Cornell, she had elevated her credentials for a teaching job. She moved back east and accepted an assignment at the Roxbury High School in a suburb of Boston. Her proximity to home and her parents' needs drew Alla into the role of serving as one of the "suffrage daughters," who cared for their aging women's rights parents and tried to keep their achievements alive.[179]

Alla lived in Boston but traveled frequently to Worcester, then out to nearby communities to fulfill her duties as her parents' representative in a world from which they were forced to retire. She served as Abby's envoy at forums, bazaars, and myriad meetings, while also standing in for Stephen, attending funerals and memorials in his place. These services and her father's precarious condition made Alla encourage him to see old friends before they—or he—died. One by one, the abolitionists were dying: Martha Wright in 1875; Helen Garrison in 1876; Angelina Grimke and William Lloyd Garrison in 1879; and Maria Child and Lucretia Mott in 1880. Wendell Phillips told Abby, "We are going away, all of us and I rejoice that I was one with you in your work."[180]

Alla welcomed visitors to the farm, eager to learn more about her parents' roles as reformers. One day, when Abby and Stephen were still strong enough to share memories about their work, William H. Channing, an abolitionist friend, visited. "Sit down with your daughter," he implored them in Alla's presence, "and tell the stories just as they suggest themselves to preserve your testimony to the grand historic import of the antislavery movement." Channing said that the resulting book would provide a unique record of what he called Puritan and Quaker convictions. The telling would leave Abby and Stephen overjoyed as they recalled the "glory and beauty" of their past. William Channing's suggestion about memorializing her parents intrigued Alla and Stephen, but Abby was less enthusiastic, and it was never even begun.[181]

On a memorable afternoon two years later, in the summer of 1879, Lucy Stone came to the farm, where she and Stephen planned a gathering on women voting in school elections. Stephen invited Alla to join them, ostensibly to take notes but more likely to tend to his many personal needs. Lucy realized how much Stephen relied on his daughter and Abby. Lucy was heartsick to see Stephen looking so old and ill, a "miserable wreck" of a man. [182]

It was difficult for Alla to preserve their lives for history when neither parent was willing to help. Abby rejected the task of writing her memoir because she saw it as a self-centered project that would merely glorify her legacy and feed the public's desire for private details. Her biographer notes that Abby always avoided personal promotion and had even refused to sit for photographs or have her daughter photographed. The last time she had consented was in 1855, and then only because Alla and Stephen wanted to have an image to remember her during long absences. Now Abby insisted that the Fosters' contribution to reform was their labor in the field rather than a story about it. Once they couldn't fight the battles, Abby had no desire to tell others how they had done it.[183]

But Alla was learning about Stephen through their many hours together. He drew her into stories of his career in antislavery and women's rights causes. She took him for rides, wrote his letters, and entertained him, watching as he became an invalid confined to his chair. Once a giant of a man, he now relied on his family for care. When Stephen realized that his ability to "better the condition of humanity" had waned, "his agony was intense." As her father neared death, Alla saw the depths of his troubled soul. She told a friend that he questioned immortality; nevertheless, he "longed to end this life of suffering, even if his spirit were to be annihilated."[184] Stephen held on for another excruciating year, dependent entirely on his daughter and wife. He never found the energy or the will to record a single sentence about his life, but Abby would attempt to a few years later.

At dawn on September 8, 1881, the old abolitionist warrior died at the age of 72. Abby and Alla complied with Stephen's wish that no funeral be held. Instead, they sent postal cards to relatives and friends, inviting them to a simple memorial service a fortnight after they buried him. The event, held in Worcester's Horticultural Hall, paid him the kind of tribute he would have appreciated. Alla placed a life-sized portrait of him, wreathed with ivy on the right side of a speaking platform and a large basket of flowers on the left. The women held center stage: two of Abby's sisters and four of

Stephen's siblings accompanying Abby and Alla. Attendees included Wendell Phillips, William Lloyd Garrison, Jr., and Lucy Stone, who delivered one of the eulogies. "He was our advisor and reprover," she insisted. "He reproved what he called our timidity. He had asked, 'Why don't you fight for your rights in the way your opponents ought to be fought?'" Lucy also lauded his marriage, which "demonstrated the possibility of a partnership of equals, neither affirming mastership, never a thought of superiority or dictation or control."[185]

Alla's extensive time with her parents reinforced her impressions about their mark on society, but it did not tempt her to join activist forces for women's rights. What she never failed to do was to respond to their needs. Abby Kelley Foster's health seriously declined over the course of the decade she lived after Stephen's death. "The scabbard of her body was almost outworn, inadequate for the keen and active brain that filled it," Will Garrison remarked at Stephen Foster's funeral in 1881, six years before Abby's death. Losing Stephen had left Abby "lonesome and saddened," but if her own health had been better, she might have resumed activist work in his memory. At 70, she endured the residual effects from her stomach surgery 13 years earlier, exacerbated by decades on the road. Abby now suffered from a previous ailment, catarrh—similar to chronic bronchitis—which rattled her breathing. Alla knew that her mother could no longer remain alone in the big, empty farmhouse on Mower Street in Worcester. [186]

For more than 30 years, Abby and Stephen had coaxed the barren acreage they still called the Cook Farm into fertility, battling drought and poor soil at home and injustice in the wider world. They had made a wise choice when they purchased the farm in 1847 and invested any extra money toward its improvement. All through Alla's youth, Abby had taught her daughter husbandry skills, along with many more important lessons. She showed her daughter how to be financially secure even on a low income. After they repaid disputed taxes, Abby sold a few acres and outbuildings. She obtained twice the $8,061 they had originally spent for the property and combined it with other savings to ensure herself an annual income of $500.[187] Abby's investments inspired Alla at age 35 to manage and invest her own money, whether she married or remained single.

Not only did this knowledge comfort Alla, it inspired her to learn from Abby how to be independent. Women had the responsibility, whether they lived with loved ones or alone, to manage and invest their money wisely with an eye to the future.

Abby persuaded the purchaser of the Foster farm to give her nearly two years to clear out her possessions. On many Saturdays in the late summer and early fall of 1883, Alla and Abby met in the attic, where they sifted through the remnants of Abby and Stephen's lives. They donated volumes of antislavery newspapers to various editors and libraries, and anti-slavery letters to the American Antiquarian Society (which still holds them as of 2020). Abby discarded some photos and adorned her new parlor with others. [188]

By the fall of 1883, mother and daughter had embarked on new, separate lives. Alla, having left her teaching job in Roxbury, relocated to downtown Boston, where she settled close to her employer, the Boston Girls' High School. At 36, she had already lived at four different addresses in the Boston area and had a clear idea of how she wanted to furnish her apartment. She became a discriminating decorator, rejecting most of Abby's offerings and advice but keeping a few of her parents' things for nostalgia: a chaise camp lounge, a desk, and a favorite painting. She boasted to Abby that she had purchased a cherry table that resembled one in Shakespeare's house at Stratford and that she was having a little bookcase made of cherry as well. Her landlord had promised her a comfortable easy chair that, with the camp chaise, would supply seating for three. Alla created a world in her own home, opened her life to new acquaintances, and launched a solid career. [189]

Living in the heart of Boston, Alla occasionally spent time with other reform daughters. Alice Stone Blackwell, editor of the *Woman's Journal*, crossed her path and the two shared at least a few excursions with other like-minded women. Alla, despite her full teaching load and copious papers to mark, spent more evenings in sociability than alone. To Alla's joy, one of her previous teaching friends from Roxbury had joined the new school before she had. She assured Abby that "the teachers are cordial, most of them, and the girls are usually well-disposed." Alla tried to respond socially when people from the reform world insisted, attending a woman suffrage fair in a friend's parlor that resembled those her mother had sponsored for the antislavery cause when she was a child. She appeared at a reception given for William Lloyd Garrison by his son, Frank, and reported to Abby, "Everybody I meet inquires very interestedly for you."[190]

Alla assumed a new role, acting rather as her mother's parent than her child. Abby moved into the boardinghouse owned by her younger sister, Lucy Barton, five miles from the Worcester farm. There she learned how to live as a widow, confined to a few small rooms, with limited mobility and a shrinking group of friends. Over the next few years, Lucy complained to Alla about her mother's behavior, however. Boarders objected that Abby was using a spit box in the common sitting room and washing her teeth in public. Alla, well accustomed to sharing living space with her mother, suggested, "In short, I find it safer, in boarding, to do all the business of my life in my own room with my door shut." She seemed to realize that her mother might perceive this as an insult because she closed the letter, "Much love (though you doubt it), Alla."[191]

If Abby resented her daughter's copious advice, she did not express it. In subsequent letters, Alla continued to make suggestions. Now that Abby was "entirely at leisure to read and had ample time to indulge in it," she noted that it was "a great pity" that her failing eyesight prevented it. Alla suggested that her mother take up knitting, which was easier on the eyes if she performed familiar patterns. "If you can knit without getting tired," Alla wrote, "that will be a good occupation." She offered several ideas for items to knit for family members. "So you see that work in abundance awaits you, should you find the occupation agreeable," suggested Alla.[192]

Abby seemed to devour, not begrudge, Alla's suggestions, perhaps because they were offered in a gentle tone. When Abby suffered from a cold, Alla suggested she gargle with very hot water, which might also help her catarrh. At age 72, Abby welcomed her daughter's suggestions about a food supplement, asked her to purchase it in Boston, and repaid her. When Abby complained of lethargy, Alla blamed it on a current lack of fresh air and on her having breathed impure air in the farmhouse for the past 20 years. "If you had given as much attention to health as to reform," scolded Alla, "it might have been better for your bodies if not for your souls." She reminded Abby that her father had been indifferent to sanitation laws, even though her mother had been interested in them. Abby assured her daughter that she did go outside for fresh air, usually in carriage rides. Alla realized that their old house was not suitably ventilated, the cellar inadequately cemented, and the plumbing failed to "trap" unhealthy gases from the house.[193]

Alla had further reason to worry about her mother when, in 1883, Abby began to fret about her memory. Abby confessed that she was frightened when she entered a "state like being half way between sleeping and waking." She told Alla, "I think this condition grows in me. I hope it is not leading to the condition I have all along feared and dreaded [senility]." The next summer, Abby repeated her concerns about her memory, but retold accounts of visits and visitors with accuracy. But she noted that "such a flickering brain is very trying." In the very next paragraph, Abby discussed a speaker at a recent convention with such clear understanding that Abby's mind seemed superior to most.[194]

Abby's physical ailments worsened. In the spring of 1884, she wrenched her back while climbing down from a carriage. "The soreness is deep into the muscle and is not yet entirely removed," she wrote, but what was worse was that her "system was so low that a slight bruise could last for weeks." She didn't trust her weakened body and "lack of firm mind" and so was reluctant to leave home or to "undertake to do anything." She ventured one final attempt at writing, penning an essay about William Lloyd Garrison, which she abandoned and which she blamed for a "dreadful attack of catarrh." "I cannot convince you of the labor and dreadful excitement it cost me," Abby told Alla. She doubted if Lucy Stone would publish it, so asked Alla to save it for another paper.[195]

Considering Abby's physical and mental state, it was remarkable that she experienced two resurgences of energy before her death. The first startled Alla—her mother accepted an invitation from Lucy Stone to attend a July 4th picnic at Lucy's Boston home, Pope's Hill. Lucy had determined to gather together all the old abolitionists while they were still alive. Abby, now 75, told Alla, "I came to the conclusion that the 'outing' would be good for my nerves."[196]

Lucy and husband Henry had hosted many relatives at Pope's Hill, but this gathering of nearly 20 acquaintances was historic. Many had not seen one another for decades. They had been active mostly during the 1840s and 1850s when they fought to end slavery. Since the Civil War, the gathered group had worked individually for freed people or for woman's suffrage but had never reunited. Alla, at ease in the midst of people she had met during her childhood, knew the special places these pioneers and their children held in Abby's heart.

The day of the picnic was capped with a fine meal, after which Lucy invited her guests to pose for a photograph. Abby, who hated photographs, was nevertheless gracious. She moved to the top step of the porch, placing herself in the back row where she might be less noticeable. As it happened, even though she wore a new dress that she thought was drab, her light shawl and central position made her stand out among her friends' dull costumes. Alla posed as straight as her body allowed, her high cheekbones, regular features, and clear eyes resembling Abby's. People called her pretty, but she hid this in a slight frown and looked away. At 40, Alla was the youngest woman present that day and the only reform daughter who had not yet taken up a public role in any reform movement. She stood at Abby's right shoulder, comfortable in the shadow of her mother. It is the only surviving photograph in which Abby and Alla appear together.

Abby's second excursion was with Alla to the White Mountains in New Hampshire, which would inspire a future home and investment for her daughter. Abby felt so well when she returned home that she began to write a portrayal of Stephen's life for the next edition of the National Cyclopedia of American Biography. The chore became an obsession as months wore

Abolitionist Picnic, July 1886 at Home of Lucy Stone and Henry Blackwell
(Sophia Smith Collection, Smith College)

on. Abby struggled over the perfect words to describe her husband. She finally borrowed from other pieces on Stephen and completed a brief essay. On January 13, 1887, Abby sent for a courier to send her essay on Stephen to the post office. For the rest of that day, exhaustion confined Abby to her bed. She ate some porridge but never dressed.

By the next morning, Abby's condition had not improved. Her sister Lucy telegraphed Alla to come to her mother's bedside. Alla rushed from her school in Boston, but the train did not arrive until late afternoon. When she entered her mother's darkened room, Abby opened her eyes. Then she gazed at Alla, smiled, and quietly closed them for the last time. She was a day short of 76.[197]

Alla knew as little about her mother's religious beliefs as she had about her father's. It was apparent that by the end of Abby's life, some kind of spiritualism had become a part of her very being and had given her a calmness and peace that "enabled her to live or die with equal resignation." Abby had long ago given up believing in a personal God. She substituted the Good, or what she had told Alla as a child, "the great first cause," for God. The Good was "a good name answering to our Christian idea of its omnipotence, omnipresence, omniscience and all beneficence." Abby believed, "we shall grow more like Him and know Him more and more." Alla knew that her mother was sure of "this continued existence" because Abby believed that a "life of labor, not of rest, could help people develop spiritual and intellectual powers."[198]

Alla arranged a private funeral service at Abby's boardinghouse for relatives and close friends. She served not as a public speaker but as a gracious daughter—comforter, competent hostess, and loving friend.[199]

Lucy Stone eulogized Abby perfectly, just as she had extolled Stephen:

> The world of women owe[s] her a debt which they can never pay. The movement for the equal rights of women began directly and emphatically with her. Other women had spoken in public but it was left for Abby Kelley to take on her young shoulders and to bear

a double burden, for the slave's freedom, and for equal rights for women. She who fought this dreadful battle is now at rest. She had no peer, and she leaves no successor.[200]

Alla inherited admirable qualities from Abby, but neither Abby nor anyone at her funeral expected that Alla would carry on her mother's work.[201] Alla devoted her life to teaching young women in the city of Boston—young women who were deprived of the privileges Alla had received. In her quiet way, Alla improved the lives of her students, in the classroom and outside it. In 1895, seven years after Abby died, Alla at age 48, was able to purchase Diamond Ledge in Center Sandwich, New Hampshire, which overlooked Squam Lake and the mountains and to which she welcomed friends in the summer. Alla eventually turned it into a lodge, where she employed promising female students from her school. It gave her great joy to nurture them, especially when they would otherwise have lacked educational opportunities. When Alla died in 1923 at the age of 76, she left the land and house to an African-American school in the South that Abby had told her about years before.[202]

Alla also worked for woman suffrage in a quiet way. Her lodge was in the town of Center Sandwich, New Hampshire, whose residents were described as "au courant" on every academic and scientific subject. Her ideals reflected what a local judge and her obituary called a "New England conscience incarnate," which was further illustrated by her founding of the town's "first socially conscious women's organization." Alla's leadership led to procuring the vote for women in Sandwich in 1903, 17 years before America ratified the Nineteenth Amendment.[203]

✳ ✳ ✳

Alla at 12 had spent fewer than two years of her life in the presence of her mother. Weaned at nine months, she was left to the care of others while Abby rejoined the antislavery movement that had long fired her furor. Abby missed Alla from the first parting, and the frequent and long separations never became easy. Had it been the 21st Century, Abby might have fought slavery from home, but in the 1840s she had to deliver her message in person. Alla's caretakers parented her well in Abby's absence. Indeed, the little girl seemed to bloom under their supervision and cope well with her mother's sporadic appearances. She cherished her farm, which provided not only a home but a place where she learned domestic and farming skills along with lessons in life. The arrangement seemed to bestow flexibility on Alla that gave her strength she needed. When Alla entered adolescence, she weathered a tax on her body that persisted for 10 years—a tax that strengthened the whole family and proved to Abby that she was perhaps a better mother than she thought. The bond this created between mother and daughter determined their relationship for the rest of their lives.

When she finally was the one to leave—for college—Alla exercised her independence with aplomb, relying on the domestic, academic, and financial tools her parents had provided. Truly a precocious student, she became a talented and devoted educator and mentor. Alla always endorsed her mother's causes but never pursued them with passion anywhere equal to that of Abby. Neither of them expected that Alla would follow in Abby's social footsteps. Gradually, mother and daughter reversed roles, subtly at first, but more and more noticeably as time and age advanced, as Abby grew to rely increasingly on Alla. Their ability to thrive in those new positions satisfied both women more than they could have imagined. Their long-distance relationship served them well no matter how close or far their separations.

A Dependence Denied

Elizabeth Cady Stanton and Harriot Stanton Blatch

Elizabeth Cady Stanton: Mothering Harriot Stanton with Ambivalence, 1856–1874

Elizabeth Cady Stanton faced the prospect of her sixth baby with misgivings. When Harriot Stanton was born on January 26, 1856, her mother and father, Henry Stanton, had been married for 15 years, the nine most recent of those spent living in Seneca Falls. Their family of five children ranged from 13-year-old Neil to 3-year-old Maggie. Elizabeth had learned how to survive in a small village, "irksome" and isolated compared to their previous "attractive" domestic life in bustling Boston. In Seneca Falls, Elizabeth lived outside of town, provided most of the family meals from raising cows, chickens, and fruits and vegetables, and relied less on markets than in Boston. Henry was rarely at home, working as a lawyer in Washington and New York, and she was in charge of all domestic arrangements, like clothing, medical needs, and education. She had "more than sufficient work to keep one brain busy, as well as all the hands I could press into service."[204]

Elizabeth, living in a home purchased by her father, tried to improve the situation as best she could. She hired Amelia Willard, a 16-year-old Quaker girl, and trained her to perform domestic skills the home required. Eventually, the family regarded Amelia as part of their household, persuading her to accompany them when they traveled to Elizabeth's mother in Johnstown for long visits and when they moved to New York City in the early 1860s. Amelia occasionally took vacations, an inconvenience to Elizabeth. But she was a devoted servant, who shared the family's interest in reform, wore bloomers, and later donated a sizeable sum from her savings to help underwrite one of Elizabeth's books. [205]

No matter how good her household help, Elizabeth had enormous responsibilities. She envied her husband's freedom, feeling "rebellious" when she saw him going where he pleased, when he pleased. In contrast, she, like most contemporary women, was held in "bondage" and forced to keep "all my noblest aspirations in abeyance."[206] Yet, for all her struggles and resentments, Elizabeth, like Martha Wright, took great satisfaction from her household and home.

Though she was initially worried that having a child at 41 would compromise her health, Elizabeth was thrilled with the birth of her second daughter, whom she dubbed "Hattie." She was "a nice baby, with plenty of dark brown hair, deep blue eyes, and a very rosy complexion," but Elizabeth was also "very happy that the terrible ordeal [was] passed and that the result [was] another daughter."[207] Just as she loved her five previous "excellent editions," Elizabeth was smitten by the sixth and realized that "it would not be in vain that Hattie held her back" from women's rights work.[208]

Elizabeth had always taken great pride in the power that motherhood presented. From her earliest months caring for children, she exerted her domestic authority and challenged the "expertise" of nurses and doctors over her own common sense. When they insisted that a baby be swaddled, she and Amelia, far more trusted than the professionals, unwound the strips of cloth that prevented movement. If nurses closed windows to keep out supposed evil substances, Elizabeth reopened them. When they suggested continuous feeding because an empty stomach caused colic and rickets, she kept an arsenal of herbal concoctions on hand and nursed on a schedule. Henry, who was not present for any of Elizabeth's births, joined the cadre of "experts" whom his wife ignored. He wrote and warned her "not to let the kiddies catch cold" or be exposed to cool breezes. He was especially

Elizabeth Cady Stanton and Harriot Stanton, 1856
(Library of Congress)

miffed when Elizabeth turned to homeopathic medical advice to treat the displaced collar bone of their oldest son. [209]

Elizabeth was happy with Harriot, but she wavered between joy and weariness during her daughter's early months. She told Susan B. Anthony, who had become a close friend in the past few years, "Day in and day out," she was "watching, bathing, nursing, and promenading the precious contents of a little crib in the corner of my room." Confined to two chambers "like a caged lion," she longed to end nursing and housekeeping cares, so that other work could proceed.[210]

During Harriot's second summer, when hot weather had "dried [Elizabeth] up," the 18-month-old baby was cutting teeth, sleeping poorly at night, and fussing during the day. Elizabeth expected visitors in August, when she was to be in charge of everything, from cooking roast beef to making dish soap because Amelia was away. The boys, who had a four-week vacation from boarding school, played pranks on her older daughter, Maggie, that complicated her life. The next year she turned to her mother for relief. She sent the younger Stanton children to Johnstown to stay with Grandmother Cady—something Harriot did not enjoy until she was older because she missed her mother. When Elizabeth came to fetch the girls after she had stayed away for weeks, lecturing or attending meetings, 6-year-old Maggie greeted her with hugs and kisses. In her memoir, Harriot recalled that, even though she was only 3, she "shyly edged toward [my mother], slipped into her lap, buried my face in her bosom, and wept as if my heart would break." This was a rare expression of feeling, for Harriot resembled her mother in hiding emotions.[211]

As Elizabeth's domestic responsibilities expanded, she increasingly appreciated relationships with other women reformers. During the Seneca Falls Convention of 1848, she planted seeds for a sisterhood that would nurture them for decades. During the winter of 1851, she welcomed Abby Kelley Foster, for "now and always," but apologized for missing her talk on antislavery because she currently "was subjected to a biennial clumsiness (pregnant with Maggie)." Martha Wright, a short train ride away in Auburn, shared afternoons with Elizabeth during which they prepared petitions for the state legislature and assigned their delivery, depending on which woman was not pregnant. "We all fell in love with Mrs. Stanton," Martha told Lucretia Mott, "a woman who talks sensibly." Elizabeth's "merry twinkle of her eye and her genuine hearty laugh would cure a misanthrope."[212]

Her door was always open to her cousin, Elizabeth Smith Miller, who brought the bloomer style to America from Europe. Both women befriended another mother, Amelia Bloomer, who lived in Seneca Falls and edited the temperance paper, *The Lily*. Her promotion of bloomer pants earned Amelia the honor of becoming their namesake. Elizabeth embraced the style of bloomer pants long before most of her associates, much to the embarrassment of her sons at boarding school. She wore them in the streets of Seneca Falls, scandalizing some townsfolk.[213]

If we can believe the artist who depicted Elizabeth's first meeting with Susan B. Anthony in a sculpture on the bridge over the Seneca Falls canal, she was sporting bloomers. Amelia Bloomer introduced the short woman with curly blond hair sporting pants to a tall, thin Quaker clad in gray with a bun anchored to the nape of her neck. It was during the spring of 1851, when Susan was staying at Amelia's home on her way back from a Syracuse meeting. They had heard of each other but had never met, nor attended the same events. Elizabeth later regretted not asking Susan home for dinner, "a neglect for which Susan has never forgiven me because she wished to see and hear all she could of our noble friends."[214] Dinner notwithstanding, Susan and Elizabeth quickly connected on their work in temperance, antislavery, and women's rights—a connection upon which they built a lasting friendship.

Within a few years, Susan and Elizabeth had forged a strong bond and working relationship. As a single woman, Susan had the freedom to travel extensively, while Elizabeth spent most her time writing articles from home, some for Susan, and sending letters to the many conventions she missed. The reformers, some not married or mothers yet, gathered at these conventions and developed a sisterhood that gravitated around Susan, and included Abby Kelley Foster, Martha Wright, Lucy Stone, Antoinette (Nettie) Brown, and eventually Elizabeth Cady Stanton.

As more women married, Susan felt abandoned. When Lucy Stone became engaged to Henry Blackwell in 1855, and Nettie Brown to his brother, Sam Blackwell in 1856, Susan resented her friends and called both women "little dunce[s]." Lucy kept her good humor, telling Susan that she should not criticize married women. If Susan married, she would find that "there is just as much of you as before." Lucy argued, "Suffrage is sure to come to women, God will wait for it, and so may you." She thought a husband might be "a great blessing" to Susan, as it had been to her. Lucy wished Henry Blackwell had a third brother for Susan. "Would we not have a grand household then?" she asked.[215] Susan was not swayed.

In the mid-1850s, Susan complained that the movement was suffering from a "rough and poor time." Lucy called her "a little naughty thing, to feel that you are left alone," as well as "a wretch" to ever "intimate that we are nothing now." After Nettie married Sam Blackwell in Cincinnati, she promised Susan that she would try to travel east to lecture but reminded her that it was more important "to be a good wife and go where my husband does." Alice Stone Blackwell, reflecting on her mother's memories years later, said, "Miss Anthony did not like to have the suffrage lecturers fall in love and marry."[216]

If Susan felt deserted when her friends married, she felt even more agitated when they had "given themselves over to baby making, and left poor brainless me to battle alone." From 1856 to 1857, Elizabeth gave birth to Harriot, Lucy gave birth to Alice, and Nettie gave birth to Florence, the first of her five daughters. "Now don't feel angry," Lucy wrote Susan. Anticipating Susan's anger, Elizabeth warned her, "let [Lucy and Nettie] rest awhile in peace and quietness and think great thoughts for the future." It was not good for any of them to be "in the excitement of public life all the time." Susan should not "keep stirring them up or mourning over their repose," but learn how to treasure her private time, work within the domestic sphere, and give mothers the dignity they had earned. "Womankind owes Lucy and Nettie a debt of gratitude for their faithful labors in the past," Elizabeth told Susan. "Let the world alone awhile. We cannot bring about a moral revolution in a day or year." Now that she had two daughters,

Elizabeth felt "fresh strength to work," but she first needed to enjoy her children.[217]

These reform mothers stayed home and cared for their babies for a few years, but they did not abandon abolition or women's rights totally. Elizabeth told Susan that in "two or three years," Harriot, her "last baby," would be old enough and she would have more time. By then her older boys would be in college or engaged in business and the three younger children would be in school. Since Susan and she would not be in their prime before 50, they had "a prospect of a good long life, twenty years at least." Susan must have courage and patience.[218]

Susan softened, though she confessed to Lucy that she had "very weak moments" and that she longed to "lay my weary head somewhere and nestle my full soul close to that of another in full sympathy." Susan wrote similar thoughts to Elizabeth, unsure how she could wait two or three years before Mrs. Stanton would join her on the "great battle field." While Susan understood the role of mothers, despite her complaints, she never failed to acknowledge the children of her friends. She was delighted when Nettie brought "darling baby Florence" to see her in Rochester. And when Nettie lost her second daughter, Mabel, at age 3, no one expressed more sorrow than Susan. She never failed to close her letters to Elizabeth with "a kiss for Maggie and Hattie and a kindly word for the boys."[219]

But Elizabeth, like Martha Wright a decade earlier, was once more surprised by a pregnancy. She found herself "with prospects" in 1859, and she had trouble mustering enthusiasm. Bob, the last and largest baby, was born at 12 and one-quarter pounds—Elizabeth's "grand specimen." She had come "through the siege once more." Just under 45 years old, she did not recover well, was unable to sleep, felt uncomfortable even when awake, and for days could hardly walk across the room.[220]

Their mother's fortitude must have impressed those Stanton children still at home in her care. Bob's birth coincided with a new resolve of Elizabeth's to spend more time lecturing, leaving the girls and baby at home, and teaching them all resiliency. Once when Elizabeth was away, Harriot injured her back in a serious fall. Her nursemaid, afraid of Elizabeth's scolding, persuaded Harriot not to tell. Over the next year, the little girl developed a chronic backache and a reoccurring nightmare about a woman "whose spine was frozen because she ate too much ice cream." Elizabeth questioned her daughter, learned the truth, and procured the medical treatment Harriot required. She encouraged her daughter to find the happy balance between fussing over small injuries and large but to always speak the truth.[221]

Henry Stanton did not approve of Elizabeth's efforts to instill courage in her daughters. He thought his sons' play was too rambunctious for the girls. Harriot, with Elizabeth's blessings, relished her brothers' antics and took vicarious pleasure watching them. One day, the children were playing in the field, which covered some 10 acres. The three older boys climbed two large cherry trees near the house and brought down luscious fruit to their younger siblings. Eventually Harriot, probably 5 or 6, joined the climbing. Henry saw his daughter high in a tree and shouted, "My daughter, come down, you will fall." Poised with confidence on the branch, Harriot retorted, "Why don't you tell Bob to come down, he's three years younger and one branch higher?"[222] Maybe Harriot thought that, like her mother, if she acted as if she could do more from her position of supposed weakness than even those perched on a higher branch, and of a different sex, you can convince your father and you can convince the world.

Elizabeth Cady Stanton spent the next few years in Seneca Falls trying to convince the world how central women were, to fight slavery and to fight it through war. After she experienced the violence of the New York speaking tour in the winter of 1861, she was ready for battle. "War is music to my ears," she told Frances Seward. "It is a simultaneous chorus for freedom." While Susan B. Anthony called war a setback for [white] women, Elizabeth insisted that if women aided the war effort wholeheartedly, the nation would reward their efforts with equal citizenship and suffrage; the emancipation of the slaves would open the way for great advances in women's rights.[223]

Some assumed that the Stantons' first and second sons had enlisted to fight for the North, but neither Neil nor Kit, eligible for the draft, actually entered military service. Elizabeth wrote William Seward seeking to enroll the third son, Gattie, in a scientific military program at West Point, but this never happened. Neil joined his father's staff at the Customs House as a clerk. By January 1862, Kit and Gattie were "under their mother's wing, never spend[ing] an evening from home and in bed at ten o'clock." Wherever her sons resided during the war, when other mothers mentioned their children's military service, Elizabeth remained silent.[224]

Besides shaping Elizabeth's politics and passions, in 1862, war moved her family from Seneca Falls to New York City, where Susan B. Anthony often shared the Stanton apartment. By March 1863, stories of battles won and battles lost seemed to be burying the war's principal aim, which, in their view, was to emancipate the slaves. In the absence of women's rights meetings, which were suspended for the duration of the war, leaders sought a vehicle to showcase their unique antislavery contributions. They looked for a strategy to reclaim women's voices and remind the country what they should be fighting for. Although reform mothers and daughters did not always agree on the war, they were unified by a vital pursuit. They organized the National Loyal Women's War League, whose goal it would be to petition for emancipation.

Susan and Elizabeth called upon Lucy Stone to emerge from semi-retirement and preside at the League's initial gathering in May 1863. She accepted, and the assembly elected her as president. The campaign drive rejuvenated the reform mothers' sense of sisterhood and went on to involve some of their daughters. They set up an office in New York, close enough to the Stanton apartment that their sons and Harriot, now 7, could help with clerical work and small tasks. Lucy worked in the New York office for two weeks, then returned to Massachusetts and gathered signatures. At home with a fragile Alice, she needed to work in a place where she had "fewer cares and nothing to vex" her.[225] Abby Kelley Foster joined the effort later that fall.

One of the most effective tools women had used throughout the 19th Century was the petition, which was the only "voice" they had. Reformers became adept at visiting women at home to persuade them and their neighbors to sign a paper. They had done so to endorse the Sabbath, to invoke temperance, and to achieve women's rights. Placing pen to paper in favor of emancipation and sending petitions to Congress on behalf of the League demonstrated that antislavery sentiment would convince the North to continue fighting—for emancipation as well as for the Union. It was an activity that women could do from and in their domestic sphere. The organization drew new, undeveloped skills from reform mothers—and daughters—that moved them out of the convention to networking among friends and relatives. Ellen Wright insisted that she and Martha join the effort of petitioning, seeing it as a way to support the war. She argued that "women as well as men must take up their packs and wander and work for the country." She persuaded her beau, William Lloyd Garrison, Jr., to take responsibility for New York State's Mohawk Valley signatures. By August 1864, the drive had procured 400,000 names—the most that had ever been submitted by any petition campaign in America's history.[226]

Life for the Stanton family presented its own war challenges when calamity struck close to home. On July 13, 1863, only a few blocks from their apartment, the worst draft riots in America's history exploded. In the wake of the Union victory at Gettysburg only 10 days earlier, Congress had passed a conscription bill that imposed a draft on all men in the North. However, any man who was drafted could commute the order by paying $300. Many New Yorkers had not joined the war against the South, usually because their incomes depended on Southern cotton. New Yorkers feared that if the war ended slavery, free blacks would come north and compete for jobs. The call for Union troops had received a tepid response from New York City. Now, the draft elicited strong opposition from many.[227]

On Saturday, July 11, the first drawing of draft numbers had been conducted without incident. But the second drawing, on Monday, July 13, provoked a crowd into fury. Led by the Black Joke Fire Engine Company 33, about 500 men attacked the office where the draft had been held. The "most brutal mob" Elizabeth had ever seen burned the Colored Orphan Asylum one block from the Stantons' brownstone, sacked the offices of Horace Greeley's *Tribune*, and hanged free black men. The rioters now turned their attention to private homes, targeting abolitionists. When the mob surged past her house, Elizabeth sent her servants and children to the fourth floor, so that they would be able to escape through the skylight if necessary. She remained at the door, preparing a speech to expel potential ruffians. Her oldest son, Neil, rescued himself by deceit, asking the rowdies to join him in a saloon, "to drink to Jeff Davis." Rob Stanton, 4, was found "happily throwing stones at a burning building."[228]

Harriot, who was 7 years old at the time, would remember the fear she felt that day for the rest of her life. Worried that the family might at any moment suffer vengeance, on the first evening, Elizabeth and Henry removed their households, along with Susan B. Anthony, to safety at the homes of relatives. The next day they all fled to Grandma Cady's in Johnstown, New York for shelter. By late summer, Elizabeth had brought everyone back to New York City. In mid-August 1863, authorities re-instituted the draft amid no opposition or upheaval, so the neighborhood was safe. The city was calm, but it had suffered 2,000 casualties and more than $1 million in property loss, about $20 million in 2020 numbers.[229]

Incidents like the riots affected the Stantons' decision about where to live in New York City. They also had to determine where to send Harriot, who had learned largely from home tutoring in Seneca Falls, to further her education. Elizabeth looked in vain for a school that would enrich her daughter. Each institution taught subjects "appropriate for young ladies" but did not offer college preparatory work or the courses Harriot would need to compete with young men seeking higher education. Fortunately, the Stanton children spent summers in Johnstown, where Harriot attended an excellent grammar school. At war's end, Elizabeth decided to move outside of New York City, where she bought a home in Tenafly, New Jersey. Harriot attended her first boarding school.[230]

Her first foray to "sleep away school" ended poorly for Harriot, enrolled at Rockland County Female Academy, 15 miles from home. She discovered on the second day that she could not possibly endure it, so she escaped and used her excellent riding skills to ride her horse home. The outrageous act persuaded Elizabeth to enroll her daughter at Englewood Academy, a small, private, all-girls school that sat only two miles from their Tenafly house. Harriot agreed; she had made her point. It was time for her to settle into school and enable Elizabeth to follow her plan to resume lecturing. But even so close to home, during the school year Harriot had trouble getting used to her mother's absence. Susan B. Anthony, a frequent presence in the Stanton home, recalled that in the spring of 1871, when 15-year-old Harriot heard that Elizabeth was considering a trip to California the next fall, she "actually cried half the day that her mother would go—too mean she said."[231]

Elizabeth, who relied on a wide network of relatives and friends, encouraged Harriot to build similar connections in their extended family. Her mother left her in Johnstown for long summer vacations. She arranged Harriot's visits to her aunts, Margaret and Tryphena, in New York City and welcomed them to her New Jersey home. Thus, Harriot learned how to be an appreciative guest and a gracious hostess. Elizabeth finally persuaded Harriot to board with her sister Maggie at Vassar's preparatory school, where she remained for three years before beginning classes at the college. When Harriot fell seriously ill in March of 1872, Elizabeth, like Abby Kelley Foster, cancelled her lecture engagements to nurse her daughter. Before she left for college in 1874, Harriot had grown accustomed to separations from her mother.[232]

Harriot Stanton: Becoming Her True Self at Vassar and in Europe, 1874–1883

Harriot continued to act out her discontent with school even after Elizabeth enlisted her in Vassar College. She tried to drop out several times, only to find herself back in Poughkeepsie after trying to enlist at Cornell, "checkmated by family authority in all attempts to escape." Harriot recalled that she disdained Vassar, objected to the absence of courses in modern history and economics, and especially protested the students' ignorance about politics and the larger world. She wrote in her memoir: "For to me in 1876 my estimate about the [Vassar] students was that 'comparatively they were a slough of despond.' It would have been such to any one coming from my home atmosphere."[233]

Harriot Stanton, early 1870s
(Vassar College)

However, Harriot eventually found satisfaction in Vassar's curriculum by developing relationships with professors she admired. Two teachers challenged her from the beginning and helped her stretch beyond the college's offerings. Math professor Priscilla Braislin "renewed that wonderful sensation of pressing my brain against that of another person." One of only two women professors at Vassar, Braislin made Harriot feel "the clear, delicately cut patterns of mathematical relations in higher algebra, spherical trigonometry, on through calculus and quaterions." Harriot encountered an equally impressive English professor, Truman J. Backus, who "inspired in his classes desire for understanding, curiosity about a subject, and willingness to work prodigiously." She described him as "tall, slender, loose-jointed, neat but disorderly, his hair always on tip-toe, his tie a bit askew." He combined a charming personality with an intriguing appearance. He had what Harriot recalled was "twinkling eyes that told the truth; he was full of wit and humor." This man, who gave Harriot the courage she needed when she later spoke at graduation, made life interesting. She recalled, "It was as good as reading an exciting novel, day by day to watch the goings and comings of such a man in a world of young women."[234]

Besides inspiring Harriot academically, Professors Braislin and Backus helped her tolerate the students whom she believed were uninterested in the wider world. Playing the card-game whist with them a few times a week helped to temper her disdain for the situation at Vassar. Harriot learned how to be patient with those whom she did not admire. She even became a popular student and was elected president of the Freshman Class and again of the Senior Class. She established a new regulation that required all students to read the newspaper for 20 minutes a day or pay a fine. Years later, at least one woman thanked Harriot for implanting this habit in her; ironically, Harriot had completely forgotten about her directive. All she recalled was an attitude that reflected the "deadly atmosphere of disapproval of all participation by the student body in the public questions of our times." She did not realize it at the time, but her professors "saved me, in the Vassar world of immature women, from a desperate end."[235]

College taught women how to navigate controversies of their campus communities, as well as of the wider world. While Alla Foster only dipped her toe into a few college disputes, Harriot embraced her family's politics, which were "hot with discussion along every line." In the summer of 1876, Harriot and her brothers Bob and Theo joined their father, Henry Stanton, after dinner for nightly debates and lively talks about the presidential campaign. The Republican Party had nominated Rutherford B. Hayes, governor of Ohio, to run against the Democrats' Samuel Tilden, New York's governor. Henry favored the Democrats' "heart and soul." Harriot and her mother, who could not vote but who had the "luxury" of expressing their thoughts, argued that the platforms of Hayes and Tilden both ignored freedmen and freedwomen, as well as woman suffrage. Nevertheless, Harriot leaned more and more toward Tilden. By the time of the election, she referred to herself as having been born and raised a loyal Democrat, attributing her political training to her father.[236]

When Harriot returned to Vassar in September 1876 for her junior year, she declared that politics had become "the breath of my nostrils," and she organized a mock presidential election. In the real world that November, Tilden received more popular votes than Hayes, but a compromise was struck, giving Hayes the election in exchange for federal troops withdrawing from the South. This compromise devastated Harriot, for the Party had abandoned freed men and women and had left their fate in the hands of Southern Democrats. Her hero had begun "to tremble on his pedestal, showing a lack of grit and courage." Tilden was Harriot's "first big political disappointment." [237]

Crushed by the election and viewing the campus as marred by "political somnolence," Harriot turned to new academic endeavors. She began an independent course in reading economics and politics, formed a debating club, and showed an interest in science. Her life took a dramatic detour when she walked into the classroom of Professor Maria Mitchell, a renowned astronomer and Vassar's prized scholar. The school's founders had lured Professor Mitchell to Vassar by promising her a fabulous observatory equipped with a state-of-the-art telescope, which was surmounted by a dome that revolved with the help of a cast-iron pulley. In no time, Professor Mitchell attracted a following among students, enlisting 17 women in advanced astronomy during her first term, more than Harvard managed to recruit for a similar course. Professor Mitchell reigned as one of Vassar's star teachers for 20 years, and her telescope resides in the Smithsonian Museum today.[238]

Maria Mitchell made Harriot's last two years at Vassar an exhilarating challenge as it opened to her the wonders of science. Had she known then that it was Mitchell who championed woman suffrage in the face of the administration's opposition, Harriot would have been even more enamored with her. To qualify for Mitchell's rigorous astronomy class, Harriot spent two years taking the required advanced mathematics courses, primarily under the tutelage of her friend and mathematician, Professor Braislin. Most Vassar students were ill-prepared to complete the classes, but Harriot triumphed and now joined a prestigious group. Mitchell insisted that her students use genuine scientific inquiry, acquiring information from experience rather than reading. She often asked her classes, "Did you learn that from a book or did you observe it yourself?" By the time she was a senior, Harriot had proven her dedication and ability, not only in inquiry but also in manipulating small telescopes and transit instruments. Mitchell rewarded Harriot's dedication with an invitation to study solar eclipses. A total eclipse was expected the summer of 1878, when Harriot would graduate. The anticipation filled her with purpose and wonder for months.[239]

If Harriot had been able to travel with Mitchell to Colorado, where the solar eclipse was to last five minutes, her life might have taken a different direction. "What a magnificent opportunity for a young student," Harriot recalled. "Oh, how I longed to go, and experience the full fruition of the two years of grind." She had "calculated every detail of the onset." But, "the home verdict was a negative, and wholly based on a matter of expense," which is a curious interpretation considering the money Elizabeth was making on the lecture circuit. Twenty years later, Harriot still regretted her parents' pronouncement that she not go, which "makes my heart stand still and my head whirl whenever I think of the utter lack of imagination in my guardians." [240]

Had Elizabeth and Henry endorsed their daughter's study of science, Mitchell might have made a scientist out of Harriot. Susan B. Anthony later remarked, "Maria Mitchell said of Harriot that she was the finest scholar in her classes." Harriot left Vassar with a lifelong interest in astronomy. For the rest of her life, she tried to comprehend figurative blockages of light, applying the scientific method to human situations. Whether she was studying the social effects of poverty or the refusal of legislators to recognize her, Harriot combined head and heart to achieve an outcome. Years later, when she viewed a total eclipse from the Vassar observatory in 1925, she was so "impressed by this deeply moving miracle of the skies that I took a vow to see every eclipse from then on that occurred within reasonable reach." Nearly three decades after her first disappointment, Harriot still "rebelled at the loss."[241]

Harriot Stanton left Vassar longing for independence and a chance to use her new degree. Her mother agreed in part but had other ideas. Elizabeth had written to her the previous summer, "Take care of yourself for my sake," so that in her old age Harriot might be a comfort and support "instead of an added load for me to carry." Elizabeth was living alone at Tenafly. Henry Stanton spent his time at his New York City apartment. Her older daughter, Maggie, had married and relocated to Nebraska. Bob was at Cornell; Theo moved to France, and the three other sons all scattered far from Tenafly, New Jersey. Looking to Harriot as "something human in shape to love," she wrote, "I have made up my mind to stick to you henceforth like a burr." Elizabeth proposed that Harriot attend Boston's School of Oratory and then join her mother on the Lyceum circuit, where Elizabeth envisioned the two would enjoy "the infinite pleasure of traveling together the remainder of my days."[242]

Elizabeth and many of her reform colleagues had made significant incomes from speaking for the Lyceum, an institution that sponsored popular public lectures on literary and scientific subjects. If Harriot could establish herself in this program, Elizabeth reasoned, she might earn enough to become financially independent, something for which her mother longed. As Harriot trained for a career in public speaking, Elizabeth encouraged and warned her to "be thoroughly prepared before making your debut so that you may feel satisfied with your own work." Harriot dismissed her mother's advice and accepted her first speaking engagement before she was well-prepared. In July 1879, she arrived at the Lyceum filled with trepidation over her topic, Edmond Burke's political thought. Whatever her motivations, Harriot failed in her debut lecture. Audiences compared her unfavorably to her mother and father, both superb speakers.[243]

Harriot did not dwell on her disaster but ended her early oratorical career before it began. She downplayed the experience, then looked to older associates, including two of her mother's confidantes, for advice. First, she called on the abolitionist Wendell Phillips, who told her to consult the expert, her own mother. William Lloyd Garrison, who had tempered his radical abolitionist politics over the decades, delivered better counsel; he warmly urged her to "seize the first bit of work that offers if it is honest and honorable." It would "lead to something better." Within a few weeks after visiting Phillips and Garrison, Harriot accepted the offer to go to Germany as the paid companion and tutor for two wealthy American girls.[244]

On May 15, 1880, Harriot boarded a ship bound across the Atlantic armed with an ample education and a few helpful experiences, unsure if she wanted a vocation or a husband. The 24-year-old, described by her biographer as "a beauty with wavy and fashionable auburn hair, medium height, a slender shape, deep violet eyes, and full lips," left the port of New York City a far different woman from the girl who had arrived at Vassar six years before. She carried herself like an aristocrat, but as soon as she spoke, she relaxed her stiff facade. Her eyes gleamed, as they had for Vassar professors, and welcomed the world, unencumbered by parental scrutiny.[245]

Harriot began her time in Germany as a companion for American girls but soon met a few young men who set her to pondering about love, a topic that her mother had hoped she would avoid for a while. Previously, she had told her diary that she should "promise [herself] not to marry," as marriage would destroy her usefulness. But she did not know how to "maintain a stern resolve against marriage." Harriot began to daydream about meeting her "counterpart" or "elect soul." She trusted that when she found him, her feelings "would be not only strong but enduring, an ideal and everlasting thing that I could worship safely, like the natural beauty I find so soul-stirring in my travels." Away from the supervision of parents and teachers, she admitted, "I am beginning to see myself in truer lights."[246]

Shortly after arriving in Germany, Harriot traveled to France to meet her brother Theo's fiancée, Marguerite Berry. The daughter of a freethinking French Protestant family, Marguerite encouraged Harriot to examine gender differences with greater intensity. Theo's wedding to Marguerite led Harriot to wonder if she would meet "someone who could allow me to love, to be loved, to marry, and yet to continue on the path of larger usefulness for which I am destined and for which I am preparing?"[247] Like Ellen Wright Garrison, Harriot expected more from marriage than her mother's generation had. She longed for a loving, intellectual partner who might allow her to exercise her own independence—surely a goal reform mothers endorsed.

At home in Tenafly, Elizabeth Cady Stanton struggled to complete a task that she, Susan B. Anthony, and Matilda Josyln Gage had set for themselves, writing *The History of Woman Suffrage*. Early in 1882, when Susan urged her fellow writers to complete the book, Elizabeth and Matilda both fell ill. Elizabeth looked to Harriot as a "girl of rare genius as a speaker, and writer, and a faithful conscientious student." She asked her daughter to come home and rescue her.[248]

Harriot's generous answer to help Elizabeth completely changed her life. She left Europe in February 1882 and endured a very chilly ocean journey to New York. Only a few days after the voyage had begun, she met a tall, dark, attractive Englishman, William Henry (Harry) Blatch. After chatting and playing whist for a week, they found significant mutual attraction. When they parted in New York, they exchanged addresses. New emotions lodged in Harriot's heart. She hoped, and expected, to see Harry Blatch again.[249]

Elizabeth welcomed Harriot home, knowing that she could rely on her daughter to serve as both nurse and secretary. She assigned her the task of proofreading copy for *The History of Woman Suffrage*. Harriot read the manuscript with a fresh eye. As a result, she noted a major omission—an account of Lucy Stone's American Woman Suffrage Association—and offered to write a chapter to be included in the history. Elizabeth offered her $100 to complete the text. Susan B. Anthony objected, worried that Harriot would be "too fair" to Lucy, but the exercise proved valuable nonetheless. It gave Harriot her first publication and showed her that her mother was willing to challenge Susan, even though they were only including one small chapter on Lucy Stone.[250]

Elizabeth, with Volume II of the *History* at the printers, sailed to vacation in France on May 27, 1882 with Harriot, who remembered that the trip was like "the joy of eloping with my mother." Pleased that their relationship had improved and expecting to see Harry Blatch, Harriot was cautiously eager. During three months in the south of France, Harriot and Elizabeth relaxed in mother/daughter camaraderie, with few demands or expectations. Elizabeth recalled, "Everything moved as if by magic, no hurry and bustle, never a cross or impatient word spoken." Proximity to Jacournassy, the family estate of Theo Stanton's wife, gave Elizabeth time with her children and her first grandchild, a daughter born to Theo and Marguerite, named for Elizabeth but called Lizette.[251]

But Harriot had more on her mind. Within a short time after their arrival, Harry Blatch asked permission to visit Jacournassy, beginning their courtship. Harriot entertained her beau whenever he could escape business concerns in England. By the end of the summer, marriage looked certain. Harriot confided to her diary, "The natural ebb and flow of life's tides moved me from France to England, and, as if without any will, toward marriage."[252]

Like 38 percent of Vassar graduates in Harriot's class, she married within 10 years of graduating. She was a bit older than the average non-college graduate bride, at 26, but followed a path similar to that of Ellen Wright Garrison and many of her sister college-graduates in marrying a man who had chosen business over higher education. Harry Blatch was, according to Harriot's biographer, "not highly educated, not particularly intellectual, and uninterested in politics and reform concerns." He managed the May

Brewery, but he was "encouraged to live the life of a gentleman, as a way to counter the family's embarrassing origins in 'trade.'"[253]

In mid-October 1882, mother and daughter traveled to Basingstoke, a small industrial town southwest of London, to meet Harry Blatch's family and plan the wedding. Harriot liked Harry's family, although wealthier and more powerful than hers. They had acquired their money through partnership in a Hampshire brewery. The entire family lived in Basingstoke, a small conservative town that had never heard the "gospel of woman's equality." In fact, Elizabeth and Harriot found themselves "quite alone in all our radical ideas, on many points" and believed that Basingstoke would benefit from being "stirred up" a little.[254]

Elizabeth found Harry worthy to be her daughter's husband, but she retained misgivings about marriage and how it would affect her relationship with Harriot. Theo Stanton's marriage had brought Elizabeth a daughter-in-law and a granddaughter; she feared that Harriot's would deprive her of her closest companion. To her, a wedding was an ending, not a beginning, and her account of it was "awash with backward looks and morbid associations."[255]

The marriage took place on November 15, 1882, in the Portland Street Chapel in London, in the presence of Harry's large family. No reason was given, but Harriot's father was unable to attend. The lavish wedding breakfast included a rich six-course repast including everything from lobster and oysters to pheasant and veal. The couple traveled from London for a three-week honeymoon at Dartmoor, then returned to "go into housekeeping," as Elizabeth told a friend.[256]

Harriot and Harry rented a home up the hill from the brewery in Basingstoke, an hour's train ride from London. The two-story brick house, named The Mount, had a library, parlor, dining room, kitchen, and four bedrooms. It also boasted indoor plumbing, a walled garden, and a small entry portico that made it look American. Like Ellen Wright Garrison, Harriot had married primarily for love and emotional support, entering a companionate marriage, but she also achieved financial security with

Harry. She assumed domestic authority in her home, including the hiring and managing servants, a task common to English and American middle-class wives.[257]

Harriot had married a man who could afford to rent a lovely house that she could furnish with beautiful things. She welcomed her mother's extended stay and took pleasure in showing Elizabeth how adept she was at managing her new home. Elizabeth, who had taken pleasure in "reigning supreme" in her own house, told her other daughter Maggie that "Hattie gets great pride and pleasure in her house and her personal appearance, all of which I heartily approve."[258]

When Harriot discovered shortly after her wedding that she was pregnant, she and her mother were delighted. It presented the perfect reason for Elizabeth to remain in Basingstoke for another nine months. Harriot had enjoyed her first weeks of marriage, including the socializing, the elegant home, and "sensual pleasures" it offered. She was intrigued by fashion as it affected women's means of self-expression and freedom, but she welcomed motherhood and greater purpose above all.[259]

Elizabeth passed the time during Harriot's pregnancy in good spirits, enjoying the countryside from the comfort of her daughter's new home. By the end of January, the weather had improved and Harriot felt healthy enough to travel with her mother. They often attended women's suffrage meetings and rallies, which provided both women with the opportunity to make companions and contacts. Elizabeth had declined public speaking engagements when she had been pregnant and believed that Harriot should do the same since she was "enceinte and suffering the usual disturbances of that condition." But Elizabeth hoped Harriot would speak in the future, since "wifehood and motherhood rightly considered are a means of development."[260]

Elizabeth placed great hope in Harriot's marriage, as Martha Wright did in Ellen Wright Garrison's. Both women regarded their sons-in-law highly. "Hattie and I are both well and our days pass happily along without the least friction," she wrote her sister. "Henry is as good as gold, his devotion to Hattie is most soul satisfying to me, and of course to her." Susan B. Anthony, who visited Basingstoke, agreed. "Darling Hattie Stanton... seems happy in the man and the lot she has chosen," she wrote in her diary. Harriot "had gotten the devoted, adoring husband she had decided would be necessary for her to carry on with her public work despite marriage and motherhood." He "provided her with a domestic existence of pleasure and luxury, a counterpoint to the sober, serious life of high purpose to which she had consecrated herself." Harry "seems a very kind hearted, loving and intelligent man, deferring in everything to her—if it will only last!"[261]

As Elizabeth anticipated the birth of her grandchild, she told Susan that she was "standing akimbo waiting for the young man or woman as the case may be"—a sentiment she never wrote to her friend when she was pregnant herself.[262]

Harriot enlisted a Quaker woman doctor for the birth, but with the experience of seven births, Elizabeth provided bedside coaching and extra assurance. Elizabeth reported to her cousin Elizabeth Smith Miller with undisguised pride that "the first bugle blast of the event was at dinner and in six hours all was over." Newborn Nora was a week old when Elizabeth told her cousin, that as she sat beside Hattie with the baby in her arms and realized that three generations of them were together, she "appreciate[d] more than ever what each generation can do for the next one, by making the most of itself and thus slowly building the Jacob's ladder by which the race shall at last reach the divine heights of perfection."[263]

Harriot Stanton Blatch: Finding Peace with Elizabeth and Motherhood, 1883-1902

Nora Stanton Blatch, whom Harriot named for the heroine of Henry Ibsen's scandalous new play, *A Doll's House*, was born on September 30, 1883. She was destined to follow in the feminist shoes of Ibsen's heroine, Nora Helmer, as well as those of her mother and grandmother. Harriot would have only two children, and in this, she was following the path blazed by her contemporary late-19th century mothers, who were having far fewer children than their mothers and grandmothers had. A reduced

Elizabeth Cady Stanton, Harriot Stanton Blatch, and Nora Blatch, c. 1886
(Library of Congress)

household gave Harriot much more liberty than her mother had to pursue her intellectual or political goals. However, birth control techniques were limited and contraception and abortion were condemned by a wide range of women, from feminists to free-love advocates to pious churchgoers, because both encouraged the sexual exploitation of women. A few years later, Harriot would research voluntary motherhood and publish an article and a book on the topic, so it is likely that she nevertheless practiced some form of birth control throughout her marriage.[264]

As far as Elizabeth was concerned, she could not have enough grandchildren. A week after Nora's birth, she wrote, "My happiness overflows that the three generations of us are together." Harriot, who had lived most of her life under Elizabeth's roof, embraced her independence, but bidding her mother farewell on November 17, 1883 wrenched both of their hearts.[265]

Harriot discovered that whatever her relationship with her mother had been, her mothering mirrored Elizabeth's. One writer argues that we are patterned after our mothers and "raise our children by reproducing the emotional dynamic we experienced as our mothers' daughters." Harriot began her public work before her mother did, when Nora was barely six months old. Her activism resembled that of her mother, but took a far more political bent than Elizabeth's. She participated in the British women's suffrage movement by signing on to the Liberal Party's campaign to amend the Reform Bill. The Liberals proposed extending voting rights to the working class; the suffragists proposed extending voting rights to women. In May of 1884, Harriot hosted a meeting in Basingstoke, where she took the podium for the first time in England to introduce the principal speaker. One impressed observer said that Harriot was a "girlish and lovely young wife with a voice at once pathetic and sympathetic, a look far-away as of one dreaming dreams of a far-away future, and a manner childlike in simplicity." She credited Harriot's "training to her eloquent mother." At the meeting, Harriot won an endorsement from her father-in-law, her most challenging critic.[266]

In order to persuade Parliament, suffragists required more than spotty support from friends and relatives. In America, Elizabeth Cady Stanton and her associates had repeatedly suffered defeat, as did Harriot and her allies in England. When Parliament passed the Reform Bill in December, it granted suffrage only to "male householders." Knowing that Harriot would be "depressed over the situation," Elizabeth suggested that she indulge herself "in the domestic retreat while the friction outside your home is more than you can stand…Shut your door and rejoice that you have one to shut."[267]

Harriot ignored her mother's advice, which might have seemed to her inauthentic considering Elizabeth's reluctance to ever shut her own door or weaken her combativeness, even from home. During 1885 and 1886, Harriot pursued a more public path than her mother had at her age, but it was no more passionate. After Harriot experienced legislative failure, she explored other avenues to promote woman suffrage. Childcare options enabled her to increase her civic activity, elevating her stature among English suffragists and reformers. Eventually, it became known that Harriot was eligible to run for one of the public offices available to women if she denounced her American citizenship. When England's Liberal Party asked her to serve, Harriot was not prepared to commit her loyalty to the queen, so she declined. Harriot looked to her mother as a model, but balanced her public political activity with private activity, such as coupling the study of history and politics with her knowledge of the new social sciences.[268]

Meanwhile, Harriot grew more visible in British politics through her writing. Elizabeth, inspired by her daughter's productivity, wrote "The Pleasures of Age," "The Woman's Bible, Introductory Comments," and a number of addresses on English politics. For this latter topic, Elizabeth turned her attention and praise to Harriot, asking her opinion of English affairs and praising her "highly complimented speeches at several parlor meetings in London."[269]

But Elizabeth's passion had turned to being Queen Mother, as her grandchildren addressed her, making them and their parents her first priority. The great distance between Elizabeth and her children's families abroad limited the number of visits, but when they did occur, they were extended and rich. Between these reunions, letters flowed both ways across the ocean. Elizabeth longed to see her babies and hear them talk; in the meantime, she relied on their parents to send her news of their lives. When Theo's daughter, Lizette, was born in 1882, Elizabeth wrote, "My precious baby, you have come at last and we are all so delighted that you belong to the superior sex. Your own Victor Hugo says this 19th century belongs to woman, now you must help to make the women grand and worthy of this glorious century." During separations from the grandchildren, Elizabeth longed for them.[270]

After three years of grandchild drought, in June 1886, Theo and Harriot, who continued to live in France and England respectively, brought their spouses and children to New York. "Mrs. Stanton's heart is full of joy," Susan B. Anthony told a friend, "for [Theo and Harriot] more fully enter into the spirit of our reform with their mother than any of the others of the seven." The fact that they brought two lovely granddaughters—Lizette, 3, and Nora, 2—sweetened the visit enormously.[271]

But the joy continued. The next fall, 1887, Elizabeth accompanied Harriot's family back to England, where she remained for nearly a year. First was a long sojourn with Nora and her parents in Basingstoke, then, in the spring there was another across the Channel to France to see Lizette and her new baby brother, Robbie. Elizabeth wrote letters to grandchildren that differed significantly from those she had written to her sons in boarding school years before. To the boys, Elizabeth had sent advice and admonitions; to Nora, she simply sent love: "Well my precious babe, I find myself often thinking of you, and all you said and did. You hold a large place in my heart." She concluded one letter to Nora with what she called her motto: "The world is my country and all mankind my countrywomen." She closed with a wish to see Nora and Lizette together, then signed, "Lovingly, Queen Mother."[272]

While in France, Elizabeth was chastened by her granddaughter for her lack of language skills. Always impressed by the multilingual skills of her grandchildren, she relished telling her niece in America that Lizette, who spoke French, German, and English, looked astonished when her grandma asked her to tell the non-English-speaking servants what she wanted. "Why grandmother, can't you talk?" she asked. "Not French or German?" Then she would laugh, and say that Robbie could and he was little. Lizette failed to understand how her grandmother "could be so large and could not talk as well as she could."[273] After reveling in Harriot's company, in March of 1888, Elizabeth returned to the United States, unaware that poor health would confine her stateside for the next two years.

Elizabeth's physical decline over the next several months paralleled an effort by Susan B. Anthony and Lucy Stone to reunite the two rival woman suffrage associations. Both women believed that Elizabeth's presence, which had been so effective in the 1888 international women's forum, was vital. However, when Harriot came to New York in the fall of 1889 and saw her mother, she was so distressed that she took her to a sanitarium for two months to prevent her friends from spending her waning energy on women's rights politics. Only after her rest did Harriot agree to accompany her mother to the 1890 unity convention, hoping to preserve her energy.

The day after the unity convention in February of 1890, Harriot bustled Elizabeth off to New York City, where they boarded the luxury steamer *Aller*, bound for Southampton, England. "We had a very pleasant, smooth voyage, unusually so for blustering February and March," recalled Elizabeth. Because she disliked tight staterooms and, perhaps, because she had gained significant weight, she remained in the ladies' salon night and day, sleeping on a sofa. They landed on March 2, 1890, after a passage of 11 days. Elizabeth delighted in having made a journey she had doubted was possible. It would, however, be her last voyage to Europe.[274]

Elated to be back in England, Harriot immersed herself in the work of the Women's Franchise League. At age 34, she had risen to honorary secretary on the Executive Committee. By now she had developed a surer sense of her own leadership and felt freer of her mother's influence. She also joined the socialist Fabian Society and continued to write articles, many directed toward American readers, highlighting British strategies and successes.

While Elizabeth was in Basingstoke, she remained vibrant, visiting her British suffragist friends. She made several speeches, entertained visitors, drafted articles, and talked on "all manner of topics, radical and otherwise."

She attended the theater in London, observing that she was one of the few people "on the shady side of seventy drinking in these worldly joys at the midnight hour." Elizabeth relished the leisure time afforded to her at Hattie's charming home.[275]

Harriot and Nora, who was now 7, loved having their Queen Mother with them in Basingstoke. During the days, Nora went to school or "played and laughed and romped as happy as a lark." In June of 1890, Lizette came over from France to spend a month, and the little girl cousins played together happily. Elizabeth later recalled that she tired of telling stories, "but grandmothers are not allowed to shelter themselves with such devices as reading the news aloud like Longfellow did. They are required to spin on until the bedtime really arrives."[276]

Harriot, now pregnant with her second child, drove around the surrounding countryside of Basingstoke with her mother. After dinner, Elizabeth napped and encouraged Harriot to do the same; Harriot, she argued, should learn the "beauty of repose, rest, the recumbent posture." People in general thought it "praiseworthy to keep their eyelids forever stretched open to their full capacity, standing on tip toe on the watch tower of mortal anxiety about some trifle."[277]

During her pregnancy, Harriot branched out in her intellectual pursuits, many of which complemented Elizabeth's more radical ideas. She wrote an essay, "Voluntary Motherhood," which she expected to appear first as an article and then as a book. In it, she recast motherhood as the source of—rather than a limit to—women's rights. She argued that maternity was not a disability but the highest and most honorable of social functions and must be considered in public policy. Solutions for mothers' lack of power lay "in according them absolute domestic liberty," including control over conception and childrearing, a solid education, and above all, financial independence.[278]

Yet a difficult pregnancy prevented Harriot from delivering the talk that would have unveiled her thesis. She had planned this baby's conception but had not counted on the problems her condition would generate. Never before had she been in such distress. Elizabeth remained in England until the late spring of 1891, telling a friend, "Hattie has been so ill I could not leave her." Harriot's sister Maggie came to stay after Elizabeth left and was present in June for the arrival of Helen Blatch. From her infancy, Helen had a weaker constitution than Nora's and required more attention from her mother.[279]

Nora described the family dynamics many years later in her autobiography: "No sooner was mother up and around than talk started about my going away to school." Once 9-year-old Nora graduated from the local grammar school, Harriot and Harry had to choose between a conventional boarding school, which his family endorsed, and a private co-educational institution. They first sent Nora to board at the Roedean School in Bristol. She hated everything about it: the rote learning, the culture of "crushes" and devotion to older students, and the separation from her family. Nora imitated her mother's previous flight from boarding school by horse but took a train instead. After a second try at Roedean, Nora escaped again and convinced her parents to allow her to study at home with a governess until they secured appropriate secondary education.[280]

Harriot and Harry Blatch reversed standard parenting roles, "her serving as the authority, he the nurturer." Nora worshiped her father but held a different kind of love for her mother, more similar to Harriot's feelings for Elizabeth. Harriot, less at ease with children than Harry was, resembled Elizabeth as a young mother. Engagement in her children's lives was more instructional than sentimental or playful. Her biographer suggests that "like her own mother, Harriot saw her primary responsibility as seeing to it that her daughters met the highest standards of achievement and self-esteem as women." Harriot urged Nora not to be cute, extra-feminine, or play with dolls.[281]

Living under these instructions, Nora became a unique young woman. "She was a superior being…brilliant, forceful, commanding, and fond of having things her own way," the daughter of Charlotte Perkins Gilman, Katharine Beecher Stetson, recalled when she met Nora at age 13. A contemporary remarked that Nora was a "slim little maid of remarkable daring and swiftness, with hair cut short like a boy's." At 11, she was the perfect traveling companion for Harriot on her trip to New York in 1894, the first visit to Elizabeth in three years. A troublesome lingering cough prevented 3-year-old Helen, whom the Queen Mother had never met, from visiting as well. Nora found America to be an "idyllic country and fell in love on first sight."[282]

During their New York reunion, Elizabeth and Harriot engaged in a rare debate over the relationship between voting and education. Up until recently, mother and daughter had agreed that educated women should receive the right to vote before uneducated men or uneducated women. Recent research among the poor classes of rural England over the past few years had swayed Harriot from the stance that they had once shared. She had conducted a study, published in the "Westminster Review," that had moved her toward granting suffrage to the uneducated working-class as well as educated middle- and upper-class women. Elizabeth still held that the woman suffrage movement should not allow what she called the "ignorant vote," and she continued to advocate for literacy restrictions on voting.[283]

After Harriot returned to England, mother and daughter transferred their private discussion to a public arena. In November 1894, Elizabeth published an article in the *Woman's Journal* that endorsed the vote for "literate" women only. Six weeks later, Harriot published "An Open Letter to Mrs. Stanton" in the same paper, strongly disagreeing with her mother. She argued that working people needed political power even more than the wealthy, precisely because "the conditions of the poor are so much harder than yours or mine." There is no evidence that either woman expressed hard feelings after they aired their differences publicly. For Harriot, it was a marker of independence and a great confidence builder.[284]

In any case, Harriot had far more to worry about on her home front than a debate with her mother. In October of 1894, just after she had returned to England, both Nora and Helen fell seriously ill with whooping cough. Nora, stronger and older at 11, was able to recover; Helen, only 3, remained weak. "The whooping cough stopped but she could not assimilate her food," Nora remembered. Harriot reduced her schedule to sporadic meetings and writing. As winter advanced, Helen's condition deteriorated so badly that she never recovered good health. Harriot hired a trained nurse to be present with Helen day and night but realized that she could not leave Helen. She wrote to Susan B. Anthony to cancel her appearance at the November 1895 celebration of Elizabeth Cady Stanton's 80th birthday. "That I must forgo the pleasure and satisfaction of being present at the celebration you are contemplating is the deepest disappointment of my life," Harriot wrote.[285]

For six more months, Harriot struggled to restore her toddler's health, "frantically consulting doctors," but "no one could save Helen." On June 11, 1896, Helen was just short of her fourth birthday. "It was not till Thursday morning about 6:30 that we saw a change in her," Harriot wrote. "In an hour the little spirit had slipped away." A grief-stricken Harriot wrote to her mother, "I had never seen anyone die before, and in [Helen's] case there was nothing but a sweet gliding away." She didn't struggle, only "breathed more and more slowly and gently, and had a sweet smile on her face." Elizabeth mourned at home. She never had seen, held, or kissed her granddaughter.[286]

Letters between Harriot and Theo indicate that the mother responded to her 4-year-old's death with restraint, an emotional posture typical of her class, her upbringing, and her personality. "Hattie broke down for a moment on meeting me," Theo wrote his mother, "but she does not look so worn out as I feared would be the case." Harriot "worked like a Trojan" on details of Helen's funeral but showed little outward emotion, which was perhaps her way of coping. She chose the greenhouse and drawing room of The Mount near their home in Basingstoke for the viewing and ceremony. Harriot placed the coffin in Helen's perambulator, then wheeled it out into the garden, followed by family, friends, and many Blatch cousins. "I love to be in the rooms where she was, and touch and handle the things she liked," Harriot wrote Elizabeth. "She seems to be there." Cremating the toddler met Harriot's need. "I am having made a silver vase for the ashes," she wrote Elizabeth, "and when I die I want dear little Helen's dust mingled with mine and buried."[287]

Susan B. Anthony wrote Harriot a poignant letter of condolence. Helen had died on the same day as another great name, Harriet Beecher Stowe. Yet, while the woman represented "the falling of ripe fruit," with "your darling there was the beginning, the promise, the ruthlessly torn blossom." Susan sent her "heart sympathies" to Elizabeth as well, "for the first great sorrow of your darling Hattie." Susan longed to see Harriot, "for you have always been closer to me than any others, save my very own blood nieces." She closed, "But darling—I only wanted to tell you I am grieving with you—that you must suffer the loss of one of your precious girls—may the other be spared to you and Mr. Blatch—give him my love and sympathy—and Nora also—and believe me ever and always affectionately, sympathetically yours, SBA."[288]

Harriot never mentioned Helen again in public, either in her speeches, her published journals, her diaries, or her letters. Only Nora, who wrote about her sister's death many years later, preserved Helen's memory publicly. Harriot failed to mark the birth of either daughter in her autobiography; it was Elizabeth who provided the few descriptions of the mother and children. Photographs were taken only at Elizabeth's insistence and always included all three generations.[289]

Harriot relied on Harry for solace but turned to the comfort of her own country and family, especially her mother, to begin the healing that the next few decades of her life would require. Elizabeth fulfilled the multiple roles expected of grandmothers: to comfort their children and their children's children. Within a year of Helen's death, Harriot parted temporarily from Harry and took Nora to New York. There on the Upper West Side, she rented a roomy apartment that eventually housed Elizabeth, Nora, Harriot and her siblings, Maggie, whose husband had died, and Bob, who had never married. Harriot, feeling out of touch with America's woman suffrage movement, began studying it intensely. She also wrote articles and expanded her network of activists. Nora attended the Horace Mann School, connected to Columbia University, whose advanced philosophy and co-ed population attracted both mother and daughter. Nora needed lightness in her life, as well as a new atmosphere. Helen's death had left her "feeling terribly old as I entered my teens."[290]

Women as confident as Harriot are more content than resentful when their mothers step in to parent their grandchildren and do it with far more interest than they raised their daughters. Elizabeth would have been the first to admit that her involvement in the lives of her grandchildren was deeper than it had been in those of her children. "Immobilized by age and weight," Elizabeth was determined to loom large in their lives, emotionally and physically. When Nora Stanton Blatch moved from England in 1897 with her mother to live under Elizabeth's roof for 10 months of the year, the Queen Mother's previous aches eased and her worries subsided. Nora, equally enamored with her grandmother, saw Elizabeth as "my guide and philosopher." One biographer writes that Elizabeth taught young Nora "the facts of life," prominent among which was "the history of woman and her long subjection." Nora thought "another feminist generation was in the making." She wanted to be part of it.[291]

Besides teaching Nora feminist goals, Elizabeth taught her and all of the family how to endure hardships. "I never encourage sad moods," she told Harriot. Like her old friend, Lucretia Mott, whenever she felt depressed, Elizabeth worked at something physical or practical, "cheating [herself] into the thought that all is well, grand, glorious, [and] triumphant." She faced blindness, an affliction her father had borne, with equal courage. At first, Elizabeth hid the condition from her family, but Harriot's move to New York coincided with a reality that she could no longer hide. "Oh what a privation," Elizabeth wrote in her diary. She faced a "sore trial, with prospective total blindness!" She could still write without glasses; however, she could not read her illegible penmanship, so she hired a personal typist and a reader to help. As her eyes "grew dimmer," she was sure her "intellectual vision [grew] clearer." She rejoiced that her hearing was "as good as ever, and I am perfectly well otherwise."[292]

Elizabeth spent the last decade of her life reunited with all of her children, living in a large apartment near Central Park with Bob and Maggie. By then, during the late 1890s, Harriot and Nora, a senior at Cornell, had moved to their own apartment nearby. Harry Blatch left Basingstoke and took up residence in a cottage on Long Island, where Harriot spent some of her time.[293]

Harriot remembered clearly the morning that Elizabeth died. She directed the maid to arrange her white hair, whose color and thickness had brought her so much pride. When she commanded the same servant, "Now I'll be dressed," her daughters protested. They refused to remove their mother's comfortable dressing gown in exchange for public attire, fearing the unnecessary strain. Elizabeth acquiesced and rested much of the day, surrounded by six children and one grandchild. Two hours before she died, she displayed a burst of energy. The 87-year-old beloved Queen Mother asked her doctor to help hoist her hefty body to a standing position.

Drawing herself up with assistance, she stood erect for seven or eight minutes with what the doctor called extraordinary muscle strength. She steadied herself, grasped the table before her, and peered out into an imaginary audience, as if delivering an address. Harriot recalled, "Mother's hair was shaped like a delicate halo of soft white curls around her death-touched face, as she pleaded the cause of the mothers of the race for the last time." Flanked by her doctor and nurse, Elizabeth endured for only a moment longer, gasped for breath, and sat down. The exertion had claimed her last lucid moments. Once eased into her armchair, she dozed. Before long, labored breathing prompted the children to ease her to a prone position. Elizabeth slept for two hours, then met a peaceful end that afternoon on Sunday, October 25, 1902.[294]

Elizabeth had always doubted whether death delivered eternal life, but she was not convinced that it didn't. She had battled with organized religion for decades, her *Woman's Bible* as a witness to her unorthodox beliefs. Yet, just the previous day, Elizabeth had informed her doctor that she hoped to die as quickly as possible. If he couldn't cure her troubled breathing, and if she was unable to "feel brighter and more like work again," she wanted him to give her "something to send me pack-horse speed to heaven." She had not required that measure; heart failure caused her death.[295]

Elizabeth had played the royal role to the hilt as she planned her own funeral. She told Maggie, "I should like to be in my ordinary dress, no crepe or black, no fripperies or fandangos of any sort, and some common sense women to conduct the services." She asked that a photo of Susan B. Anthony be placed at the head of the coffin and a second one, picturing both women, nearby. The table where she wrote the *Declaration of Sentiments* stood close to the casket and displayed *The History of Woman Suffrage*. The service, held in Elizabeth's apartment, was an intimate one, closed to all but family and friends. The Reverend Moncure Conway presided. Rev. Nettie Brown Blackwell assisted him and delivered one of the tributes. The Reverend Phebe Hanaford, co-author of *The Woman's Bible*, led the graveside service at Woodlawn Cemetery.[296]

Harriot had wired Susan a terse message immediately after her mother died: "Mother passed away at three o'clock." In Rochester, though she had expected the news, Susan sank into deep sorrow. A secretary described Susan as "a piteous thing, though none of us would have dared tell her so." Harriot sent a second cryptic telegram in the early evening of the same day: "Private funeral for you and ourselves only, Wednesday, eleven, apartment full. Trained nurse. Maggie ill. Hattie."[297]

Susan told inquiring reporters, "I am too crushed to say much," and sat silent throughout the funeral proceedings, sad eyes riveted on the photo of her and her dearest friend. From an armchair, she "looked with aching heart into the face which with the crown of beautiful, snowy hair was so grand in the majesty of death." When the casket was closed and covered with flowers for the final prayers, the photo remained in Susan's heart. Seven months later, she told Theodore Stanton, "It was a great going out of my life when she went."[298]

Susan wrote in her diary, "Life continues. It is all at sea … It goes right on and on—no matter who lives and who dies." So, too, the struggle for woman suffrage would continue. Susan placed hope for Elizabeth's successor in Harriot Stanton Blatch, "a splendid woman who will say and do a great many good things." Susan observed in the wake of Elizabeth's death, "I am waiting and watching to see what she will accomplish in an organized way."[299]

Elizabeth Cady Stanton and Susan B. Anthony, c. 1890
(Library of Congress)

Twenty-two years before she died, Elizabeth told Harriot, "I do want you to love and work for humanity, to go on with my work when I am done, to make life easier in any direction for those who come after you."[300] Within a few years of Elizabeth's death, it was obvious that Harriot would follow the essence of her mother's wish but diverge slightly from Elizabeth's goals to pursue her own calling. Harriot, initially feeling a pull back to America from her mother and eager to join the women's rights movement, distinguished herself in 1909 by working with New York City's working-class women, then extended her efforts to spearhead woman suffrage parades, which became her trademark. She supported the parades but eventually left the organizing to others. Her daughter, Nora Stanton Blatch, a Cornell University engineering graduate, continued to represent the family. Harriot spent a few months in a new venue in Kansas, a state still struggling to win suffrage for women in 1916. There she encountered women who recalled Elizabeth. For her skills and in fond remembrance of her mother, they gave Harriot a standing ovation.

✳ ✳ ✳

Harriot remained at home with Elizabeth for longer than the other reform daughters, perhaps an indication of how much she and Harriot needed each other. Elizabeth provided her with basic skills through tutoring, then found a school that would enrich and continue Harriot's learning. Elizabeth celebrated the independence Harriot experienced at Vassar but was not prepared for her daughter's desire to relocate across the ocean. During the next few years, the women enjoyed rich visits that led to a new appreciation of each other. Elizabeth taught Harriot how to seize moments of intellectual exploration while also allowing herself necessary respite from work and study. Meanwhile, Harriot showed her mother how to embrace a new culture and enter its politics with confidence.

In time, Harriot would launch a life that reflected her mother's in many ways but imitated it only from time to time. She and Elizabeth had embarked on the journeys of motherhood and public activism in different ways; while Harriot combined domestic and public roles from the beginning, Elizabeth focused her concentration on parenting seven children prior to venturing fully into the larger world. Elizabeth published essays and occasionally left home to deliver a speech but remained largely near the hearth. Harriot's life, carpeted with financial ease but hampered by a strange land and culture, took her to unexpected personal and political destinations. She had married into a conservative family, who might have stunted her work, but she never hesitated to express her voice. Continually influenced by the distant hand of Elizabeth, Harriot was embarking on the most substantial part of her profound journey. When Elizabeth left for home after her daughter's first child was born, she had become more than a mother—she was a mother-in-law and grandmother who embraced her new title, Queen Mother, with glee. To Harriot, Elizabeth was a friend and role model. They both agreed that the greatest achievement was the launching of a third generation of women to follow whatever legacy she chose.

Partners for the Cause

Lucy Stone and Alice Stone Blackwell

Lucy Stone: Mothering Alice Stone Blackwell Joyfully, 1857–1870

Henry Blackwell, who was at home for Alice's birth, boasted that the cry of his "brave, vigorous little girl with dark blue eyes and black hair" made it clear that she was declaring, "I will be heard." Alice sounded her first exclamation on September 14, 1857. Lucy's labor was aided by her sister-in-law, Dr. Emily Blackwell, making little Alice the only reform daughter whose birth was assisted by a physician.[301]

Lucy's experience in motherhood differed from most women in the 19th Century. They became sexually active in their 20s soon after they married and became pregnant at more or less regular intervals until menopause. Lucy alone among the reform mothers had graduated from college, resisted marriage until she was 37, and retained her maiden name. She did not conceive until she was nearly 40, the age at which most women bore their last babies. Martha Wright and Elizabeth Cady Stanton married in their 20s and had seven children each, while Lucy and Abby Kelley Foster, also an older bride, had only one child. Age at marriage certainly determined the number of children borne, but some women began to limit the size of their families by exercising domestic authority.

Like all reform mothers, Lucy looked to other mothers to network, both to pursue their reform work and to bond as parents. She met Antoinette (Nettie) Brown at Oberlin Collegiate Institute, where they numbered among a few female students. At the age of 20, Nettie arrived at Oberlin in 1845 with an advance warning to avoid a woman named Lucy Stone, who was seven years her senior and a Garrisonian abolitionist with "strange and dangerous opinions." On her first night in the dining room, Nettie heard the "clear-cut tones of Lucy's voice arguing some point with earnestness," then saw the "small, fresh, round-faced girl in a neat calico frock." Her hair was cut just above her smooth, white collar, which, Nettie soon learned, Lucy always washed and ironed herself.[302]

Before long, defying earlier advice, Nettie had forged a close friendship with Lucy, sharing a passion for public speaking and protesting because Oberlin banned women from all podiums. Each woman ignored the rules and prepared for her chosen career, Lucy as a lecturer on slavery and Nettie as a minister. The friends wrote each other endearing, encouraging letters after they returned home: Lucy in West Brookfield, Massachusetts and Nettie in Henrietta, a Rochester, New York, suburb. These letters expressed affectionate physical longing for one another, helping shore them up in the face of adversity. Before Lucy delivered her first paid speech, Nettie wrote, "Don't be afraid of anybody but speak as though you had a right to."[303]

The bond that Lucy and Nettie shared as single women only deepened when they married a pair of brothers. Later, motherhood further strengthened their domestic ties as they trained their daughters for adulthood. Many of the women in the Blackwell family formed a unique network of support for each other. Young Alice was one of its major beneficiaries.

When Alice was just under 2 months old, Lucy tried to continue her former activities. She hired a young woman to help with housework and baby care while she resumed a modified speaking schedule, though she kept her engagements near home. Lucy, who had always been nourished by her audiences, found that they did not fulfill her in the way Alice did. Nor was she comfortable being away from her daughter. In addition, Lucy's health was suffering; a persistent headache, something she had experienced during

Lucy Stone and Alice Stone Blackwell, 1857
(Library of Congress)

her courtship and early in her marriage, returned, accompanied by a severe case of boils. The conditions forced her to cancel most of her speeches and stay home mothering, at least for a few months.[304]

Lucy found great satisfaction and purpose in raising her daughter, but she recognized its hardships. One day Lucy wrote about Alice poetically: "I never feel [my baby's] little cheek beside of mine, never hear her quick coming breath—or her sweet baby voice without the earnest purpose to gather to myself more symmetry of being—to sustain all my relations better." But the next day, she expressed her frustration that mothering burdened her. Like the other reform mothers, she regretted that Henry, who left mother and baby soon after Alice's birth to work as a bookseller in Chicago, missed "the miracle of the unfolding child." Lucy marveled at her baby's "radiant little face," skillful crawling, and growth that was so rapid she claimed Henry "will scarcely believe his eyes." At 7 months, Alice was smart enough to understand when Lucy asked her to send Henry 10 kisses and a half in every letter. She told Henry, "Every day I love [my baby] more."[305]

After a break, Lucy tried again to deliver a lecture. She ventured into New York City, leaving a neighbor in charge of 6-month-old Alice. With her hair combed in the old-fashioned, smooth, simple style, only the mole above her lip marked her face with distinction. Dressed in a plain black dress with a black basque, open in front, and edged with white ruffling passing around the neck, Lucy presented her talk, "The Future of Woman in America." It attracted a good audience and brought her $50. She stayed in the city with Henry's sister, Elizabeth, but kept awake all night, worrying about Alice. The next day, Lucy reported to Henry, "I was thinking of the dear child, and vowing I would never leave her again. She took a dreadful cold, which has made me very anxious." For Lucy, the sacrifice had been too great.[306]

Unlike Ellen Wright or Harriot Stanton, who grew up in stable homes among many siblings, Alice spent her youth as an only child, migrating from house to house. Lucy longed for a permanent home during her first two years of marriage to Henry, who held jobs all across the country. When Alice was born, Lucy purchased a cottage in Orange, New Jersey, from her lecture fees and land investments, but she soon found that the responsibilities of housework in Henry's absence overwhelmed her. Even though her mother had trained her in housewifery, Lucy found it demanding, and she could not afford to hire regular help that Martha and Elizabeth employed.[307]

Lucy felt exhausted and misunderstood. When she told Henry, whom she called Harry, "I get tired—arms, feet and back every day," he insisted she take a break. "But, Harry, no one who takes care of a baby can rest," she wrote. If Henry tried to take care of Alice for even one day, he would sympathize. If he also performed all of her other duties—sewing, mending, washing, and ironing—he would understand that there is "no time to rest." Lucy might have reduced her household tasks, but she ignored Henry's admonition to slow down when it came to cultivating her first spring crops. Overruled by his wife's passion for farming, Henry suggested she engage help and not break her back by planting. With the couple living largely on Lucy's money, he suggested she spend $25 on yard help. This expense "would more or less not affect" him, but if she suffered a strain, a cold, or any personal injury, it would.[308]

When Susan B. Anthony, with whom she had organized many conventions, asked her to lecture, Lucy refused because she could not "speak well while I nurse the baby." She compared their lives, insisting that even if Susan had measles and whooping cough plus all of her work, Lucy's fatigue was worse. Lucy insisted that the occupation of mothering was "vastly more important than that of the merchant or manufacturer or any other." No one thought it strange that men in those professions did not "carry on a world of other business," so why should mothers? When her children were old enough to know that they were well taken care of, Lucy told Susan, "I hope to be a better world worker than before, but until then, you need not ask me to lecture."[309]

Once considered an inspired and natural public speaker numbered among the best in America, Lucy now shied away from the podium, either because of a long absence or a distance from issues she had once championed. She kept close to home, protecting Alice—and perhaps herself, as well. Years later, Alice praised Lucy for being what she called a "best mother." In her mother's biography, she wrote, "Neither mobs nor matrimony had been about to 'shut up the mouth of Lucy Stone,' but mother love did it, for a time. In her, the maternal instinct was very strong and deep."[310]

Lucy told Nettie, "I wished the old impulse and power to lecture would come, both for the sake of cherished principles and to help Harry with the heavy [financial] burden." Dread of failure and of missing Alice overwhelmed her. On the rare times she ventured out to hear a talk, Lucy came home, and "looked in Alice's sleeping face and thought of the possible evil that might befall her if my guardian eye was turned away." Then she "shrank into its shell and saw that for these years I can be only a mother— no trivial thing either." She confessed to Nettie, "I am afraid and dare not trust Lucy Stone."[311]

Lucy was exhausted, missed speaking, and hungered for her husband. She wanted to reunite the family and hoped to have one more baby. When Henry returned to Chicago to sell books, she and 1-year-old Alice moved there to join him. The family boarded in nearby Evanston, Illinois, in an apartment that lacked most amenities. Early in 1859, Lucy was elated to discover that she was pregnant again. In June, though, her joy turned to sorrow when she gave birth prematurely to a baby boy who died. Heartbroken, she wrote Henry, who was away, that if she had had a nurse at the first call of labor, they would not have lost their little one. She concluded, "We are liable to sickness and death everywhere."[312]

After living in Illinois with Henry for a year, Lucy and Alice returned East and moved to their third home, in Roseville, New Jersey, near current day Newark. This pleased Lucy initially, but the size of the house and 20 acres of planted crops demanded she acquire a new skill: becoming landlord to tenant farm workers. Lucy relied on former talents to graft fruit trees and cultivate gardens with the aim of selling their produce. Henry finally joined them and took a new job managing a real estate company in New York City. He spent little time with Alice, but they all lived in the same house.

In the late summer of 1860, Lucy was called home to West Brookfield to nurse her mother. She and Alice were at Hannah Stone's bedside when she died on Alice's third birthday, September 14, 1860.[313] Because Lucy was in Boston for her mother's funeral, she took the opportunity to meet with former colleagues, officers of the New England Antislavery Society. She thereby began to re-enter the world of antislavery and women's rights advocacy, finally ready to reaffirm principles she had long promoted.

Lucy had aligned herself with the radical Garrisonian sector of abolitionists, which Abby Kelley inspired, since her college years at Oberlin in the 1840s. She had never accepted political solutions to end slavery, which usually embraced the formation of an antislavery political party. Lucy, instead, insisted on immediate and total emancipation of slaves, not the gradual freedom the new Republican Party promoted.

During the fall of 1860, as the nation contemplated a presidential candidate, all four reform mothers in this book—Martha Wright, Abby Kelly Foster, Elizabeth Cady Stanton, and Lucy Stone—agreed that Abraham Lincoln insufficiently furthered the cause of antislavery to merit their support. After he took office, war became inevitable. Lucy was back in Roseville, where she faced domestic problems that distracted her from national ones. The house and farm was burdened by mortgage payments, taxes, and hired farm labor—none of which she and Henry could afford. Taking a big risk, Henry left his real estate business to join a new venture reinforced by his antislavery beliefs: growing sugar beets to provide an alternative to slave-raised sugar cane. His partners required that he live near the premises, so he rented an apartment near the beet distribution headquarters in New York City.

The Blackwell family once again lived separately. In April 1861, a few days after the war began, Lucy was called back to West Brookfield, this time to help her ailing father, and she and Alice spent the summer there. Over the next two years, Lucy and Henry split their time among the Roseville farm, West Brookfield relatives, and Henry's apartment in New York City. Soon, they rented out the farm, after which Alice and Lucy moved temporarily to Massachusetts. Once again, Henry became a rare visitor to his own home.

When the Union instituted a draft in 1863, Lucy Stone insisted that Henry, 38 years old and nine years her junior, avoid fighting this "infernal war" and "buy a substitute at any price." Even if he had to draw on her credit or travel west to sell their property in Wisconsin, he must not serve. He agreed. She remained in the east with Alice, missing her husband. "We shall be glad, when [the separation] is past," she wrote to him, "that we braved it through, or if not, we shall at least feel, that we tried to get safely over a bridge that, after all broke."[314]

Like other reform mothers, Lucy educated Alice, not only in domestic skills, but also in school work. During the summer of 1864, while living in West Brookfield with her ailing father, Lucy enrolled 7-year-old Alice in the local grammar school. Alice's physical constitution, which had been weak, worsened. Her limbs ached, and her eyesight began to fail. Lucy tutored Alice at home when she appeared especially tired to prevent any strain or infection from other children when scarlet fever or other diseases threatened.[315]

Lucy reported Alice's strengths along with her frailties to Henry, noting that her shyness was waning. Alice was a good child who "trotted to school night and morning, enjoyed herself, and learned rapidly." Soon she could read anything. She sent Henry her first sentence, as well as many "kisses with long tails." Lucy did not want to interrupt their contentment by moving back to New Jersey, so they went to stay with her sister in nearby Gardner, Massachusetts. Lucy, who planned to throw Alice a very small party, reminded Henry that it was his daughter's birthday and that he should send her a letter of greeting. When Lucy hinted to Alice that Henry might come for her birthday, she "danced first on one foot, and then on the other, and ended with a vigorous clapping of hands." Henry did not come, but Alice forgave him. When she received academic rewards, she saved a colored certificate for him.[316]

By the spring of 1865, the family, happily united, returned to their farmhouse in Roseville, New Jersey and remained for five years, the longest period they had consistently resided in any one place. Still longing for another child, Lucy adopted a 5-year-old orphan girl named Annie Gleason, ostensibly for a playmate for Alice. Henry described the child as "an active, noisy, hasty-tempered, impulsive, rollicking affectionate young girl," who nevertheless "did not prove a congenial companion to Alice." Lucy became deeply attached to the child, however, and her letters during the period are peppered with references to "our children." The girls, unfortunately, did not get along, so after a while, Annie went to stay with other Massachusetts families until she sadly died of meningitis at age 10.[317]

"Lucy had hoped for a large family," Alice recalled later, "but this hope was disappointed." She reserved "all her wealth of deep maternal tenderness" for her one little daughter. Her comments resemble those of Alla Foster, who admired the way her mother shaped her character. Lucy's love was not "blind and unreasoning, such as makes some mothers side with their own offspring, right or wrong." She was more anxious that Alice "should do right by everybody than that everybody should do right by me." If she got into trouble, there was strict and close inquiry. If she was in the wrong, "I had to make apology and reparation." Like Alla, Ellen, and Harriot, Alice appreciated her mother's love and lessons. She was grateful that her mother nursed her at her breast and that she made her mind: "She nourished me with her soul as well as with her milk."[318]

With the end of the Civil War and parenting obligations eased, Lucy anticipated reuniting with her reform friends in the antislavery and women's rights work that she had left for nearly a decade. A large question loomed: which cause—suffrage for freed black men or suffrage for white and black women—would enlist the dedication of former advocates? Elizabeth Cady Stanton and Susan B. Anthony were central to Lucy's sisterhood and would be in the forefront. In January 1866, they all attended a meeting of the American Anti-Slavery Society in Boston, where they proposed that anti-slavery and women's rights leaders combine in a new organization whose goal they called "universal suffrage." To their dismay, their long-time hero and ally, Wendell Phillips, blocked a vote, preventing its formation. Like many former abolitionists, Phillips was seeing violence against freed enslaved people in the South and worried that suffrage was more crucial for black men than for white women. Reformers could not condone combining the causes but must stick to one—it was the Negro's Hour.[319]

Having failed at their first effort to form a new organization, Lucy and her colleagues did not give up. In May 1866, they attended the first Women's Rights Convention held after the Civil War, in New York City, where Susan B. Anthony moved and Martha Wright seconded a resolution to form the American Equal Rights Association (AERA), whose goal was universal suffrage. When their friend Abby Kelley Foster opposed the proposal, Lucy told her, "O Abby, it is a terrible mistake you are all making. The tears are in my eyes, and a wail goes through my heart akin to that which I should feel, if I saw my little daughter drowning before my eyes with no power to help her." Abby insisted with Wendell Phillips that they should help freedmen first before turning their attention to white women.[320]

The new state of Kansas provided a stage for the drama to play out. There, two separate bills were up for a vote in the fall of 1867; one proposed suffrage for white women and the other proposed suffrage for black men. In the spring before the vote, Lucy and Henry felt called to act upon their new conviction to fight for universal suffrage. They left Alice without a parental guardian for the first time, placing her in the care of Henry's sisters, to campaign in Kansas for both bills. Lucy's speeches, filled with all of her old force and fire, rejuvenated her passion for lecturing and led Kansas farm women to adore her.[321] Shortly after Lucy and Henry returned east, Elizabeth Cady Stanton and Susan B. Anthony also traveled to Kansas, but they were less passionate about suffrage for black men than for white women. In November 1867, Kansas voters defeated both bills, confining suffrage privileges to white men alone.

Frustrated at the defeat and desperate for financial backing, Elizabeth and Susan made a decision in Kansas that might have altered the women's rights movement for a generation. They accepted the assistance of a flamboyant English man, George Francis Train, whom they had met on the campaign trail. The women entered the association with open eyes; they knew that Train was a racist but they compromised to win his support for white woman suffrage. Elizabeth, Susan, and Train spent December 1867 traveling from Kansas back to New York, making dramatic appearances along their route. Lucy was appalled at the alliance her friends had entered, leading her to seriously question where she would place her energy to pursue women's rights for the next several years.[322]

After months of discord, when the AERA met in the spring of 1869, a small faction led by Elizabeth Cady Stanton and Susan B. Anthony broke off and organized the National Woman Suffrage Association. In the fall, Lucy founded the American Woman Suffrage Association and began to publish its official voice and her life's legacy, the *Woman's Journal*. It outlived Elizabeth's *The Revolution*, which had been funded by Train, by nearly 50 years. The National and American associations both advocated for woman suffrage but differed in beliefs and tactics. The National opposed the Fifteenth Amendment, which gave black men (but not women) the vote, but believed a federal amendment was the best route to achieve woman suffrage. The American supported the Fifteenth Amendment and believed a state-by-state campaign of legislatures was the best route to gain woman suffrage. Martha Wright did not participate in the formation of either the National or American Suffrage Associations and was rather impatient with the disagreement, comparing the sides to Kilkenny cats, a contemporary term for tenacious fighters. She finally affiliated herself with the National Association and was appointed as its president in 1874.[323]

"The break up [of the women's rights movement] began in Kansas [in 1867]." Alice later wrote. "The facts hitherto have been largely suppressed. Now they can be told. Both the race question and the sex question entered into the causes of disagreement." Lucy would not have disagreed with her daughter. At home in New Jersey, Lucy watched her friends' activity with Train closely, read the speeches they all delivered, and tried to find a school for Alice.[324]

Lucy found Miss Jane Andrews' Boarding School in Newburyport, Massachusetts, to be a perfect fit. She enrolled 12-year-old Alice in the fall of 1869, launching a flow of letters between mother and daughter that spanned nearly 30 years. Like Martha Wright, Lucy wrote endless advice to her adolescent but offered it in softer tones. Initially, politics and reform issues were rarely mentioned. What Alice could expect to read were four kinds of instructions—academic tips, domestic expectations, personal lessons, and social suggestions.

For her academic tips, Lucy maintained that Alice should practice excellent penmanship and spelling, get good lessons, learn how to record her accounts in a blank book, and "do your very best every day." "Be very brave and good, my darling child, and conquer the lessons while you are trying to do the same for other things." When Alice had trouble learning music, Lucy urged her to play drums to "do the tunes."

In terms of domestic expectations, Alice should know how to harvest peaches, make blackberry preserves, keep the indoor plants healthy, and evaluate hired help.

As for her personal lessons, Lucy instructed Alice to care for her own welfare. When her light-sensitive eyes kept her from school, she should buy a veil to shade them from the snow glare. Knowing her propensity to lose track of belongings, she advised her to take care of her shoes, gloves, and cloak, hang up all clothes, and use a sponge to wash. For cold weather, Alice must be "well wrapped up" in leggings, rubbers, warm coat, muff, and furs. In the summer, she should wear a "layered" shirt over a sleeveless waist and white stockings with any outfit.

Finally, Lucy offered social suggestions to her pupil. When Alice protested that she lacked privacy, Lucy wrote, "You must try, Alice dear, to make the best of the small room and bed, and crowded arrangements." In short, Lucy suggested Alice simply find a way to cope. Furthermore, Alice should obey social decorum: "Dress neatly...and go home early." Lucy summed it up beautifully: "You know, my dear, I expect a great deal of you," and I will always take "care of my little girl Alice," whom she called "Cubby" until Alice was nearly 40.[325]

Alice Stone Blackwell: Experiencing Adolescence, 1870–1881

In December 1870, Alice, 13, and her parents moved into the first house they ever owned to fulfill a dream they all shared. Named Pope's Hill for the slope on which it was built, the large home was located in Dorchester, just outside Boston, a city Alice would call home for the rest of her life. The family spent one year settling in, during which time Lucy and Henry managed the new American Woman Suffrage Association and launched the *Woman's Journal*, which the family published for decades. Disaster struck when a fire destroyed much of their precious house the next December. This misfortune removed them to quarters that resembled those the three had inhabited for much of Alice's childhood—a small, temporary cottage on the edge of their damaged property.[326]

A bright future dawned, though, as soon as Alice began classes at the Harris Grammar School in February 1872. She used this new experience to begin writing a personal journal, a gem replete with the triumphs and disappointments of her emerging adolescence. It sets the themes for Alice's life during these years, reflecting Lucy's influence, as well as her own independence. In its pages, Alice relates her deep interest in women's rights, her persistent search for a spiritual life, and a determination to establish meaningful personal relationships. From the earliest entries, written when Alice was 14, she demonstrated a willingness to shock her classmates.

Alice's story opens in February 1872, when she is an awkward and untested student at Harris Grammar School. It is George Washington's Birthday celebration, but Alice is not enthused. Feeling like an outsider, she ignores the class singing of "God Bless America," intoning "God Save the Queen" instead. This elicits a "battle royal" among the girls at recess, each assuming the role of a British or American general in the Revolutionary War. Those with muffs use them as weapons. Later that afternoon, the argument continues. On the walk home, Alice, lacking social skills, calls her schoolmate, Hattie Mann, a bad girl, whereupon Hattie replies, "You are the bad one because you sewed on Sunday."

Alice Stone Blackwell, 1877
(Boston Athenaeum)

"You are worse," Alice says, "as you don't believe in women's rights."

"Why Alice Blackwell!" she cries, "Do you mean to say you think it's as wicked not to believe in women's rights as to sew on Sunday?"

Alice says, "I think it's quite as much of a mistake. Don't turn this into a women's rights meeting, just learn your lesson."

The next day, Alice continues to press her point about women's rights, horrifying a second friend, who asks, "Do you stand up for them?"

Alice answers, "Of course."

"I do not," is the reply.

"I supposed so."

"I don't want to vote, anyway."

"You would not have to."

"I thought every man had to vote unless he could get a substitute."

Alice explains to her uninformed friend that this is not so.[327]

Alice continued to assert her outspoken opinions at Harris, but her academic achievements won her more admiration than her wit. In March, Alice received her first public honor, a citywide award for the best student essay written about "Kindness to Animals." The preparations to dress her for the Boston Music Hall ceremony earned more space in her journal than the event itself. Alice's cousin Emma Lawrence, the niece currently residing under Lucy's tutelage and someone who was central to the Blackwell family for decades, helped dress Alice in her first formal gown. It even had a train, which was the easiest part of her elaborate costume to handle because Alice was tall for her fourteen years.

At the awards service, Alice almost fainted when the Unitarian minister, Mr. Robert Collyer, came to the podium to deliver the opening prayer. Having read his sermons, she was thrilled to be in his presence. From this moment on for the next two years, Alice followed Reverend Collyer, whose accessible and simple themes of a personal religious life attracted her, a child of parents who never had joined a church or attended services with any regularity. Alice hungered for his sincere, enthusiastic, and eloquent message.[328]

Alice frequently mentioned in her journal how reluctant her parents were to participate in formal religion, suggesting that faith like the one she held might ease what she saw as "Mama's blues" and "Papa's lack of belief." Her mother relied on a "guiding Influence, and gets along somehow," Alice wrote. "As for Papa, I don't know what he does believe; I think he supposes that creation is a sort of machine, set going once for all." Alice found it a "special Providence" when Lucy and Henry suggested they all attend one of Mr. Collyer's services. After the talk, Alice was amazed when Reverend Collyer found her parents in the crowd and approached them. When Collyer asked her to kiss him, Alice complied, but she regretted her rash action and was so embarrassed that once "Mama began to take him up on the subject of woman's rights I cleared out with my girlfriends."[329]

Later in the summer, Alice, continuing to feel plagued with questions of faith, took advantage of a rare opportunity to discuss religion with her mother. Their conversation, though, proved less than satisfying. "Set spinning and let go is Mama's theory," Alice reported. "I'd rather be blue orthodox and believe in hell than believe what she does. She'll have a pleasant surprise when she dies."[330]

During the spring, summer, and fall of 1872, besides expanding her spiritual devotion through studying the work of Reverend Collyer, Alice spent a considerable amount of time making friends with the girls in her class. The starkest example of this effort was her love/hate relationship with one of her first new acquaintances, Mary Fifield. Their communication ranged from warm exchanges when they were getting along to nasty poems when they were enemies. At 14, the girls, who still loved games, agreed to have it out with a pretend duel, which Alice arranged.

Mary arrived at the Blackwell house on a late April afternoon and greeted Alice with laughter and bad names. Alice brought her in and displayed a syringe in a pail of water, a horsewhip, a pair of tongs, and a carving knife made of paper, which "almost sent Mary into convulsions."

What followed was an outside battle, with water as the primary weapon, between "a pair of cheerful lunatics." They ended the session in the Blackwell kitchen, chatting with Lucy, while they ate maple sugar, "discussed books, recounted scrapes, and enjoyed ourselves." The rest of the spring Alice and Mary shared a tumultuous friendship, sprinkled with minor and major spats and spiced with teases but always tempered with gifts. A favorite trick of Alice's was to salt a banana and present it to Mary after they had completed a rather violent physical fight. Although Alice seemed to take all of this in her stride, in the spirit of her adolescent turbulence, she sometimes expressed doubts to her journal.

Alice's relationships with girls like Mary Fifield were often conflict-laden, but those with boys were even more complex. Her friendship with Harry Spofford, son to old family friends of her parents, was particularly complicated. While Mary was predictable, Harry kept Alice guessing. The day he arrived at Pope's Hill in the summer of 1872 to work on the grounds, Alice, almost 15, described him as "thin, pale, dark, rather ugly, astoundingly tall, and the picture of his mother." Harry greeted her with a kiss, which pleased her. The two worked well together for the most part, spending their hours digging up flowerbeds and planting seeds; both children were skilled at gardening. Just as Alice was warming up to Harry, though, he pulled a prank on Annie, the servant, scaring her with a garter snake. "Harry, who I always have quoted as the one exception to the rule of total boy-ine depravity, is as bad as the rest," Alice complained to her journal.

Harry raised sympathy in Alice one afternoon when he was stricken with a throbbing headache. It afflicted him so strongly that he retreated indoors. Alice recalled in her journal that he "lay around in chairs with his eyes shut, looking white and miserable, which distressed me." She made him a cup of sage tea, which he drank with "unexpected meekness." Then she "soaked his feet and bayrum-ed his head."

Two days later, Harry was feeling much improved, again full of his teasing banter. They were transplanting a row of violets to the side of the summerhouse and pruning rose bushes when he began to irritate Alice with his comments about married women who kept their fathers' names.

"I would get a divorce from my wife unless she took my name," he declared.

Alice saw this as an insult aimed toward her mother, whose retention of her maiden name had caused those who imitated her to call themselves Lucy Stoners. Henry, she thought, had no right to decide what his wife might call herself. She liked him but did not know how to show it, especially when he was so obnoxious about female issues. Unaccustomed to simple boy-girl repartee, Alice overreacted to his mockery by becoming verbally sharp-edged and assertive; then, she hid her uncertainty behind a facade of bravado. Alice thought Harry would take her remarks as jokes. Unfortunately, he took them seriously, and "got it into his head [goodness knows how] that I hated him and was abusing and insulting him." When he left the household at the end of the summer, Alice ended up feeling disgusted with him and with herself.[331]

Lucy advised her daughter on all subjects, but it was only after a year had passed since this encounter with Harry that Alice mentioned any motherly hints about boys in her journal. During the summer of 1873, she and Lucy found time to talk privately during a long train ride to visit a sick aunt in northern Massachusetts. "Mamma told me all sorts of queer things about boys," she wrote, "how if you show them any attention they immediately think you want to marry them, and that they would like to marry you. How very inconvenient!"[332]

Alice's confusion about boys increased the fall that she turned 16. Her parents insisted against her will that she leave the Harris School and begin classes at a new private school named Chauncey Hall. Located in downtown Boston, it promised to prepare young men for Harvard and young ladies for Boston University. When Alice arrived, she was "both interested and appalled by this great hall full of boys," whose numbers overwhelmed those of the girls. At sixteen, Alice towered over most of her male schoolmates and found herself "a watermelon among peaches."

Before long, however, Alice adjusted to the situation well, finding that the classes at Chauncey Hall engaged her more than those she had taken at the Harris School. "I like it better at school, but it is very unpleasant that I, who would about as lief have a garter snake near me as a boy, should be the one girl in a class of from 20 to 50." Alice appreciated serious subjects, in school and outside, so she grew to value boys with aptitudes similar to hers. She remained at Chauncey Hall from September of 1873 until May of 1874. If anything, her experience among so many boys enhanced her interest in women's rights. She began to spend hours in the office of the *Woman's Journal* and welcomed the chance to meet her mother's many friends in the field.[333]

One distinct advantage reform daughters had was the opportunity their mothers afforded them to meet prominent leaders in the community. Ellen, Alla, and Harriot were all exposed to various women pioneers in the women's rights field. Alice attended a tea party to raise money for the New England Woman Suffrage Association, an auxiliary of the American Woman Suffrage Association that Lucy and Henry managed. There she met "lots of people, among them Miss [Louisa] Alcott, whose looks greatly disappointed me. I didn't expect her to be handsome, but she is positively unpleasant looking, and I think laces [wears a corset, something reform women rejected]." Henry introduced her to women's rights advocate, Parker Pillsbury, to whom she acted "cordially" even though he favored the radical Victoria Woodhull for President of the United States. After a full evening of meeting men and women in the Women's Movement, Alice concluded, "It's saltier than I thought—the world, I mean."[334]

However, Alice welcomed the salt, delved deeper into reform events, and grew in her respect for Lucy's role. To prepare for the tea party, Alice hung evergreens that she had woven into a huge motto—"Taxation without representation is tyranny"—behind the speaker's platform in Faneuil Hall, where Lucy and other luminaries would speak. Alice sat in the gallery, eyes riveted on her mother. "Mama made the most eloquent speech I ever heard from her...We all thot [sic] it had been a great success."[335]

Although she infrequently discussed her health in her journal, throughout her adolescence Alice endured nagging problems. She and Lucy, along with most of the other reform mothers and daughters, believed in the Graham theory to maintain wellbeing. Still, Alice had suffered from dysentery during the warm months and bronchitis and whooping cough in the cold, illnesses that had detained her at home and caused extended absences from school. Her worst affliction was her eyes, which caused pain and precluded sight at close distance for long periods. In the spring of 1874, she missed five weeks of classes but was able to make up her work. College would demand even more, which made Alice and her parents wary of proceeding with her enrollment.

Alice graduated with distinction from Chauncey Hall and began to prepare for college while trying to conserve her health. In the meantime, she also worked to build up the network of relatives she and Lucy treasured. Alice saw Lucy's side of the family, based in Gardner and West Brookfield, Massachusetts. This is where the beloved Emma, the daughter of Lucy's sister Sarah, lived. Only a few years older than Alice, Emma held a special place in Lucy's heart because when the child had been born, newlywed Lucy lived so nearby that she was able to treat Emma like her own baby. Alice later observed that "Emma was Mama's baby—her first, I believe; and slept with her the first night of her life." As a young woman, Emma often came to help out in Lucy's household. During 1875, the family was thrilled when Henry's younger brother, the consummate bachelor George Blackwell, married their beloved Emma. Trips to the Somerville, New Jersey home of her aunt, Antoinette (Nettie) Brown Blackwell, Lucy's sister-in-law and best friend, were especially gratifying. Alice also visited unmarried Blackwell aunts at their homes in New York City and England or at the family enclave in Martha's Vineyard.

Like the other reform mothers, Lucy Stone was able to afford college for her daughter and proudly sent her, even though she had mixed emotions about Alice beginning higher education. She worried for her daughter and wondered if, even at age 20, she was physically and mentally prepared to leave home. When Alice made the decision to enroll in the fall of 1877, the first year that Boston University opened its doors to women, Lucy resigned herself. She exclaimed, "You ought to be congratulated...Is my little girl really a member of Boston University? And ready to go on four years more?" She hungered for details about he daughter's classes, grades, and teachers, which Alice readily shared. "I wish I knew how your examination passed off though I feel sure you had no trouble," Lucy wrote after hearing about Alice's "exam jitters." She reminded Alice about her "previous success in the Arristoceans and Homer," and congratulated her for being a good pupil.[336]

Even though Alice lived with her parents and commuted by familiar trains and routes to college, she entered a new environment from Chauncey Hall. She experienced many of the same aspects of separation that Alla and Harriot did. She "ventured forth, psychologically if not always geographically," at a coeducational college in which she was one of only two women among 26 men in her class. Initially, her letters to traveling parents demonstrate concerns about running the house in their absence. Eventually, though, like students of that era, she pulled away and let campus matters dominate her daily life. One historian suggests that "in this intense period of personal growth, students questioned family values and absorbed new viewpoints from professors and other students."[337]

Lucy worried about Alice's loneliness, but she vacillated about encouraging her daughter to entertain friends, echoing Martha Wright's earlier advice to Ellen about dating. She suggested that Alice invite a woman or two to be a companion, but her advice about male guests wavered between "no" and "maybe." At first, Lucy said Alice should never ask a man over except, perhaps, one she already had invited home, which was tricky. "This is not a prohibition, but I think it has a better look not to [invite a stranger]," she advised. Then she backtracked and told Alice, "Follow your own performance when bringing out guys of your class." Five days later, Lucy changed her mind: "I am too far away [to judge] but I still advise you not to bring out gentlemen." Henry also traveled periodically but was home more than she, so Lucy advised Alice to "ask your father."[338]

Since Alice lived at home, Lucy imposed domestic management chores on her when she and Henry traveled. While attending college, Alice supervised the house's servants, a skill Lucy had instilled years before. Although Lucy extended the power of the purse to her daughter, she kept a short leash on Alice's authority. She allowed her to pay everyone but imparted detailed directions about their work. Lucy also expected Alice to spend time at the *Woman's Journal* office, so that she might learn about editing. While there, Alice could consult with Miss Fogg, Lucy's personal and business book-keeper, about household expenses. Lucy assured her daughter that she was "of course entitled to money for your meals and your allowance and you will also have to have a new pair of boots."[339]

Lucy Stone and Henry Blackwell, who were on the road for woman suffrage for much of Alice's college years, believed that their daughter would benefit from her own travel. The summer after her freshman year, in 1878, Alice embarked on her first trip to Europe, which Lucy supervised from a distance. "I don't see quite how you are to get along," Lucy wrote, but Alice got along fine. She played the perfect houseguest when she visited relatives' homes, serving as a family ambassador. Alice followed the hosts' routine, using the mornings to read or write in her room or to walk in the woods. Lucy suggested that Alice should offer to help with any family chores but not insist "lest you may be more in the way than your help will do good." Finally, Alice must "get the happiest times you can," as long as she saved her fragile eyes. Lucy concluded, "Little Cub I cannot tell you how much we wish you a delightful time of real rest and enjoyment." Finally, she advised Alice that, on the trip home, she should be punctual, choose a stateroom near the middle of the ship, pack her trunk efficiently, and, most importantly, "be very discreet."[340]

After her sophomore year, in 1879, Alice returned to Europe, this time with her father, Henry. Lucy, home alone, took pleasure in thinking of the joy the two would share. "Make the most of it, dear Little Cub," Lucy wrote, "and if possible get Papa not to hurry but to take it easy. There is

Lucy Stone, 1878
(Boston Athenaeum)

no need to fret about me." Lucy relished Alice's letters, saving them "for dessert with my dinner."[341]

Lucy kept Alice up to date on stateside concerns through rich correspondence. She reported on suffrage meetings, her work at the *Journal*, and domestic activities. Her garden was gay with gladioli, four o'clocks, geraniums, and berries, enhanced by string beans ready to eat. Lucy loved warming food over her little oil stove and making treats for herself. She teased that she could be employed as anyone's servant. She always closed her letters sounding content, invariably planning domestic projects like canning peaches that would be ready when her daughter and Henry returned. Whenever travel separated Lucy and Alice, they expressed deep feelings for each other. "With hosts of love for you, darling dear, and with love to the cousins, I am, Little Cub, Your Mother," she signed one letter. Lucy read and reread Alice's letters, "putting them against my cheek, for love of the fingers that lay along the paper as they traced the words." After Lucy received Alice's card on the occasion of her 60th birthday, she thanked "Little Alice" for her "letter written in haste and for the sixty kisses that came in good time."[342]

Alice interrupted her studies during her junior year when Lucy was diagnosed with a bleeding lung. When the illness became life-threatening in May of 1880, Alice took a leave of absence to nurse her, just as Lucy had nursed her own mother. Alice accompanied Lucy to Wilmington, Delaware and settled her mother in for a long recuperation alongside her beloved niece, Emma Blackwell, and her husband, George. Alice completed her degree from Boston University at the age of 23 and graduated with her class the following June in 1881. Of all the reform daughters, Alice could best predict her future.[343]

Alice Stone Blackwell: Writing Her Public Life, 1881–1893

When Alice graduated from Boston University, her mother declared, "She might do what she chose; all the professions were open to her and she could enter any line of business." But did she really have a choice? Alice's parents had been preparing her to take over the *Woman's Journal* since she had been a young girl. There is no indication that Alice ever refused or resented the position, but she initially doubted her ability to fulfill it. Many contemporary New Women would have envied her opportunity. Publishing the *Journal* gave Alice an entrée into a world whose management ranks were normally closed to women.[344]

Alice became editor of the *Woman's Journal* on September 10, 1882, a few days before she turned 25. Home alone and in charge, Alice wondered if she was up to the task. Lucy and Henry were in Madison, Wisconsin, attending woman suffrage meetings that they expected Alice to report among her first stories. "Use your discretion" to decide what to print, Lucy wrote. That said, she must never omit any articles her mother sent her. When she did not have enough copy, Alice was directed to include selected articles from other sources. She must acknowledge subscribers and donors and pay attention to Lucy's instructions.[345]

Lucy sometimes praised Alice, especially for her ability to handle the pressures of the job. "This is Thursday," Lucy wrote from Grand Island, Nebraska. "We always think of you on that day as busy and tired, but more and more getting used to it." After Alice served as editor for a month, Lucy congratulated her on a good job. She and Henry read Lucy's *Journal* with pride and expressed satisfaction with her editorial comments.[346]

Besides qualifying as a New Woman by virtue of her college education and career, Alice personified the description by remaining single. It is presumed that both she and Alla Foster never married because their careers and independence offered an engaging life, and no man had presented a compelling reason to alter it. Both of their mothers had resisted marriage until their mid-30s, an unusually advanced age for that era. Neither Lucy Stone nor Abby Kelley Foster indicated any concern in regard to their daughters' choices to remain unwed. Historian Nancy Woloch claims that by the late 19th Century, even the word spinster, which had once signified a marginal member of society, had "moved from the periphery of history to center stage." Single New Women who assumed prominent roles in various professions, reform, and women's education were increasingly common. They might have been lesbians, never found the right man, or were determined to be self-supporting and not passively accept marriage as their only option in life.[347]

Women like Alice and Alla chose lives that were, as historian Barbara Solomon notes, no longer "predetermined as a simple transition from daughter to wife to mother." Undergraduate experiences had strengthened women's independence, allowing many of them to think of themselves as individuals who would not be forced into any particular pattern. In this and many other ways, the reform daughters enjoyed the liberties for which their mothers had fought. Alice and Alla did not marry, but lived lives that they controlled, exercising authority that stemmed from their professions. They, in turn, acted as examples to other women that life held more opportunities than previously imagined as the 19th Century progressed.[348]

On the summer morning of July 21, 1884, Lucy offered Alice another opportunity to ensure her future. Alice was at the home of her Aunts Ellen and Emily Blackwell when a letter arrived from Lucy, written on *Woman's Journal* stationary. Only two pages drifted out when she opened the onionskin envelope, covered with her mother's distinct, nearly illegible handwriting. This letter brought news of Lucy's will for Alice, who would turn 27 in two months.

"My dear child," Lucy began, "I have today written my will and I have given you the bulk of what I have." As Alice read, she learned the details. Lucy would leave her holdings that included $4,000 in stocks, their house in Boston, and a house in Montclair, New Jersey. Henry would have the use of the Boston house as long as he lived. Alice would have the proceeds of the stock and rent from the Montclair property, to share with Henry if she had no husband or children and to support her for life; it amounted to $12,000 a year.

Lucy wrote, "But whether here or there, darling little child of mine, my heart will always be warm to you. Be sure you are right and then never fear. Try and get an intelligent conscience." Alice's first thought was that Lucy, now 66, was dying. Perhaps it was only natural that Lucy would have bequeathed this sizable sum to Alice, assuring her independence for life. But why wasn't she giving more to Henry, who had never earned a steady income or accumulated savings and was healthy at age 59? He would probably live well past Lucy. She was stunned but pleased that Mama had placed so much trust in her.[349]

Over the next few years, Alice monitored her mother's health as Lucy limped through the late fall and early winter. By February of 1886, Lucy's rheumatism, heart troubles, and stomach ailments convinced her to retreat to a warm climate. As she had done in 1880, Lucy recuperated in Thomasville, Georgia for three months with her niece, Emma, and her husband, George. Meanwhile, Alice managed the *Journal* and oversaw the house. Alice expected her usual instructions, but they never came. Lucy had already begun to turn over the reins to Alice.[350]

Alice marked her new independence at the *Journal* with her personal stamp, which reflected an avid interest in woman suffrage. In January 1887, she began publishing the "Woman's Column," which she sold separately to newspapers looking for suffrage items. After a few months, it was thriving, but her mother worried. "I do not want my sole daughter to be drawn to death in it," Lucy wrote from Georgia. Alice assured her she was handling the work well, though she missed her terribly. "Darling little mother," she wrote, "I love you so much it makes me ache."[351]

Alice's editorial work connected her to other New Women, who formed "a dedicated corps of leaders who wrote and spoke frequently and kept the [woman suffrage] movement alive." Between 1870 and 1890, 33 woman suffrage periodicals were launched, but only the *Woman's Journal* endured. It was the most successful of all women's rights periodicals, and although it required support from Lucy's personal funds, by 1883 it boasted 30,000 readers. The periodical acted as a consciousness-raiser by taking every scrap of news on the suffrage front, from abroad as well as in the United States, and compiling them conveniently into one collection. At the same time, it promoted expanding opportunities for women's self-development. Over the years, Alice's column, later titled "What Women are Doing," publicized breakthroughs in women's educational and work opportunities and celebrated female "firsts." Innovations like these made Alice's and Lucy's *Journal* superior to its competitors.

Alice's confidence as an editor of the *Woman's Journal* faced a challenge in 1887, a few years after she had assumed the job. Rachel Foster, a rising star in the woman suffrage movement and Susan B. Anthony's "niece," had begun to publish a suffrage news service as a voice of the American Woman Suffrage Association's rival, the National Woman Suffrage Association. Alice wrote in dismay to her mother, seeking her counsel. With the help of Susan, Rachel had convinced the Pennsylvania affiliate of the National Association to drop its subscription to Alice's paper and subscribe instead to Rachel's comparable and competitively cheaper newsletter.[352]

"You should not let Rachel trouble you, dear," Lucy said, "but I am glad you wrote me about it." Instead of sympathizing with Alice, Lucy invited her daughter to advance beyond the acrimony of the woman suffrage conflicts of the past two decades. Alice should welcome "any real help" that her rivals gave to the cause, "even the worst of them." It was time to be conciliatory and perhaps bring about a union between the two factions. Lucy told Alice, "I am ready to "rejoice in good work no matter who did it.""[353]

The leaders of the National and American associations had been personally out of touch for most of the duration of the rift. Lucy had not seen Elizabeth for 10 years; she had occasionally encountered Susan but had not shared a stage with her for two decades. Most of the younger suffragists, though cognizant of the split, found friends in both factions. Alice and Rachel Foster, acquaintances before the recent problem, typified the new generation, being better educated, more financially secure, and more sophisticated than their older counterparts, but they were influenced by senior leaders. Lucy believed that Elizabeth's National Association was doing "very good work" and that there was "no reason why we should not unite." Merging would remove grievances that both sides felt.[354]

Lucy's American Association took the first step in reconciling with Elizabeth's National Association. It invited representatives from the two sides to convene in October 1887 to lay the groundwork for reunification. Next

Alice Stone Blackwell, 1880s
(Library of Congress)

was a meeting between Lucy and Susan in Boston. Susan was suspicious at first and worried that if she refused the overture, everyone would blame her for the failure, but she finally agreed. Susan requested that Alice and Rachel be present as well, so "that each of us may have a suffrage daughter to help bring about the desired end." She signed the letter, "Yours hopefully, Susan B. Anthony."[355]

The day of the meeting, December 21, 1887, dawned cold and wet in Boston. Alice and Lucy waited at the *Journal* office for Susan and Rachel to join them. Some historians would later contend that the success of the encounter was because of Alice. But before the gathering, Alice had told a friend that she "dreaded these people even more than" her mother did. Alice had felt insulted by Rachel. Even so, once the meeting started, she found that the younger participants were more willing to work together than their older counterparts. In her memoir, Alice remarked, "When I began to work for a union the elders were not keen for it," but "nothing really stood in the way except the unpleasant feelings engendered during the long separation." Alice believed those could be overcome for both sides were "sincerely devoted" to the cause.[356]

It required the presence of Elizabeth, Susan, and Lucy to complete unification. In March of 1888, Susan persuaded Elizabeth to leave her grandchildren in England to attend the first meeting of what they were calling the International Council of Women. The gathering was also intended to celebrate the 40th anniversary of the Seneca Falls Convention of 1848, which Susan and Elizabeth saw as the beginning of the women's rights movement. Elizabeth arrived in Washington during a severe snowstorm, reportedly wrote her talk while Susan confined her to her hotel room, and delivered one of the most spectacular speeches she had ever written. "Through suffering," Elizabeth said, women held the key to understanding one another. Women shared the bondage of their sex, whether they were "housed in golden cages with every want supplied, or wandering in the dreary deserts of life, friendless and forsaken."[357]

Lucy Stone presented an equally riveting talk, the second of the forum. For the sake of unity, she agreed to 1848 being marked as the founding year, but she recognized 1850 as the formal beginning of the movement, for that was the year the first National Women's Rights Convention was held in Worcester. Now 70 years old, stout, and crippled with rheumatism, Lucy told her story of the pioneer women's rights movement, capturing the attention of her listeners within minutes of her opening remarks. Alice, in the audience with her father, recalled her mother's wrinkled face as radiant but strained. Elizabeth, enormous in her black silk gown capped with a white lace collar and her white hair rolled in fat, cigar-shaped curls, dominated the stage with her attention riveted on Lucy. Susan sat on the podium next to her, polite, listening as if Lucy's words prescribed only one version of the history of woman suffrage. They were all pioneers, but as historian Lisa Tetrault claims, each pioneer had a different version of what actually happened.[358]

Lucy succeeded in her aims. She had given credit for women's advances to disparate elements and lessened some of the friction between the factions. As the ovation ebbed, she settled, exhausted, into her chair, one of seven people on the platform, showing more fatigue and pain than joy. She sat still for two more hours of short talks by 20 other "valiant old soldiers of the cross."[359]

Three years of behind-the-scenes work were required to make the unity meeting a reality; it opened February 15, 1890, in Washington, D.C. with a gala celebration of Susan B. Anthony's 70th birthday. Alice and Henry did not arrive until the following day and illness kept Lucy Stone away altogether. Ellen Wright Garrison and her sister, Eliza Wright Osborne, to the "delight" of Susan B. Anthony, attended the first meeting they had graced in decades. Elizabeth came from a sanatorium with daughters Harriot and Maggie, who were more concerned about her health than about the well-being of the woman suffrage movement. Maggie Stanton Lawrence, a reluctant speaker, paid tribute to Susan at the grand supper, which was served in a decorated dining room. Elizabeth confessed, "I am ashamed to say that we kept up the festivities till after two o'clock."[360]

On the following morning, challenging business began. Elizabeth sat on the podium with her daughters; she invited Harriot to speak for a few moments about England's radical woman suffrage movement. At this juncture, the delegates were not about to endorse extreme tactics; they had gathered to compromise and to form a new group called the National American Woman Suffrage Association.[361]

Alice focused on the election of officers for the new association. It was she who had drafted the procedural rules. She worried that the election process might not follow the officers' agreement, about which most delegates were uninformed. Alice had reason to fret because even though the organizers had agreed that neither Susan nor Elizabeth would serve as the new association's president, when Elizabeth was nominated, she did not withdraw her name. Lucy had foreseen possible betrayal, writing Alice, "I fear you may have had a tough time with the enemy." It seemed unlikely that Lucy would have the strength to travel from Boston to join them the next day. Elizabeth was quickly elected president and Susan vice president of the new organization; Lucy was unanimously elected to head the executive committee. When Alice was awarded the position of recording secretary, only graciousness and the certainty that the American Association would have a voice compelled her to accept.[362]

The meeting left Alice and Henry stunned. At day's close, they returned to their rooms where they found letters waiting from Lucy that informed them that she could not make the trip because her "cough is hard and doesn't get better." She called it a "real grief to me not to go, where I should so much like to be among our friends." Having witnessed the jubilation of Anthony and Stanton, Alice wondered whether Lucy would have been able to keep up the pretense of goodwill regarding the union. Perhaps it was best that she had stayed home.[363]

The following day, the last of the convention, attendees voted to form the new National American Woman Suffrage Association (NAWSA). Alice's unification work was done. She now had to write about the event for the *Woman's Journal*, continuing her role as recorder, rather than maker, of history. When historians insisted that Alice had played a central role in the reunion, she denied it, acknowledging only that her mother had inspired her and that a few friends had kept her steadfast.[364]

Alice and Lucy's relationship matured, but in many ways mother continued to treat daughter like a child. Nevertheless, they worked together for woman suffrage and the *Woman's Journal*. When Alice turned 33, Lucy wrote Henry, "This is astonishing! And I am very grateful for her good intellect, her good conscience, and for HER."[365]

As time went on, Alice cultivated her editing and writing. She saw women's rights in a broader landscape, taking interest in what her Aunt Nettie Blackwell called "collateral issues." Although she never considered marriage, she wrote about the inequality of matrimony. When addressing suffrage, Alice made it her special responsibility to counter the growing arguments of "anti's," who fought vehemently against the vote for women. Alice exercised her position as secretary of the NAWSA, corresponding with Elizabeth Cady Stanton about annual meetings and programs for the conventions, but the two women were never close.[366]

In the summer of 1892, Lucy's health was failing. She confessed to a friend, "I have never been so miserable with rheumatism as more pain, keen like a hard digging knife into my joints." She exercised financial independence from Henry; it was time for the couple to keep their money separate. On May 1, 1893, their 38th anniversary, she revealed the frustration she had been feeling throughout their marriage. Having assured him in an earlier letter that she had provided for him in her will, Lucy would help him out occasionally, but she had "never liked having my money put in your bank." She had supplemented his meager income throughout their marriage, largely because he had contributed "so much for women." It was time now "that we will let it go into my bank."[367]

Lucy had earned most of her money through her lecturing skills, which satisfied her but drained her energy. On May 15, 1893, at the World's Columbian Exhibition in Chicago, she delivered the last speech in her stellar public career. Her small, slightly bent figure moved at a touchingly slow, feeble pace. Her talk, rewarded by wave upon wave of applause, taxed her severely. Stomach pain prevented her from enduring more than a few moments of congratulations. Henry missed the event because of miscommunication. Lucy, like her pioneer colleagues Elizabeth, Martha, and Abby, had enjoyed a long public career. Her husband was not often in the audience. What mattered to Lucy was the presence of Alice, who proudly assisted her to and from the podium, marveling at her mother's continuing ability to stun her listeners.[368]

Lucy and Alice remained in Chicago for two weeks while mother introduced daughter to congressional representatives and groomed her, not only to continue editing the *Woman's Journal*, but also for a significant role in the legislative arena. Lucy paved the way for what she imagined would be her daughter's future. When Lucy returned to Pope's Hill after obligatory visits to relatives in Massachusetts, she and Henry both knew "my working days are over."[369]

The next few months acted as a testament to a mother-daughter relationship marked by trust. Lucy now required a full-time caretaker, but both she and her daughter knew Alice would serve Lucy better at the editor's desk than her bedside. The beauty of this bond was how closely the women knew each other, in weaknesses and strengths. Lucy loved Alice, but she longed for her niece Emma, who had spent so many months under their roof as a young woman. This did not mean that Lucy loved Alice any less, nor that Alice failed to cater to her mother's needs, even though George felt it inappropriate for his wife to take what should have been Alice's place. Emma understood that she was no threat to her cousin and felt cherished and privileged to accept the job of nursing her aunt. She "loves her mother and wants to help her, but feels inadequate—she isn't heartless or indifferent." Emma argued that "women with none of her aunt's public skills have been miserable homemakers." Alice perhaps had "an absolutely different temperament," but for this she could not be blamed. Henry had meanwhile consulted other doctors besides his physician sister Emily about Lucy's condition. One diagnosed her distress as stomach cancer and warned that the prognosis was poor. Medical tests at the time described the ailment as inoperable and incurable. Treatment to ease the pain included gastric lavage—literally the washing out of digestive organs—and the administration of alkalies, or basic salts, for relief. These palliatives were viewed as more atrocious than the symptoms.[370]

Emma was Lucy's nurse until late August, when Alice returned from the annual camping trip her parents insisted she take. When Emma left, they hired a professional nurse to help Alice with her mother's physical care. Within a few weeks, Lucy asked that Emma return. Only her cool hand soothed. It wasn't that Alice didn't try to comfort—she simply lacked the bedside manner for which the gravely ill long.[371]

"Do you expect Emma today?" Lucy asked her daughter every day. Alice pleaded with her cousin to return to Pope's Hill. "Mama keeps expressing the wish to take ether or something that would painlessly end her life," Alice wrote Emma before her visit. "When Dr. Emily was here, I told her that if Mama should get into distress and want it done, I mean to do it for her." The extreme measure remained unnecessary.[372]

Emma finally returned to nurse Lucy for her last few days. Visitors and flowers poured into the house. Nothing could keep death at bay; on the evening of October 18, 1893, Lucy lifted her head slowly and leaned forward, her stomach pulsing in paroxysms of agony. She motioned to Alice to come closer, to lean in.

"Make the world better," she quietly commanded her daughter.

Then she sank back into her bed. Finally, she escaped her pain, falling into a coma. Twenty minutes later, the 75-year-old women's rights leader exhaled her last breath.

Alice and Henry sat for a while near Lucy's bed in the parlor at Pope's Hill, her beloved home. They had moved Lucy to the veranda, encircling her bed with screens for privacy from the household but keeping the windows within sight.

"She has left us," Emma wrote her mother, Sarah, minutes after Lucy died. "I am glad for her that it is finished, but it leaves the others here bitterly bereft."[373]

Alice was stricken, as much from her mother's death as from her final words: "Make the world better." For the past three weeks, mother and daughter had been more preoccupied with gastric lavage or alkali salts than with the suffrage campaign and *Woman's Journal*. During the rare hours that Lucy's pain abated, she had given Alice detailed instructions about editorials, donations, and hopes for her reform legacy. She had directed Alice on domestic responsibilities as well, from the care of the house and the education of the cousins to the luncheon menu to be offered at her funeral. Now Lucy could say no more; she had left her daughter the care of the world.

Alice spent a few years engaged in her mother's work on woman suffrage before she began to work for causes to help care for the world. She served as the recording secretary of the National American Woman Suffrage Association until 1908 and became one of its auditors in 1909 and 1910, maintaining the Blackwell presence in the new organization. She continued to edit the *Woman's Journal* until 1917, when it briefly became the *Woman Citizen* before resuming its original title. She made countering the anti-suffrage campaign a major goal of her journalistic work, and after the Nineteenth Amendment granted women the vote in 1920, she persisted in championing political rights. She was instrumental in the founding of the League of Women Voters and prominent in the Woman's Christian Temperance Union.

Alice ventured into international arenas, first as a translator of Spanish material. Then, Russia claimed her attention, leading her to reorganize the Society of Friends of Russian Freedom in Boston in 1903 and write a biography of the Russian figure, Catherine Breshkovsky. The Armenian massacres in Turkey around World War I arrested her attention and led her to study that language and become a translator of Armenian poetry into English.[374] Perhaps Alice's greatest tribute to Lucy's legacy was her biography of her mother, published in 1930, the only book by a reform daughter that leaves us her memory of her mother's life. Though she, like Elizabeth Cady Stanton, went blind in later life, Alice continued her many endeavors until her death in 1950 at age 92. Without a doubt, she had "made the world better."

✳ ✳ ✳

Motherhood altered the life of Lucy Stone more dramatically than that of the other reform mothers. Before Alice arrived, Lucy had decided to take only a short break from her outstanding career as one of the best antislavery and women's rights speakers of the day. However, adoration for Alice, fear for her daughter's welfare, her own physical ailments, and a growing insecurity about her ability to speak publicly altered Lucy's priorities. Though she had planned to resume her lecturing after Alice's birth, like Abby Kelley Foster had, she reversed her decision and remained at home for most of her daughter's first 10 years. Alice developed as a confident young girl with enormous affection for both parents and a willingness to learn the skills and values they taught her.

Through her example, Lucy demonstrated how to lead the difficult life of a woman but included lessons on joy as well. Alice's personal journal reflects the exuberance and sense that the young woman brought to life. Her willingness to accept Lucy's tutelage in domestic skills reflects her parents' work ethic and general good nature. Aunt Lucy had trained all of her nieces in housewifery but left the most thorough and enduring lessons for her daughter. Treasuring her own education from Oberlin, Lucy made sure that Alice received a similar experience, sending her daughter to grammar schools, boarding schools, excellent day schools, and the recently coeducational Boston University. She assumed Alice would be able to edit the Woman's Journal. Lucy had prepared Alice for much more than managing a house or newspaper. She imparted the importance of being a true friend and valued family member. Lucy also tried to instill ideas about male-female relationships, however clumsily, and offer an ear to Alice's blossoming spirituality. She insisted her daughter reserve time to relax and care for her fragile health.

Following the path set before her by Lucy, Alice expanded women's rights and suffrage in her life's work—especially in the international arena—beyond that that had been previously achieved by other reform daughters.

Conclusion

On Saturday, October 23, 1915, 40,000 women and 10,000 men took part in a great suffrage parade and mass meeting—the fifth of its kind in New York City and one of the most remarkable street pageants ever seen. Unique among the parade vehicles was a horse-drawn carriage whose every inch was covered with flowers in the new suffrage colors: white, purple, and green. The snowy-gloved hands of an erect young woman held the reins. Dressed in a crisp white suit accented by a sash emblazoned with the phrase "Votes for Women," she stared ahead through unblinking bespectacled eyes. She sported a huge helmet-shaped bowler designed with a white, purple, and green emblem. A skilled driver, she carried precious cargo.

Antoinette (Nettie) Brown Blackwell and her niece, Alice Stone Blackwell, rode behind the anonymous chauffeur. Nettie was continuing her fight for woman suffrage even at age 90. A warm white cloak was draped over the shoulders of her wool dress to help shelter her from the brisk fall air. An elegant though modest bonnet embellished with copious purple and green ribbons adorned her naturally white head, completing the trio of suffragist colors. Next to Nettie sat her beloved niece, Alice, the 58-year-old daughter of Lucy Stone, her oldest friend and school chum, who had died more than 20 years before. Alice appreciated her position in the honored place next to Aunt Nettie. Her small stern face was nearly entirely hidden by a hat whose ample flowers could have served as a handsome centerpiece. She presented an incongruous image—her severe features set off by a soft bouquet, her small body enrobed in swathes of white flannel.

Although Nettie had attended many of New York City's parades, lately she had been less than enthusiastic, writing to Alice, "The whole thing is so tiresome I half regret planning to go to New York. Such is life."[375] Alice, living in Boston, had never been present at a parade but always reported them in the *Woman's Journal.* As secretary to the co-sponsor of the National American Woman Suffrage Association, this year Alice had determined to show her support in person for this event. With her sense of the parade's historical significance, Alice made sure the wagon she and Aunt Nettie rode in would mark the occasion and find a place in Washington's Smithsonian Museum.

The parade had expanded in size nearly four-fold since the first of its kind in 1910. Harriot Stanton Blatch had conceived the idea a few years after her mother, Elizabeth Cady Stanton, had died. "Convinced as I was that mankind is moved to action by emotion, not by argument and reason," Harriot had written Alice Stone Blackwell at the *Journal,* "I saw the possibilities in a suffrage parade." Harriot could not imagine anything "more stirring than hundreds of women, carrying banners, marching—marching—marching! The public would be aroused, the press would spread the story far and wide, and the interest of our own workers would be fired."[376]

Harriot was not present for this fifth parade in New York City. After the New York Legislature had defeated a woman suffrage resolution for the fourth time in 1913, she re-directed her activism toward other projects. Instead, she passed down the obligation of parade organization to her daughter, Nora Stanton Blatch, a Cornell University engineering graduate who often drove the automobiles for older riders. Nettie and Alice rode in one of few horse-drawn carriages, feeling at home in a fashionable crowd. More importantly, they were militant leaders, fearful of nothing, who liked the idea of propaganda.[377]

Alice Stone Blackwell and Nettie Blackwell traveled back to New York City later that month to attend a second momentous event focused on woman

Alice Stone Blackwell & Antoinette Brown Blackwell at
NYC Woman Suffrage Parade, 1915
(Courtesy of Blackwell Family Papers, Schlessinger Library)"

suffrage—the 100th anniversary of Elizabeth Cady Stanton's birth. Harriot Stanton Blatch, now 59, had spent six weeks arranging the Saturday, October 30, gala at New York's Hotel Astor. "Intended solely for propaganda purposes," Harriot insisted the event would "not be a meaningless laudation of a life that is passed."[378] Instead, it would draw attention to the fact that women still did not have the right of the vote in the United States.

Every suffrage association in America sent representatives to the Centennial celebration. Harriot had chosen members of the Honorary Committee with care to demonstrate that her mother was a "many-idea'd woman," as well as one who "underlined the breadth of the suffrage coalition" that Harriot was helping to forge. She expected 1,000 people, and the pictures of the event show more than 100 tables of eight. Among the guests sitting in that huge crowd were some of the reform mothers and daughters. It's hard to imagine that Alice did not have some feelings of resentment toward the woman in whose honor the lunch was being held. Her mother and Elizabeth Cady Stanton, close allies when they had launched the women's rights movement in the 1850s, grew so far apart that two separate woman suffrage organizations emerged during their later years. They had died without a full reconciliation; it remained for Alice and Harriot to carry on and mend the rift.

Harriot's family surrounded her at the head table. Her daughter, Nora Stanton Blatch, had been at her side for all of the parades and public demonstrations over the past five years. Her sister, Maggie Stanton Lawrence, assumed a less public stand on suffrage but helped from behind the scenes.

Ellen Wright Garrison, 75, also had many relatives in her midst. Her mother, Martha Wright, had tried to mend the rift between Elizabeth and Lucy. She had died on congenial terms with both but was unable to bridge their gap. As the wife of William Lloyd Garrison, Jr., Ellen hosted women descended from friends of Elizabeth, as well as Lucy. Ellen herself had become a life-long member of the National American Woman Suffrage Association in 1900. Her daughter, Eleanor Garrison, had never met her grandmother Martha, but in 1912, she became an organizer for Carrie

Chapman Catt, who headed the New York State campaign for woman suffrage.[379]

The reform mothers would have been extremely proud to see their daughters and granddaughters gathered together to remember them and continue the fight for suffrage. They would have been surprised and saddened to learn that only one of the pioneers, Antoinette Brown Blackwell, would be alive when in 1920 America finally granted women the vote after a 72 year struggle. What would not have surprised the reform mothers was that their daughters had moved into arenas besides women's rights. Each would probably vote when finally given the opportunity, but they did not see that as their mothers' major hope for them. Ardent as they were, Martha, Abby, Elizabeth, and Lucy did not view their political struggle as the quintessential purpose of their daughters' lives. Acquiring women's rights was only one aspect of being a woman and only part of the legacy they wished to leave.

Reform mothers held expectations like those of their contemporary 19th Century peers. They hoped their daughters would learn how to achieve satisfaction not only as they themselves had—from reform and activism—but also from acquiring skills to maintain their independence. Their young women should pursue education, housekeeping, friendships, love, and motherhood, but only if they wished. If reform daughters dipped into their mothers' pioneer work in women's rights, this would be a satisfying surprise; it certainly was not expected.

They held simple goals for their daughters, not unlike the desires of all mothers in all eras. They hoped, first, that the young women knew how to survive—alone or as a member of a family. They taught their daughters how to master basic housewifery: how to milk a cow, gather eggs, plant a vegetable garden, make bread, hire honest kitchen help, and balance the books. Reform mothers showed young girls how to accept responsibility to help other children and to anticipate the needs of unhappy or lonely companions and schoolmates or relatives. The young women must understand how to communicate within their families to help members reach their greatest contentment.

Reform mothers savored sharing pleasure with their daughters but also taught them how to cope with life's challenges. During their youth, three of the four daughters experienced illness, which their mothers helped them manage. The reform mothers left a legacy of advice that seems more commonplace than revolutionary. They all wanted their daughters to make their marks on the world, as clearly indicated by deathbed wishes like that of Lucy Stone to Alice: "Make the world better." However, they expected the younger women would satisfy that goal in their own manner.

When Ellen Wright, Alla Foster, Harriot Stanton, and Alice Blackwell looked at their mothers' lives, they did not see reform mothers. Instead, each viewed her mother as a source of creativity and inspiration, then determined how to shape and fit a life that suited them. Their mothers made it clear that they never sought to reproduce themselves in their daughters. Martha Wright, Abby Kelley Foster, Elizabeth Cady Stanton, and Lucy Stone served not as reform mothers to their daughters but simply as mothers.

Ellen Wright Garrison and Harriot Stanton Blatch, although they raised children in two different eras, copied many elements of their mothers' parenting. They stressed skills in domesticity, networking, and obtaining educations, but because they were raising children who were born nearly 20 years apart, were able to present different opportunities to their respective children. What held firm among all the mothers and grandmothers was a continued belief in finding justice for freed peoples and rights for women. How each person exercised those ideals varied over their lives. When granddaughters embraced their grandmother's causes, the sweetness multiplied. But love between generations never relied on the level of participation. One scholar contends that grandmothers give their grandchildren, rather than children, the "physical affection, the indulgence and praise, approval and affection beyond our chastened dreams—all are transferred to our children." Grandmothers might give this love to "strangers," but they actually are passing it to their daughters.

When reform mothers died, they may have left legacies of writings, statues, portraits, and achievements named for them, but they also left so much more. They left the legacy of their precocious daughters, who realized the dreams their provocative pioneer work for women had made possible.

Bibliography

Primary Sources, Unpublished

Abby Kelley Foster Papers, American Antiquarian Society, Worcester, Massachusetts

Abby Kelley Foster Papers, Worcester Historical Museum, Worcester, Massachusetts

Blackwell Family Papers, Schlesinger Library, Radcliffe Institute of Study, Harvard University, Cambridge, Massachusetts

Blackwell Family Papers, Library of Congress, Washington, D.C.

Elizabeth Cady Stanton Papers, Vassar College, Poughkeepsie, New York

Elizabeth Cady Stanton Papers, Library of Congress, Washington, D.C.

Garrison Family Papers, Sophia Smith Collection, Smith College, Northampton, Massachusetts

Harriot Stanton Blatch Papers, Vassar College, Poughkeepsie, New York

Harriot Stanton Blatch Diary, in Rhoda Barney Jenkins Papers, Greenwich, Connecticut

Selected Primary Sources, Published

Barney, Nora Stanton. "Spanning Two Centuries: The Autobiography of Nora Stanton Barney." History Workshop, no. 22. Autumn 1986.

Blackwell, Alice Stone. *Lucy Stone: Pioneer of Woman's Rights*. Boston: Little, Brown, and Company, 1930.

Blatch, Harriot Stanton, and Alma Lutz. *Challenging Years: The Memoirs of Harriot Stanton Blatch.* New York: G.P. Putnam's Sons, 1940.

Gordon, Ann, Tamara Gaskell Miller, Susan I. Johns, Oona Schmid, Mary Poole, Veronica A. Wilson, and Stacy Kinlock Sewell, eds. *Selected Papers of Elizabeth Cady Stanton and Susan B. Anthony, Volumes I-VI.* New Brunswick: Rutgers University, 1997-2013.

Stanton, Elizabeth Cady. *Eighty Years and More: Reminiscences 1815-1897.* n.p.: T. Fisher Unwin, 1898; reprint, Boston: Northeastern University Press, 1993.

Stanton, Elizabeth Cady, Susan B. Anthony, and Matilda Joslyn Gage. *The History of Woman Suffrage, Vol. 1.* New York: Fowler & Wells, 1881.

Stanton, Theodore, and Harriot Stanton Blatch, eds. *Elizabeth Cady Stanton as Revealed by Her Letters, Diary and Reminiscences, Volumes I and II.* New York and London: Harper Brothers Publishers, 1922.

Secondary Sources

Alonso, Harriet. *Growing Up Abolitionist: The Story of the Garrison Children.* Amherst: University of Massachusetts, 2002.

Arcana, Judith. *Our Mothers' Daughters.* Berkeley: Shameless Hussy Press, 1979.

Bacon, Margaret Hope. *I Speak for My Sister: The Life of Abby Kelley Foster.* New York: Thomas Y. Crowell Company, 1974.

Bacon, Margaret Hope. *Valiant Friend: The Life of Lucretia Mott.* New York: Walker and Company, 1980.

Barry, Kathleen. *Susan B. Anthony: A Biography of a Singular Feminist.* New York: Ballantine Books, 1988.

Burkett, Nancy H. *Abby Kelley Foster and Stephen Foster.* Worcester, Massachusetts: Worcester Bicentennial Commission, 1976.

Cazden, Elizabeth. *Antoinette Brown Blackwell: A Biography.* Old Westbury, New York: The Feminist Press, 1983.

Daniels, Elizabeth. *Main to Mudd and More: An Informal History of Vassar College Buildings,* revised edition. Poughkeepsie, New York: Vassar College Press, 1996.

Degler, Carl. *At Odds: Women and the Family from the Revolution to the Present.* Oxford: Oxford University Press, 1980.

DuBois, Ellen Carol. *Harriot Stanton Blatch and the Winning of Woman Suffrage.* London and New Haven: Yale University Press, 1997.

Ginzberg, Lori. *Elizabeth Cady Stanton: An American Life.* New York: Hill and Wang, 2009.

Ginzberg, Lori. *Women and the Work of Benevolence: Morality, Politics, and Class in the 19th Century United States.* New Haven and London: Yale University Press, 1990.

Graham, Sara Hunter Graham. *Woman Suffrage and the New Democracy.* New Haven, Connecticut: Yale University Press, 1996.

Griffith, Elisabeth. *In Her Own Right: The Life of Elizabeth Cady Stanton.* New York and Oxford: Oxford University Press, 1984.

Horowitz, Helen Lefkowitz. *Alma Mater: Design and Experience in the Women's Colleges from their Nineteenth-Century Beginnings to the 1930s.* New York: Knopf, 1984.

Kerr, Andrea. *Lucy Stone: Speaking Out for Equality.* New Brunswick, New Jersey: Rutgers University Press, 1992.

Kraditor, Aileen. *Up from the Pedestal: Selected Writings in the History of Feminism.* New York: Quadrangle, 1975.

Lasser, Carol and Marlene Deahl Merrill, eds. *Friends and Sisters: Letters Between Lucy Stone and Antoinette Brown Blackwell.* Urbana and Chicago: University of Illinois Press, 1987.

Lebsock, Suzanne. *The Free Women of Petersburg: Status and Culture in a Southern Town, 1784-1860.* New York: Norton and Company, 1984.

Matthews, Jean. *The Rise of the New Woman: The Women's Movement in America, 1875-1930.* Chicago: Ivan R. Dee, 2013.

McMillen, Sally. *Lucy Stone: An Unapologetic Life.* Oxford and New York: Oxford University Press, 2015.

Merrill, Marlene Deahl, ed. *Growing Up in Boston's Gilded Age: The Journal of Alice Stone Blackwell, 1872-1874.* New Haven: Yale University Press, 1990.

Million, Joelle. *Woman's Voice, Woman's Place: Lucy Stone and the Birth of the Woman's Rights Movement.* Westport, Connecticut: Praeger Press, 2003.

Penney, Sherry H. and Livingston, James D. *A Very Dangerous Woman: Martha Wright and Women's Rights.* Amherst: University of Massachusetts Press, 2004.

Smith-Rosenberg, Carol. *Disorderly Conduct: Visions of Gender in Victorian America*. New York: Oxford University Press, 1985.

Soloman, Barbara. *"In the Company of Educated Women": A History of Women and Higher Education in America*. New Haven and London: Yale University Press, 1985.

Sterling, Dorothy. *Ahead of Her Time: Abby Kelley and the Politics of Antislavery*. New York: Norton and Company, 1991.

Tetrault, Lisa. *The Myth of Seneca Falls: Memory and the Women's Suffrage Movement*. Chapel Hill: University of North Carolina Press, 2014.

Venet, Wendy Hamand. *Neither Ballots Nor Bullets: Women Abolitionists and the Civil War*. Charlottesville: University Press of Virginia, 1991.

Wellman, Judith. *The Road to Seneca Falls: Elizabeth Cady Stanton and the First Woman's Rights Convention*. Urbana: University of Illinois Press, 2004.

Wellman, Judith. "The Seneca Falls Women's Rights Convention: A Study of Social Networks." *Journal of Women's History 3*, no. 1 (Spring, 1991): 9-37.

Wheeler, Leslie, ed. *Loving Warriors: A Revealing Portrait of an Unprecedented Marriage*. New York: The Dial Press, 1981.

Woloch, Nancy. *Women and the American Experience*, third ed. Boston: McGraw Hill, 2000.

Abbreviations

AAS	American Antiquarian Society, Worcester, Massachusetts
AB(B)	Antoinette Brown (Blackwell)
AD(H)	Anna Davis (Hallowell)
AERA	American Equal Rights Association
AH	Agnes Harrison
AK(F)	Abby Kelley (Foster)
AF	Alla Foster
ASB	Alice Stone Blackwell
ASBJ	Alice Stone Blackwell Journal
AWSA	American Woman Suffrage Association
BFPLC	Blackwell Family Papers, Library of Congress
BFPS	Blackwell Family Papers, Schlesinger Library, Radcliffe Institute, Boston, Massachusetts
CF	Callie Foster
DW	David Wright
ECS	Elizabeth Cady Stanton
ECS Diary	Elizabeth Cady Stanton Diary
ECSPLC	Elizabeth Cady Stanton Papers Library of Congress
ECSPVC	Elizabeth Cady Stanton Papers Vassar College, Poughkeepsie, New York
ELB	Emma Lawrence Blackwell
ESM	Elizabeth Smith Miller

EW(G)	Ellen Wright (Garrison)
EWJ	Ellen Wright Journal
EWO	Eliza Wright Osborne Memoir
GFP	Garrison Family Papers Smith College, Northampton, Massachusetts
GWB	George Washington Blackwell
HBB	Henry Brown Blackwell
HS	Henry Stanton
HEG	Helen Eliza Garrison
HS(B)	Harriot Stanton (Blatch)
HS Diary	Harriot Stanton Diary
LM	Lucretia Mott
LS	Lucy Stone
LMcK(G)	Lucy McKim (Garrison)
MCW	Martha Coffin Wright
MDH	Maria Davis Hallowell
MCW Diary	Martha Coffin Wright Diary
NWSA	National Woman Suffrage Association
NAWSA	National American Woman Suffrage Association
MSL	Margaret Stanton Lawrence
NSB	Nora Stanton Barney Autobiography
PBM	Priscilla Bright McLaren
Rem	Alla Foster Reminiscences
SBA	Susan B. Anthony
SBA Diary	Susan B. Anthony Diary
SP I-V	Selected Papers, Volumes I-V
SSF	Stephen Symonds Foster
WHM	Worcester Historical Museum, Worcester, Massachusetts
WLG, Jr.	William Lloyd Garrison, Jr.
WLG, Sr.	William Lloyd Garrison, Sr.
WP	Wendell Phillips

Endnotes

1. Elizabeth Cady Stanton Diary, November 15, 1883, in Theodore Stanton and Harriot Stanton Blatch, eds., Elizabeth Cady Stanton, As Revealed in Her Letters, Diary, and Reminiscences, Vol. II (1922), 212.

2. In the Quaker style, which many of the women's rights leaders followed, I have chosen to use the first (Christian) forms of adult names throughout the text to avoid the terms "Mrs." or "Mr."

3. Sherry H. Penney and James D. Livingston, *A Very Dangerous Woman: Martha Wright and Women's Rights* (2004).

4. Dorothy Sterling, *Ahead of Her Time: Abby Kelley and the Politics of Antislavery* (1991), Margaret Hope Bacon, *I Speak for My Slave Sister: The Life of Abby Kelley Foster* (1974), Nancy H. Burkett, *Abby Kelley Foster and Stephen Foster* (1976).

5. Elisabeth Griffith, *In Her Own Right: The Life of Elizabeth Cady Stanton* (1984); Lois Banner, *Elizabeth Cady Stanton: A Radical for Woman's Rights* (1980); Lori Ginzberg, *Elizabeth Cady Stanton: An American Life* (2009), Elizabeth Cady Stanton, *Eighty Years and More: Reminiscences 1815-1897* (1898).

6. Alice Stone Blackwell, *Lucy Stone: Pioneer of Woman's Rights* (1930), Andrea Kerr, *Lucy Stone: Speaking Out for Equality* (1992), Carol Lasser and Marlene Deahl Merrill, eds. *Friends and Sisters: Letters Between Lucy Stone and Antoinette Brown Blackwell* (1987), Sally McMillen, *Lucy Stone: An Unapologetic Life* (2015), Joelle Million, Woman's Voice, Woman's Place: Lucy Stone and the Birth of the Woman's Rights Movement (2003), Leslie Wheeler, ed. *Loving Warriors: A Revealing Portrait of an Unprecedented Marriage* (1981).

7. Martha Coffin Wright to Lucretia Mott, March 11, 1841, Garrison Family Papers, Smith College, Northampton, Massachusetts, hereinafter GFP.

8. Eliza Wright Osborne Memoir, GFP, hereinafter EWO.

9. MCW to LM, Nov. 19, 1841, GFP.

10. MCW to LM, Feb. 17, 1848, Mar. 12, 1844, Sept. 23, 1844, Feb. 17, 1848, April 23, 1844, Sept. 12, 1844, and April 23-29, 1845, GFP.

11. MCW to LM, Dec. 11, 1845, in GFP; Penney and Livingston, 66.

12. MCW to LM, April 23-29, 1845, GFP.

13. EWO; MCW to LM, Jan. 18, 1843, GFP.

14. MCW to LM, April 23, 1848, GFP.

15. Elizabeth Cady Stanton to Elizabeth W. McClintock, July 14, 1848, in *Selected Papers, Vol.* I, 69 hereinafter SPI; LM to ECS, July 1,1846, Elizabeth Cady Stanton Papers Library of Congress, hereinafter ECSPLC; Judith Wellman, "The Seneca Falls Women's Rights Convention: A Study of Social Networks," *Journal of Women's History* 3, No. 1 (Spring, 1991), 16-17, 32.

16. Judith Wellman, *The Road to Seneca Falls: Elizabeth Cady Stanton and the First Woman's Rights Convention* (Urban, Illinois: University of Illinois Press, 2004), appendix; Ginzberg, *Elizabeth Cady Stanton*, 65.

17. MCW to LCM, Oct. 29, 1848, GFP.

18. Penney and Livingston, 92; MCW to LCM, Jan. 21, 1849, GFP.

19. EWO; MCW to LCM, Dec. 9, 1850, in GFP.

20. *The Daily Journal* agreed, concluding that "the convention was the most dignified, orderly, and interesting deliberative body ever convened in this city." Penney and Livingston, 101-02, 106, 89; MCW to David Wright, Oct. 23, 27, Dec. 4, 25, 1853, in GFP.

21. MCW to LM, June 29, 1851 and April 17, 1853, in Penney and Livingston, 95. 117; Martha experienced two storms at sea, when she was first married to Peter Pelham and a drowning when her fiancé was drowned in the Genesee River in Rochester, NY, so she feared Tallman drowning in the Owasco Creek near their Auburn home. The Auburn Daily Advertiser, Oct. 11, 1854; MCW to Ellen Wright, Oct. 20, 1854, GFP.

22. Benjamin P. Thomas, "The Gospel Truth, Theodore Weld: Crusader for Freedom," 1950, 16 www.Eagleswood.com – accessed January 2015.

23. MCW to EW, April 20, 25, June 7, Oct. 20, 27, Nov. 17, 24, 1854; EW to MCW, May 10, 21, 31, 1854, GFP.

24. MCW to EW, April 25, 1854, Oct. 24, 1854, May 12, April 25, June 20, 1854, Dec. 15, 1854, June 19, 1854, Nov. 17, 1854, Aug. 4, 1855, in GFP.

25. MCW to EW, Oct. 24, May 12, 1854; EW to MCW, May 31, 1854, in GFP.

26. MCW to EW, June 19, Oct. 27, 1854, in GFP.

27. MCW to EW, Nov. 3, 10, 17, 24, Oct. 24, 1854, Aug. 27, Sept. 1, Dec. 8, 1855, in GFP; Penney and Livingston, 118; MCW to EW, Dec. 8, 1854, GFP.

28. MCW to EW, June 15, Oct. 10, 27, Nov. 3, 10, 24, 1854; EW to MCW May 10, Oct. 8, 17, 24, Nov. 14, Dec. 3, 1854, Jan 28, Mar. 1, April 7, 11, Aug. 20, Dec. 7, 1855; EW to Anna Davis, Aug. 20, 1855; MCW to EW, Aug. 27, 1855, Feb. 8, 1855, in GFP.

29. EW to MCW, April 4, 11, 1855, MCW to EW, April 23, 1855, in GFP.

30. https://www.lifeinthefingerlakes.com/coming-full-circle-the-clifton-springs-sanitarium-clifton-springs-hospital-clinic.accessed July 10, 2018; EW to MCW, Aug. 3, 4, 5, 8, 1855; EW to Anna Davis, Aug. 20, 1855, in GFP; Penney and Livingstone, 110; Margaret Hope Bacon, *Valiant Friend: The Life of Lucretia Mott* (1980), 157.

31. EW to AD, Aug. 20, 1855; MCW to EW, Sept. 1, Nov. 13, Aug. 27, 1855, May 8, 1856, in GFP.

32. MCW to EW, Nov. 27, 1855, in GFP.

33. Ellen Wright's Journal, Dec. 7, 1855, in GFP, hereinafter EWJ.

34. EWJ, Feb. 2, 5, 8, and 10, 1856, [March 21, 1856]; EW to LM, Dec. 11, 1856, EW to MCW, March 3, 1856; MCW to EW, Jan. 1, 1856, in GFP; Penney and Livingston, 118.

35. EWJ, Feb. 4, 1856; EW to MCW, Jan. 24, 1855. For other references to Ellen's hesitation to speak, see EWJ, Dec. 7, 1855, EW to MCW, Oct. 26, 1856 and Dec. 10, 1855; EW to John Plumly, Oct. 11, 1855, EWJ, March 12, 31, 1856; EW to MCW, April 29, 1858, in GFP.

36. MCW to EW, Nov. 13, 1855; EW to MCW, Nov. 16, 25, 1855; EWJ, Nov. 30, 1855, in GFP.

37. EWJ, Nov. 30, 1855, in GFP.

38. EW to MCW, Oct.14, 1856, in GFP.

39. MCW to EW, Nov. 12, 21, 1856; EW to MCW, Nov. 15, 1856, in GFP.

40. EW to MCW, Dec 11, 14, 1856; Penney and Livingston, 117-18; EW to AD, Aug. 20, 1855; EWJ, Feb.15,1857, GFP.

41. EWJ, Feb. 15, 1857, in GFP.

42. MCW to EW, Feb. 13, 1858; EW to MCW, April 23, 1858, in GFP.

43. EW to MCW, April 29, 1858, in GFP.

44. MCW to Susan B. Anthony, Nov. 2, 1855, SBA to MCW, July 6, 1856, in GFP.

45. Lori Ginzberg, *Women and the Work of Benevolence: Morality, Politics, and Class in the 19th Century United States* (1990), 105-06.

46. Harriet Alonso, *Growing up Abolitionist: The Story of the Garrison Children* (2002), 187-89.

47. EW to MCW, Dec. 13, 1858, Dec. 6-9, 1855; Jan, 19, 1855; EWJ, Nov. 30, 1855, in GFP.

48. EWJ, Dec. 19, 25, 1857, Jan. 12, 1858, in GFP.

49. EW to MCW, Jan. 20, 1859, in GFP;

50. EW to Anna Davis, Dec. 21, 1859, Jan. 6, 1860, in Alonso, 188-89.

51. SBA to MCW, Jan. 7, 1861, in SPI, 453. Twenty times $60, or $1200 in today's money. www.Measuringworth.com, accessed August 2016; Henry Brewster Stanton to Elizabeth Cady Stanton, January 12, 1861 in SPI, 454.

52. Penney and Livingston,134-35; MCW to EW, Jan. 27, Feb. 10, 11, 1861; EWJ, Feb.10, 1861, in GFP..

53. EW to Willy Wright, April 23, 1861, in GFP.

54. MCW Diary, March 15, 1863, hereinafter MCW Diary; MCW to David Wright, March 17, 1863, in GFP; Penney and Livingston, 160-61.

55. EW to Rev. Thomas Wentworth Higginson, 1858, in GFP.

56. EW to Eliza Wright Osborne and David Munson Osborne, August 17, 1862, in GFP; EW to SBA, Sept.18, 1862, in GFP.

57. EW to Lucy McKim, Jan. 10, 24, 1863, in GFP.

58. William Lloyd Garrison, Jr. to EW, April 11, 1863; William Lloyd Garrison, Sr. to WLG, Jr., Oct. 26, 1858, in GFP.

59. EW to WLG, Jr., June 13, 1863; MCW to Frank Wright, April 30, 1863, in GFP.

60. MCW to LM, June 25, 1865; WLG, Jr. to EW, July 22, Oct. 25, and Dec. 3, 1863, in GFP.

61. WLG, Jr. to EW, Feb. 19, 1864; MCW to EW, March 1864, in Penney and Livingston, 167; WLG, Jr. to MCW, Feb. 26, 1864, in GFP; www.Measuringworth.com, accessed August 2016.

62. WLG, Jr. to EW, July 22, 1863; LM to EWO, Aug. 1, 1862; EW to EWO, Aug. 17, 1862, in GFP.

63. EW to LMcK, Feb. 12, June 13, 1863, Aug. 29, Feb. 18, 1864, in GFP.

64. EW to LMcK, June 24, July 21, Aug. 29, 1864, in GFP.

65. EW to LMcK, June 24, 1864, in GFP.

66. MCW to LM, Aug. 20, 1864; SBA to EW, Aug. 9, 1864, in GFP; Penney and Livingston, 167.

67. EW to LMcK, July 21, Oct. 14, 1864; EWG to MCW, Sept. 21, 25, Oct. 2, 1864, in GFP,

68. EWG to LMcK, July 21, 1864, in GFP.

69. WLG, Jr., to MCW, Oct. 23, 1864, Nov. 13, 1864, in GFP.

70. Penney and Livingston, 224.

71. MCW to EW, Feb. 8, and Aug. 27, 1855; EWJ, Oct. 21, 1859, in GFP; MCW to Will Wright, July 14, 1869, in Penney and Livingston, 173.

72. EWG to LMcK, Oct. 14 and Dec. 11, 1864, in GFP.

73. WLG, Jr. to MCW, Sept. 28, 1864, Oct.10, 1864, Nov. 2, 1864, and Jan. 29, 1865, in GFP.

74. WLG, Jr. to MCW, Nov. 13, 1864, in GFP.

75. WLG, Jr. to MCW, Nov.13, 1864, in GFP.

76. WLG, Sr. to EWG, May 23, 1866; WLG, Jr. to MCW, Sept. 28, Oct. 6, 10, 13, 18, 20, 23, Nov. 2, 13, 21, 29, 1864; June 6, 1869, in GFP.

77. WLG, Jr. to MCW, Oct. 13, 1864; EWG to Agnes Harris, March 29, 1870, in GFP.

78. WLG, Jr. to MCW, Sept. 28, Oct. 6, 13, 1864; EWG to LMcK, Oct. 14, 1864, in GFP.

79. WLG, Jr. to MCW, Oct.10, 1864, in GFP.

80. WLG, Jr. to MCW, Oct. 23, Nov. 2, 13, 21, 29, 1864, in GFP.

81. EWG to LMcK, Dec., 1865, in GFP.

82. WLG, Jr. to MCW, June 6, 1869, WLG, Jr. to David Wright, Dec. 26, 1869, in GFP.

83. Ibid.

84. EWG to LMcKGarrison, Sept. 1, 1866, in GFP.

85. Frank J. Garrison to Fannie Garrison Villard, June 17, 1866; Helen Eliza Garrison to EWG, Aug. 18, Sept. 14, 1866, in GFP.

86. HEG to EWG, Aug. 18, Sept. 14, 1866; EWG to MCW, Dec. 3, 1866, in Alonso, 233.

87. EWG to LMG, Sept. 1, 1866, WLG, Jr. to MCW, May 10, 1867, all in GFP.

88. WLG, Jr. to MCW, May 10, 1867; MCW to EWG, May 19, 1867, in GFP.

89. EWG to MCW, Dec. 3, 1854, MCW to EWG, Sept. 6, 1867, in GFP.

90. EWG to LMG, May 12, 1868; MCW to Anna Davis Hallowell, May 15, 1868; EWG to ADH, Aug. 10, 1868, in GFP.

91. EWG to LMG, July 10, 1869; EWG to AH, March 29, 1870, in GFP. Alonso, 233, suggests that Helen Garrison did not approve of Ellen's mothering skills.

92. EWG to HEG, Sept. 3, 1871, in GFP.

93. EWG to LMG, Nov. 16, 1871, in GFP.

94. EWG to LMG, Nov. 16, 1871, in GFP, Penney and Livingston, 201.

95. MCW to LS, Dec. 21, 20, 1874; MCW to Eliza Wright Osborne, Dec. 15, 1874, in GFP.

96. William Lloyd Garrison, Sr., to his son, Wendell Garrison, Jan. 4, 1875, in GFP.

97. MCW to ADH, Dec. 25, 1874; Martha Coffin Wright's Diary, December 28, 1874; MCW to DW, Dec. 25, 1874, in Penney and Livingston, 218.

98. EWG to Maria Davis Hallowell, Jan. 28, 1875, DW to MCW, Dec. 29, 1874, in GFP; Penney and Livingston, 218; *Woman's Journal*, January 8, 1875.

99. EWG to MDH, Jan. 28, 1875, in GFP; Penney and Livingston, 220.

100. Penney and Livingston, 219; SBA to EWG, Jan. 22, 1875, in GFP.

101. SBA to EWG, Jan. 22, 1875, in GFP.

102. EWG NAWSA Certificate in GFP.

103. Stephen Symonds Foster to Abby Kelly, Aug. 10, 1843 and March 18, 1844; AK to SSF, July 30, 1843, April 24, 1844, and Jan. 3, 1845, in American Antiquarian Society, Worcester, Massachusetts, hereinafter AAS.

104. AKF to SSF, Aug 18, 1847, in AAS.

105. AKF to SSF, April 7, 1847, in AAS.

106. AKF to SSF, Sept. 3, 1847, in AAS.

107. AKF to SSF, April 7, 1847, Sept. 3, 1847, in AAS.

108. AKF to SSF, Sept. 3, 1847, in AAS.

109. AKF to SSF, Aug. 18, Sept. 3, 1847, in AAS; Bacon, 138.

110. AKF to SSF, Sept. 3, 1847.

111. AKF to SSF, Sept. 3, 1847, Sept. 9, 1847, Sept. 28, 1847, in GFP..

112. AKF to SSF, Sept. 9, 1847, in GFP.

113. AKF to SSF, Sept. 9, 1847; Bacon, 45-46; Alla Foster's Reminiscences of Abby Kelley Foster, hereinafter Rem.

114. AKF to SSF, Sept. 11, 28, Aug. 26, 1847, in AAS.

115. Jane Lizzie Hitchcock Jones to AKF, Jan. 23, 1848, in Burkett, 26.

116. Lizzie Gay to AKF, Sept. 24, 1847, Feb. 11, 1848, in AAS; Susan Cabot to AKF, Jan. 16, 1848, in Burkett, 26.

117. *Woman's Journal*, July 4, 1874.

118. Callie Foster/Alla Foster to AKF, July 6, 1849, in AAS.

119. CF/AF to AKF, July 6, 1849, Jan. 27, 1850, in AAS.

120. SSF to AKF, Aug. 5, Aug. 15, 1850, in AAS.

121. AKF to SSF, September 3, 1847, Aug. 11, 1850.

122. Sterling, 275.

123. Million, 106; Sterling, 265.

124. Bacon, 157-59; Sterling, 268-69.

125. Susan B. Anthony to AKF and SSF, April 20, 1857; Sterling, 285, 284.

126. SSF to AF, Oct. 5, 1854, in ASS.

127. AKF to AF, Jan. 5, 1854, in ASS.

128. SSF to AKF, April 6, 1854, in ASS.

129. SSF to AKF, Oct. 31, 1854, in AAS; Rem; Sterling, 296.

130. AKF to AF, April 17, 1852, Sept. 14, 1855, in AAS and Jan. 5, 1854, in Worcester Historical Museum, Worcester, Massachusetts, hereinafter WHM.

131. Rem.

132. Wendell Phillips to AKF, May 31, 1855, in ASS.

133. Sterling, 299.

134. SSF to AKF, Sept. 15, 1855, in ASS.

135. AKF to Wendell Phillips, March 29, 1857, in Sterling, 304.

136. AKF to SFF, Aug. 1, 1857; SSF to AKF, Aug., 1857, in AAS.

137. AKF to SSF, Winter 1858, in AAS.

138. SSF to AKF, Feb. 14, 1858, in AAS.

139. AKF to Maria Weston Chapmen, Feb. 11, 1858, in Sterling, 316.

140. Sterling, 329-30.

141. Sterling, 326-30, 334-35; Bacon, 189, 193.

142. Sterling, 329-30, 335.

143. Sterling, 335-36; SSF to George Thompson, March 16, 1862, in AAS.

144. Ibid.

145. Sterling, 347; AKF to WP, July 28, 1866, in AAS.

146. Sterling, 344; AKF to WP, July 28, 1866, in AAS.

147. Sterling, 345-47.

148. Vassar Alumnae Quarterly, Aug. 1, 1923; Sterling, 350; AKF to AF, Sept. 22, and Oct. 14, 1868, in AAS.

149. AKF to AF, Dec. 9, 1870, in AAS.

150. http://www.vassar.edu.on_matthew.htmlwebsite, accessed April 1, 2015; Elizabeth Daniels, *Main to Mudd and More: An Informal History of Vassar College Buildings,* revised edition (1996), 7.

151. AKF to AF, Sept. 22, 1868, in AAS.

152. Ellen Carol DuBois, *Harriot Stanton Blatch and the Winning of Woman Suffrage* (1997), 25; Helen Lefkowitz Horowitz, *Alma Mater: Design and Experience in the Women's Colleges from Their Nineteenth-Century Beginnings to the 1930s* (1984), 37-38; AKF to AF, March 9 and Dec. 9, 1870, in AAS.

153. Daniels, 12, 21.

154. "Overview of Original Faculty," Vassar Encyclopedia; co-educational institutions at the time included Oberlin, Cornell, Boston College, and the University of Rochester.

155. Daniels, 12, 15, 32; DuBois, 25.

156. Sterling, 360; AKF to AF, Oct. 14, 1868, in AAS.

157. AKF to AF, Sept. 22, 1868, in AAS.

158. Ibid.

159. AKF to AF, Sept. 22, 1868, in AAS; SSF to George Thompson, 1870, quoted in Bacon, 209.

160. AF to AKF, May 3, 1869, in AAS.

161. AF to AKF, Feb. 20, 1870, March 5, 1870, in AAS.

162. AF to AKF, Feb. 26, 1871; AKF to AF, March 5, Dec. 9, 1870, in ASS.

163. AF to AKF, May 3, 1869, Feb 20, 1870.

164. Bacon, 206 and 207; Rem; AF to AKF, Feb. 26, 1871, in AAS.

165. AF to AKF, Feb. 26, 1871, in AAS.

166. Ibid.

167. Ibid.

168. AF to AKF, Feb. 20 1871, in AAS.

169. Ibid.

170. "History of Vassar College," Vassar Encyclopedia.

171. SSF to Mr. Robison at Cornell University, Dec. 20, 1872, in AAS; Sterling, 359.

172. Vassar Alumni Quarterly, Mar. 1, 1928; Carole Smith-Rosenberg, "Hearing Women's Words: A Feminist Reconstruction of History," 46, "Bourgeois Discourse and the Progressive Era: An Introduction," 176, and "The New Woman as Androgyne," 247, in *Disorderly Conduct* (1985).

173. Sterling, 368-72. AF to AKF, Feb. 20, 1871, in AAS.

174. AKF to (William Lloyd Garrison's son) Frank Garrison, March 15, 1875, in Sterling, 374.

175. Barbara Solomon, *"In the Company of Educated Women": A History of Women and Higher Education in America* (1985), 116-17; Sterling, 368.

176. Smith-Rosenberg, "The New Woman as Androgyne," 247, in *Disorderly Conduct.*

177. AF to AKF, Oct. 14, 1883, in AAS; Sterling, 381.

178. Sterling, 372; $2400 would be $48,000 in 2016. www.measuringworth.com, accessed Jan. 2016; Abby Kelley Foster address to Jubilee meeting, Worcester 1880, quoted in Sterling, 373.

179. Sterling, 374; William Lloyd Garrison, Sr., to AKF, Nov. 8, 1877, in AAS.

180. WP to AKF, July 26, 1880, in Sterling, 374.

181. William Channing to the Fosters, July 4, 1877, in WHM; Sterling, 374.

182. LS to ASB, Aug. 17, 1879, in BFPLC.

183. Sterling, 374-75.

184. Sterling, 375.

185. Sterling, 375-76.

186. *Woman's Journal,* Jan. 22, 1887; AKF to Frederick Douglass, Nov. 9, 1881, in Sterling, 377.

187. Sterling, 377-78; Bacon, 135; SSF to AKF, Feb. 7, 1847, in AAS. $500 annual income in 1880 was worth $12,000 today. www.MeasuringWorth.com, accessed Aug. 2016. www.worcesterhistoryproject.com, accessed January 2015.

188. AKF to AF, Aug. 14, 1883; AF to AKF, Sept. 23, 1883, in AAS.

189. AF to AKF, Oct. 14, 1883, in AAS.

190. AF to AKF, Oct. 14, 1883, Sept. 23, 1883, in AAS.

191. Sterling, 377, 379; Lucy Barton to AF, Oct. 14, 1883, in AAS.

192. AF to AKF, Nov. 11, 1883, in AAS.

193. AF to AKF, Nov. 11, 1883, Feb. 26, 1884, in AAS.

194. AF to AKF , June 7, 1884, Nov. 2, 1885, in AAS.

195. AKF to AF, June 11, 20, 1884, Jan. 29, 1886, in AAS.

196. AKF to AF, June 21, 1886, in AAS.

197. Sterling, 386.

198. Ibid.

199. Ibid.

200. *Woman's Journal,* Jan., 1887.

201. Sterling, 380.

202. Worcester History Project.

203. "Points of Interest," Twenty-First Annual Excursion of the Sandwich Historical Society, Aug., 1940, 15, www.allafosterdiamondledge.com, accessed May 2016.

204. Stanton and Blatch, 142-43.

205. *The History of Woman Suffrage* by Elizabeth Cady Stanton, Susan B. Anthony, and Matilda Joslyn Gage. See "Sketch of the Stanton family from 1835-1920," in SPI, 190.

206. Elizabeth Cady Stanton to Susan B. Anthony, July 4, 1858, in Kathleen Barry, *Susan B. Anthony: A Biography of a Singular Feminist* (1988), 131; ECS to Elizabeth Smith Miller, Sept. 20, 1855, in ECSPLC.

207. ECS to ESM, Jan. 24, 1856, in ECSPLC.

208. ECS to Elizabeth Neall, Nov. 26, 1841, SPI, 26. As Elizabeth did at the time of each child's birth in Seneca Falls, she raised a flag when Harriot was born.

209. Banner, 28; Henry Brewster Stanton to ECS, June 23, 1842, in SPI, 35; ECS to ESM, Feb. 10 or 11, 1851, in SPI, 178.

210. Banner, 32; ECS to SBA, Feb. 10, 1856, in Griffith, 88.

211. ECS to SBA, July 20, 1857, in ECPSLC; Blatch and Lutz, 5-6; DuBois, *Harriot Stanton Blatch and the Winning of Woman Suffrage* (1997), 11.

212. AKF to ECS, Jan. 11, 1851, in SP1, 176; ECS to AKF, Jan. 11, 1851, in AAS; MCW to DW, Oct. 23, 27, Dec. 4, 25, 1853; Penney and Livingston, 106.

213. ECS to Lucretia Mott, November 12, 1849, in SPI, 149.

214. Stanton, 163.

215. Blackwell, 198, 169; LS to SBA, Jan. 16, 1856, in BFPLC.

216. Blackwell, 198.

217. LS to SBA, Jan. 15, 1857, in BFPLC; ECS to SBA, June 10, 1856 and July 12, 1857, in SPI, 325 and 349.

218. ECS to SBA, [Aug. 20?, 1857].in SPI, 351.

219. SBS to ECS, Sept. 29, 1857, in SPI, 352.

220. ECS to SBA, April 10, 1859, in SPI, 387.

221. Harriot Stanton Blatch and Alma Lutz, *Challenging Years: The Memoirs of Harriot Stanton Blatch* (1940), 25-27.

222. Blatch and Lutz, 4-5.

223. ECS to Frances Seward, September 21, [1861], in ECSPLC; Griffith, 110.

224. Ginzburg, Elizabeth Cady Stanton, 101; Griffith, 110.

225. Blackwell, 200; Lucy Stone to Henry Brown Blackwell, July 22, 1864, in Wheeler, 195.

226. EW to MCW, May 21, 1863; WLG, Jr. to EW, May 21, 1863, Oct. 25, 1863, in GFP. Wendy Hamand Venet, *Neither Ballots Nor Bullets: Women Abolitionists and the Civil War* (1991), 103, 106, and 120.

227. The "real price" of $300 in 1862 would be $6,000 in 2015. www.Measuringworth. com, accessed August 2016.

228. Elizabeth Cady Stanton to Mrs. Gerrit Smith, July 1863, in Stanton and Blatch, Vol. II, 94-95.

229. Griffith, 109.

230. Dubois, 20, Blatch and Lutz, 10-17.

231. Dubois, 23; SBA Diary, May 14, 1871, in SPII, 430.

232. Dubois, 23-25.

233. Blatch and Lutz, 35

234. Blatch and Lutz, 33-34.

235. Blatch and Lutz, 36.

236. Blatch and Lutz, 37; DuBois, 28; Stanton, 309-14.

237. DuBois, 28-29, 38; Blatch and Lutz, 39.

238. Blatch and Lutz, 39. Daniels, 16-19; Horowitz, 61; Solomon, 89.

239. DuBois, 27 and 28; Daniels, 18.

240. Blatch and Lutz, 39.

241. DuBois, 27; Blatch and Lutz, 39.

242. ECS to Harriot Stanton, Aug. 1877, March 12, 1878, in DuBois, 30-31.

243. DuBois, 31-32; ECS to HS, March 25, 1879, in Elizabeth Cady Stanton Papers, Vassar College, Poughkeepsie, New York, hereinafter ECSPVC; Margaret Lawrence, "Life of Harriot Stanton Blatch," in ECSPVC.

244. Blatch and Lutz, 45-46; DuBois, 33 and N287.

245. DuBois, 34-36.

246. Harriot Stanton Blatch Diary, Nov. 26, 1880, Rhoda Barney Jenkins Papers, Greenwich, Connecticut, hereinafter HS Diary. Elizabeth Cady Stanton married at the age of 25.

247. HS Diary, March 31, 1881.

248. ECS to Theodore Weld, Feb. 2, 1881, SPIV, 46; ECS to Harriet Hanson Robinson, Oct. 26, 1881, in SPIV, 118.

249. DuBois, 47-49, 290, N61; Blatch and Lutz, 61.

250. Blatz and Lutz, 61-62; DuBois, 49.

251. DuBois, 51; Blatch and Lutz, 63; Stanton, 349, 337-38; ECS to Lizette Stanton, May 3, 1882, SPIV, 164.

252. HS Diary, Sept., 1882; Blatch and Lutz, 62 and 65.

253. DuBois, 54.

254. Priscilla Bright McClaren to ECS, Oct.29, 1882, in SPIV, 191; DuBois, 52-54; Blatch and Lutz, 62 and 65; ECS to Anna M. Priestman, Jan. 30, 1883, in SPIV, 215.

255. Priscilla Bright McLaren to ECS, Nov. 14, 1882, in SPIV, 199; DuBois, 53; Stanton, 351.

256. Blatch and Lutz, 65; ECS to Elizabeth Pease Nichol, Nov. 16, 1882, in SPIV, 202.

257. Nora Stanton Barney, "Spanning Two Centuries: The Autobiography of Nora Stanton Barney," History Workshop, no. 22, Autumn 1986, 2; DuBois, 56, hereinafter NSB.

258. ECS to Maggie Stanton Lawrence, Oct. 15, 1890, in DuBois, 57; Stanton, 136.

259. DuBois, 56-57.

260. ECS to Elizabeth Pease Nichol, Jan. 10, 1883, in SPIV, 212. ECS to Anna M. Priestman, Jan. 30, 1883, in SPIV, 215.

261. ECS to Harriet Cady Eaton, July 10, 1883, in SPIV, 266. SBA Diary, March 11 and 12, in Dubois, 54.

262. ECS to SBA, Aug. 20, 1883, quoted in DuBois, 57; ECS Diary, Sept. 9 and 18, 1883, in Stanton and Blatch.

263. ECS to ESM, Oct. 13, 1883, in DuBois, 58.

264. Griffith, 328; Carl Degler, At Odds: Women and the Family from the Revoltion to the Present (1980), 150; HSB, "Voluntary Motherhood," in Aileen Kraditor, ed., Up from the Pedestal: Selected Writings in the History of Feminism (1968), 167-75.

265. ECS Diary, Oct. 7, 1883, in DuBois, 58; ECS Diary, Nov. 17, 1883, in DuBois, 58.

266. Judith Arcana, Our Mothers' Daughters (1979), 193; Women Suffrage Journal, June 2, 1884, in Dubois, 61.

267. ECS to HSB, Dec. 15, 1884, in DuBois, 63.

268. DuBois, 64-65.

269. DuBois, 66; ECS to Marguerite Stanton, Mar. 8, 1885, in ECSPLC; ECS to Ellen Dana Conway, after Dec. 13, 1885, in SPIV, 468.

270. ECS to Lizette (Elizabeth Cady) Stanton, May 3, 1882, in SPIV, 164-65.

271. SBA to Elizabeth Herbert, June 3, 1886, in SPIV, 506; WLG, Jr. to EWG, Feb. 14, 1865, in GFP.

272. ECS to Nora Blatch, April 16, 1887, in SPIV, 31.

273. ECS to Flora McMartin Wright, June 15, 1887, in SPIV, 31.

274. Stanton, 421; Griffith, 197.

275. DuBois, 70; Griffith, 200; ECS Diary, Feb. 25, Aug. 30, and Nov. 4, 1890, in Stanton and Blatch, 262, 264, 268, 591.

276. Stanton, 429.

277. ECS to MSL, Oct. 15, 1890, in DuBois, 58 and Griffith, 200.

278. DuBois, 77; HSB, "Voluntary Motherhood."

279. ECS to Ida Harper, Mar. 21, 1891, in DuBois, 68.

280. NSB, 13, 14, in Rhoda Barney Jenkins Papers, Greenwich, Conn, in DuBois, 68.

281. DuBois, 68; NSB, 14; Interview with Rhoda Barney Jenkins.

282. Katharine Stetson Harris to Harriet de Forest, April 17, 1971; E. Silphia Pankhurst, "The Suffragette Movement: An Intimate Account of Persons and Ideals," 1931, 111-12, both in DuBois, 68; NSB, 16, in DuBois, 72.

283. HSB, "Another View of Village Life," *Westminster Review*, Vol. 140, Sept. 1893, 318-24, in DuBois, 72.

284. *New York Times*, May 5, 1894; *Woman's Journal*, Nov. 3, 1894, in DuBois, 73.

285. NSB, 16c; HSB to SBA, Dec. 28, 1895; HSB to Mrs. McIlquham, n.d. (between Dec. 1895 and Jan. 1896) in DuBois, 82.

286. NSB, 16c and HSB to ECS, June 24, 1896; in DuBois, 82-84.

287. Theodore Stanton to ECS, June 14, 1896 and HSB to ECS, June 24, 1896, in DuBois, 84. Cremation has been a burial custom common for 1,000 years in the Western world, but periodically practiced.

288. SBA to HSB, July 2, 1896, in ECSPLC.

289. NSB, 16, in DuBois, 84.

290. NSB, 17-18, in DuBois, 84-85.

291. Nora and Harriot spent every summer with Harry Blatch while he worked in Basingstoke. DuBois, 84-85; Elizabeth Cady Stanton told her cousin Elizabeth Smith Miller, "I was weighed yesterday and brought the scales down at 240...I intend to commence

dieting. Yet I am well; danced the Virginia reel with Bob. But alas! I am 240! Pray for your lumbering Julius." ECS to ESM, Sept. 11, 1888, in SPV, 140.

292. ECS to HSB, Aug. 20, 1880, March 11, 1877; ECS to Theodore Stanton, Oct. 25, 1896; ECS Diary, Feb. 4, 1899, in Griffith, 216; ECS Diary, April 1, 1897, in ECSPLC; Elizabeth's granddaughter, Nora Stanton Barney, also lost her eyesight in her old age.

293. DuBois, 85.

294. HSB to Helen Gardener, n.d., in Griffith, 217.

295. ECS Diary, Oct. 22, 1902; Griffith, 217-18.

296. ECS to Margaret Stanton Lawrence, ECS Diary, Oct. 9, 1895 in Griffith, 217–21.

297. Telegram from HSB to SBA, Oct. 25, 1902, Griffith, 218; Kathleen Barry, Susan B. Anthony: A Biography of a Singular Feminist (1988), 340-41; Second Telegram from Harriot Stanton Blatch to Susan B. Anthony, Oct., 25, 1902.

298. SBA to Ida Husted Harper, Nov. 1902, in Barry, 340-41; Griffith, 218; SBA to Theodore Stanton, May 18, 1903, in ECSPLC.

299. SBADiary, in Sara Hunter Graham, *Woman Suffrage and the New Democracy* (1996), 44.

300. ECS to HSB, July 15, 1880, in DuBois, Blatch, 33.

301. Henry Brown Blackwell to George W. Blackwell, Sept. 16, 1857, in Blackwell Family Papers, Schlesinger Library, Radcliffe Institute, Boston, Massachusetts, hereinafter BFPS; Wheeler, 173.

302. Kerr, 57.

303. Antoinette Brown to Lucy Stone, June 28, 1848, in BFPLC.

304. LS to HBB, Mar. 3, 7, 1858, in Wheeler, 178.

305. LS to HBB, April 1, May 9, 21, 1859, in Wheeler, 178 and 181-82.

306. $50 in 1850 would be about $1000 today; LS to HBB, April 25, 1858.

307. LS to HBB, March 3, 1858, in Wheeler, 174-75; LS to HBB, March 7, 1858 and March 8, 1858, in BFPLC.

308. $25 in 1860 was about $500 in 2019 money; www.Measuringworth.com, accessed August 2016; LS to HBB, April 1, 1858, in BFPLC; LS to HBB, April 4 and June 2, 1858, in Wheeler, 178 and 183; HBB to LS, March 25, 1858 in Wheeler, 177-78.

309. LS to Susan B. Anthony, April 1, 1858, in Kerr, 106; LS to SBA, Aug. 26, 1858, BFPLC.

310. Blackwell, 199.

311. LS to Antoinette Brown Blackwell, Feb. 15 or 20, 1859, BFPS.

312. Million, 269; LS to HBB, June 14, 1859, in BFPLC; Kerr, 142, 109.

313. LS to HBB, Sept. 14, 1860, in Kerr, 112.

314. LS to HBB, June 14, July 31, 1864 in Wheeler, 191, 197.

315. LS to HBB, June 21, 1864, in Wheeler,192-93; Million, 270; LS to Hannah Blackwell, Oct.23, 1864, in Wheeler, 203-04.

316. LS to HBB, July 22, 31, Oct. 10, 1864, in Wheeler, 196-98, 203.

317. Kerr, 127.

318. Blackwell, 203.

319. Wheeler, 212; Million, 272.

320. LS to Abby Kelly Foster, Jan. 24, 1867, in Wheeler, 215.

321. Blackwell, 207.

322. Blackwell, 210.

323. Kilkenny cats are fabled fighters from the county of Kilkenny, Ireland that appear in nursery rhymes.

324. Blackwell, 206.

325. LS to ASB, Jan. 21, Feb. 26, 1870, Nov. 9, 20, 21, 30, 1869, in BFPLC.

326. Wheeler, 235-36.

327. Alice Stone Blackwell Journal, Feb. 19, 21, 1872, hereinafter ASB Jrnl.

328. ASB Jrnl, March 27, 1872.

329. ASB Jrnl, May 6, June 2, 1872.

330. ASB Jrnl, Aug. 26, 1872. I assume "blue orthodox" connotes a "true blue" loyalty.

331. ASB Jrnl, May 7, 8, 9, 10, 11, 14, June 11, 1872; ASB to Kitty Blackwell, Oct. 29, 1872, in BFPLC.

332. ASB Jrnl, June 14, 1873.

333. ASB Jrnl, Sept. 16, 17, 1873.

334. ASB Jrnl, May 28, 1873.

335. ASB Jrnl, Dec 1873.

336. Kerr, 106 and 119; Wheeler, 184-89; Merrill, *Growing Up in Boston's Gilded Age*, 1-11; LS to ASB, Aug. 24, 26, Sept. 5, 7, 21, 1877; LS to ABB, July 15, 1877, in BFPLC.

337. Solomon, 95-97. Elinor Rice Hays, *Morning Star: A Biography of Lucy Stone* (1961), 162, reports that in the summer of 1865 Henry and Lucy took Alice to the Blackwell cottages in Martha's Vineyard, beginning a tradition father and daughter loved.

338. LS to ASB, Feb. 2, March 1, 6, 11, 1880, in BFPLC.

339. LS to ASB, March 1, 11, 1880, in BFPLC.

340. LS to ASB, July 30, 18, Aug. 9, 7, 17, 1878, in BFPLC.

341. LS to ASB, July 30, Aug. 14, 1878, Aug. 14, 15, 1879, in BFPLC.

342. LS to ASB, Aug. 14, 15, 1879, Aug. 5, 1875, Aug. 24, Sept. 21, 1877, July 18, Aug. 4, 14, 1878, in BFPLC.

343. LS to ASB, March 6, 10, 1880, in BFPLC.

344. Jean Matthews, The Rise of the New Woman: The Women's Movement in America, 1875-1930 (2013), 40, argues that, like many New Women, "Alice worked in a woman's milieu, even if a newly created one;" Lasser and Merrill, eds., *Friends and Sisters*, 238, write, "Neither mother nor daughter seemed to question that Lucy Stone's only daughter would establish herself a public career closely linked to her mother's lifelong work."

345. LS to ASB, Sept. 1882, Sept. 7, 21, 24, 1882, in BFPLC.

346. LS to ASB, Oct. 12, 1882, May 9, 1883, in BFPLC.

347. Nancy Woloch, Women and the American Experience, third ed. (2000), 280-281.

348. Solomon, 115-16.

349. Suzanne Lebsock, *The Free Women of Petersburg: Status and Culture in a Southern Town, 1784-1860* (1984), 78, argues that many women left estates to female relatives and friends, adding an economic dimension to the portrait of their relationships. Most often the "grants were from mothers to their daughters because women understood what it was to be legally and financially vulnerable; more often than men, they tried to see to it that their daughters were spared." LS to ASB, July 21, 1884, in BFPLC; $12,000 in the 1880s would be about $240,000 in 2015; www.Measuringworth.com accessed January 2016.

350. HBB to GWB, Feb. 13, 1887, in BFPSL; Kerr, 223.

351. LS to ASB, March 31, 1887, in Wheeler, 301.

352. LS to ASB, April 11, 1887, in SPIV, 57; Kerr, 224.

353. LS to ASB, April 12, 1887, in BFPLC.

354. LS to ASB, April 12, 1887, in Wheeler, 303-04.

355. LS to ASB, April 22, 1887, in BFPLC. LS to SBA, Nov. 7, 1887 and SBA to Rachel Foster, Nov. 11, 1887, SBA to LS, Dec. 13, 1887; Minutes of the meeting prepared by Alice Stone Blackwell, SPV, 52-53, 57, 59-6; Wheeler, 311.

356. Blackwell, 229; SBA to LS, Dec. 13, 1887, SPV, 59-64.

357. ECS to HH Robinson, Sept. 30, 1886, in SPIV, 519; SBA Diary, February 1, 2, 3, 6, and 14, 1888, SBA to Frederick Douglass, Feb. 6, 1888, in SPV, 42,85, and 83; Griffith, 192; Lisa Tetrault, *The Myth of Seneca Falls: Memory and the Women's Suffrage Movement* (2014), 146-47.

358. SPV, 83-109; Tetrault, 146-54.

359. SBA to Caroline Dall, Jan. 20, 1888, in SPV, 78, 59-64; SBA to Francis J. Garrison (William Lloyd Garrison's youngest son), May 8, 1888, in SPIV, 122.

360. Kerr, 226; SBA to Eliza Wright Osborne, Feb. 5, 1890 in SPV, 236; William Lloyd Garrison, Jr. to Ellen Wright Garrison, Feb. 14, 16, and 21, 1890; EWG to Family, Feb. 14, 1890; Agnes Garrison to EWG, Feb. 16, 21, and 24, 1890; EWG to Agnes Garrison, Feb. 19, 1890; EWG to William Lloyd Garrison, Jr., Feb. 19, 1890, in GFP.

361. DuBois, 70; Anthony, Stanton, and Gage, *History of Woman Suffrage*, Vol. IV, 166-67.

362. Minutes of the meeting prepared by Alice Stone Blackwell, SPV, 42, 57N, 59-64, 85; LS to HBB and ASB, Feb. 19, 1890, in BFPLC; ECS, "Address to the National American Woman Suffrage Association," Feb. 18, 1890, SPV, 249-63.

363. LS to HBB and ASB, Feb. 19, 1890, in BFPLC.

364. In SPV, 55, Ann Gordon writes, "Alice Blackwell later took most of the credit for overcoming her parents' resistance to union, but Lucy's letters belie that role in the early stages. The mother tried to teach her daughter how to rise above personal dislike for the competition and serve the cause."

365. LS to HBB, Sept. 14, 1890, in Wheeler, 340.

366. ABB to LS, April 20, 1892, in Lasser and Merrill, 261; ASB, *Woman's Journal*, Jan. 11, 1890, answers an anti-suffrage letter by asking if matrimony was the chief end of the writer's existence.

367. LS to HBB, May 1, 1893, in Wheeler, 345.

368. HBB to LS, May 15, 1893, in Wheeler, 348.

369. LS to Sarah Stone Lawrence, July 14, 1893, in Kerr, 240; LS to HBB, Aug. 15, 1893, in Wheeler, 352.

370. HBB to LS, Aug. 30, 1893; Emma Lawrence Blackwell to George Washington Blackwell, Sept. 6, 8, 1893, all in Kerr, 241.

371. Kerr, 242; McMillen, N313.

372. ASB to Emma Lawrence Blackwell, Oct. 10 and 11, 1893, in Kerr, 244.

373. ELB to Sarah Stone Lawrence, Oct. 18, 1893, in Kerr, 245.

374. Kerr, 247.

375. ABB to ASB, n.d. in Elizabeth Cazden, Antoinette Brown Blackwell: A Biograpbhy (1983), 262.

376. DuBois, 140-46.

377. DuBois, 201.

378. DuBois, 175.

379. Fanny Garrison Villard, Ellen Wright Garrison's sister-in-law, also attended, as did Martha Mott Lord, daughter of Lucretia Mott. Original program, Centennial Luncheon, ECSPV.

Index

A

Abolition/abolitionists, 3, 4, 5, 27, 29, 31, 52, 56, 58, 59, 89, 99, 102, 141

Abortion, 117

Alcott, Louisa May, 151

American Antislavery Society (AAS), 2, 4, 56, 67, 75, 141

American Equal Rights Association (AERA), 4, 7, 142

American Woman Suffrage Association (AWSA), 7, 8, 49, 112, 143, 145, 151, 160, 164, 168, 172, 174

Anthony, Susan B., 17, 22, 23, 26, 29, 32, 36, 48, 49, 50, 58-59, 60, 62, 67, 96, 97, 99, 100, 101, 103, 104, 108, 111, 112, 115, 119, 120, 124, 125, 128, 137, 139, 141, 142, 143, 160, 162, 163, 164

"Antis", 7, 165

Armenians, 7

Auburn, New York, 2, 3, 12, 13, 18, 25, 28, 35, 39, 42, 43, 45, 46, 47, 48, 96, 110

B

Barney, Nora Stanton, 5, 115, 117, 119, 121, 122, 123, 124, 125, 126, 130

Barton, Lucy Kelley, 86, 90

Basingstoke, England, 113-115, 117, 119-121, 124, 126

Birth control, 117

Blackwell, Alice Stone, 1, 6, 7, 85, 98, 101, 133-169, 171, 172, 176

Blackwell, Antoinette Brown, 17, 22, 23, 97, 98, 99, 133, 138, 152, 172, 175

Blackwell, Ellen, 158

Blackwell, Elizabeth, 136

Blackwell, Emily, 133, 158, 166, 167

Blackwell, Emma Lawrence, 147, 152, 156, 159, 166, 167

Blackwell, George, 152, 156, 159, 166

Blackwell, Henry, 7, 88, 98, 133, 136, 137, 138, 139, 140, 142, 145, 148, 151, 154, 156, 158, 159, 163, 164, 165, 166, 167, 169

Blackwell, Sam, 98
Blatch, Harriot Stanton, 1, 5, 93-
132, 136, 141, 151, 153, 163,
172, 174, 176
Blatch, Helen, 122
Blatch, William Henry (Harry),
111-115, 122, 124, 125, 126
Bloomers, 62, 94, 97
Boston Girls' High School, 85
Boston University, 151, 153, 156,
169
Burns, Anthony, 61

C

Cady, Daniel, 5
Cady, Margaret Livingston, 94, 96,
103
Catt, Carrie Chapman, 49, 175
Catherine Sedgwick's Music
School, 31
Centennial Celebration of
Elizabeth Cady Stanton's
Birthday, 174-175
Center Sandwich, New
Hampshire, 91
Channing, William H., 82
Chauncey Hall, 150-153
Child, Maria, 82
Cincinnati Young Ladies' School,
80
Civil War, 4, 7, 28, 29, 31, 32, 34,
50, 66, 67, 89, 139, 140, 141,
142
Collyer, Rev. Robert, 148
Cornell University, 67, 71, 78, 81,
93, 104, 109, 126, 130, 172

D

Davis, Anna, 9, 28
Davis, Paulina Wright, 51, 59
Declaration of Sentiments, 5, 16,
128
Diamond Ledge, New Hampshire,
91
Douglass, Frederick, 16
Draft riots, 102-103

E

Eagleswood School, 18, 21, 22, 24,
25, 32, 33
Eighty Years and More, 6
Englewood Academy, 104

F

Fifield, Mary, 148, 149
Fifteenth Amendment, 7, 75, 143
Forten, Charlotte, 27
Foster, Abby Kelley, 1, 3, 4, 6,
51-92, 96, 97, 98, 101, 104, 133,
139, 141, 142, 157, 165, 169,
175, 176
Foster, Alla, 1, 3, 4, 5, 51-92, 106,
107, 141, 151, 153, 157, 158,
176
Foster, Caroline "Callie", 57, 58,
60, 61, 66
Foster, Rachel, 160, 162
Foster, Stephen Symonds, 51, 52,
53, 55, 56, 57, 58, 59, 60, 61, 63,

65, 66, 67, 72, 73, 74, 77, 78, 81,
    82, 83, 85, 87, 89, 90
Fugitive Slave Law, 61
Fugitive slaves, 14

G

Gage, Matilda Josyln, 6, 111
Garrison, Agnes, 41, 42, 43, 45,
    46, 49
Garrison, Charley, 41
Garrison, Eleanor, 2, 49, 174
Garrison, Ellen Wright, 1, 2, 11-
    50, 101, 111, 112, 113, 114, 136,
    141, 151, 153, 163, 174, 176
Garrison, Fanny, (see Villard,
    Fanny Garrison)
Garrison, Frank (son of William
    Lloyd Garrison, Sr.), 42
Garrison, Frank (son of William
    Lloyd Garrison, Jr.), 46
Garrison, Helen, 36, 37, 39, 42, 43,
    45, 46, 62, 82
Garrison, Lucy McKim, 33, 34, 35,
    38, 41
Garrison, Wendell, 33, 35, 38
Garrison, William Lloyd, Jr., 2, 33,
    34, 35, 36, 40, 46, 49, 62, 84,102,
    174
Garrison, William Lloyd, Sr., 2, 4,
    33, 36, 39, 41, 42, 43, 47, 58, 62,
    66, 67, 82, 86, 87, 110
Garrison, William Lloyd, III, 47
Garrisonian Abolitionism, 2, 120,
    134, 139
Gettysburg, Pennsylvania, 34, 102

Gleason, Annie, 140-141
Graham, Sylvester, diet, 71, 74,
    152
Grimke, Sarah and Angelina, 3, 18

H

Harris Grammar School, 145-151
Higginson, Rev. Thomas
    Wentworth, 22, 23, 24, 25, 26,
    32
History of Woman Suffrage, 6, 111,
    128, 163
Homeopathy, 34, 96
Hunt, Mary Ellen, 14
Hydrotherapy, 53

I

International Council of Women,
    162

J

Jane Andrews' Boarding School,
    143
Jacournassy Estate, 112
Johnstown, New York, 94, 103,
    104

K

Kansas, 7, 130, 142, 143

L

Lawrence, Emma, (see Blackwell, Emma)
Lawrence, Margaret "Maggie" Stanton, 93, 96, 99, 101, 104, 109, 114, 121, 122, 125, 126, 128, 163, 174
League of Women Voters, 168
The Liberator, 33
Liberty Farm, 52
Lincoln, Abraham, 139
Lucy Stoners, 7, 134, 150

M

Martha's Vineyard, 152
McClintock, Mary Ann, 14
Miller, Elizabeth Smith, 97, 115
Mitchell, Maria, 107-109
Mott, Lucretia, 2, 11, 12, 13, 14, 16, 17, 23, 32, 38, 82, 97, 126
Mott, Marianna Pelham Wright, 11, 13, 26, 46, 48

N

National American Woman Suffrage Association (NAWSA), 7, 49, 164, 165, 168, 172, 174
National Loyal Women's War League, 101
National Woman Suffrage Association (NWSA), 6, 7, 48, 143, 160, 174

National Women's Rights Convention, First, 7, 163
National Women's Rights Convention, Second, 59
National Women's Rights Convention, Third, 3, 17
"The Negro's Hour", 141
The New England Antislavery Society, 139
New England Woman Suffrage Association Tea Party, 151, 152
New Woman, 78, 80, 81,157, 159
Non-resistance, 33, 66

O

Oberlin Collegiate Institute, 6, 134, 169
Orange, New Jersey, 136, 139
Osborne, Eliza Wright, 11, 12, 17, 21, 42, 46, 48, 49, 163

P

Pelham, Peter, 18, 36
Philadelphia, Pennsylvania, 2, 21, 23, 24, 25, 26, 31, 32, 35, 37, 67
Phillips, Wendell, 82, 84 110, 141, 142
Pillsbury, Parker, 151
Pope's Hill, 88, 145, 149, 166, 167
Purvis, Robert, Jr., 26-29

Q

Quaker, 2, 3, 13, 17, 18, 82, 93, 97, 115

R

The Revolution, 6, 143
Rockland County Female Academy, 103
Roseville, New Jersey, 138, 139, 140, 143
Roxbury High School, 82
Roxbury, Massachusetts, 36, 39, 41, 42, 45, 85

S

Saratoga, New York, 22, 23
Schism in Woman Suffrage Movement, 3, 6, 107, 127, 128, 138, 143-146, 160-164, 174
Seneca Falls, New York, 14, 17, 59, 93, 96, 97, 100, 101, 103, 162
Seneca Falls Wesleyan Chapel, 16
Seneca Falls Women's Rights Convention, 3, 5, 16, 59, 96, 162
Seneca Falls Women's Rights Park, 14
Seward, Frances, 100
Seward, William, 101
Sharon Female Academy, 22, 23, 24
Solar eclipse, 108-109
Spofford, Harry, 149-150

Stanton, Daniel "Neil", 93, 96, 100, 101, 103
Stanton, Elizabeth Cady, 1, 4, 5, 6, 14, 16, 29, 48, 59, 67, 93-132, 133, 137, 139, 141, 142, 143, 162, 163, 164, 165, 165, 168, 172, 174, 175, 176
Stanton, Gerrit "Gat", 101
Stanton, Harriot "Hattie" (see Blatch, Harriot Stanton)
Stanton, Henry Brewster, 5, 93,94, 100, 103, 107, 108,109, 113
Stanton, Henry "Kit", 100, 101
Stanton, Lizette, 112, 119, 120, 121
Stanton, Margaret "Maggie," (See Lawrence, Margaret Stanton)
Stanton, Marguerite Berry, 111, 112
Stanton, Robbie, 119, 120
Stanton, Robert "Bob", 99, 100, 103, 107, 109, 125, 126
Stanton, Theodore "Theo", 100, 107, 109, 112, 113, 116, 119, 124, 128
Stone, Hannah, 139
Stone, Lucy, 4, 6-8, 17, 22, 23, 25, 50, 57, 58, 67, 80, 82, 84, 87, 88, 90, 97, 98, 99, 101, 112, 120, 133-169, 171, 174, 175, 176

T

Temperance, 5, 13, 97, 102, 168
Tanafly, New Jersey, 103, 109, 111
Train, George Francis, 142, 143

Truth, Sojourner, 59
Tubman, Harriet, 39

U

Underground Railroad, 14, 39, 61
The Union, 28, 32, 34, 102, 140
Universal Suffrage, 5, 6, 141, 142

V

Vassar College, 5, 70-74, 76-78,
  80, 104, 106-110, 112, 130
Villard, Fanny Garrison, 37, 49, 62
"Voluntary Motherhood", 117, 121

W

Water cure, 22, 34, 53, 62
Weld, Theodore, 18, 21, 25
West Brookfield, Massachusetts,
  134, 139, 140, 152
White Mountains, New
  Hampshire, 89
Willard, Amelia, 94, 96
The Woman's Bible, 6, 118, 127
"Woman's Column", 159
Woman's Journal, 85, 87, 123, 143,
  145, 151, 154, 156, 157, 158,
  159, 160, 162, 164, 165, 166,
  168, 169, 172

Woman suffrage parade, 116, 130,
  154, 172
Woman's (note typo, not
  Women's) Christian
  Temperance Union, 168
Women's Franchise League, 120
Woodhull, Victoria, 151
Worcester High School, 78
Worcester, Massachusetts, 7, 51,
  52, 58, 59, 61, 66, 72, 78, 80, 81,
  82, 83, 84, 86
World Antislavery Convention, 4
World's Columbian Exhibition, 8,
  165
Wright, Charley, 16, 17
Wright, David, 2, 32, 36, 39, 43,
  47, 48
Wright, Eliza (see Osborne, Eliza
  Wright)
Wright, Ellen (see Garrison, Ellen
  Wright)
Wright, Martha Coffin, 2, 4, 11-
  50, 60, 61, 94, 96, 97, 99, 102,
  114, 133, 137, 139, 142, 143,
  153, 165, 174, 175, 176
Wright, Marianna Pelham (see
  Mott, Marianna Pelham
  Wright)
Wright, Tallman, 11, 18
Wright, Willy, 18, 32, 33, 47

Acknowledgments

Iacknowledge two sources as the idea for this book: my students and my friends. The more engaged I became in teaching women's history, the more I wanted to share the private lives of the leaders whom we studied. I looked for stories about women's rights and woman suffrage told from personal points of view—stories that would engage a broad spectrum of students. These stories also would invite the general public to learn this vital history.

During the same time, I deepened my friendship with a woman activist leader in my community, a mother of three daughters and three sons. I watched the family as they interacted, each admiring their mother but always seeing her primarily as their mother rather than as a public figure. Did the children mimic the life of their mom, who spent hours away from them as babies, went to jail for her causes, and seemed to expect the same from them? The clear answer was no. Instead, they took lessons from her about being a good person, a loving parent, and a responsible citizen. Each, especially the women, demonstrated that they had inherited traits from their mother that might have resembled, but never duplicated, her actions. They absorbed her example but responded in ways that worked for them. When their passions coincided with shared actions, it was extra sweet. But when they each took a different path, one informed by their mother's example but far from the same, all was well. Individuality was accepted, indeed encouraged.

Motivated by these two incentives, I began to look for nineteenth-century mothers who told the story of women's rights through their private as well as their public actions. My rewards were rich. After I found four "reform mothers" and "reform daughters" who left a huge volume of accessible letters and diaries, I set my goal. Then I took to the road, driving to archives throughout the Northeast to uncover their fascinating stories.

I begin my acknowledgments to these rich resources in my home, Rochester, New York, where Susan B. Anthony lived. Here I took advantage of the Anthony home for inspiration and the University of Rochester Archives for letters. I made day trips to Syracuse University's collection of the William Lloyd Garrison and Munson Osborne Papers. Before long, I traveled to Vassar College in Poughkeepsie, New York, where I experienced the school that inspired two of the reform daughters and used the Stanton and Blatch collections. When my first grandchild was born, I had the happy opportunity to combine babysitting with days at the Library of Congress, where I uncovered more Stanton and Blackwell papers.

Then off to Cambridge, Massachusetts, where my son Jeremy Schnittman was completing a graduate degree. During the day, he studied physics while I worked on the Blackwell Family Papers at the Radcliffe Institute's Schlesinger Library. In the warm evenings, we painted his apartment. I came to know Worcester, Massachusetts, just as well as Cambridge. Here I spent weeks at the American Antiquarian Society and the Worcester Historical Museum. Next, I traveled to nearby Northampton, where Smith College's Collection led me to a larger Garrison Family collection, whose treasures include locks of hair preserved and saved by many of my subjects. When I broke my arm in the midst of research, my husband, Michael Schnittman, drove me back to Northampton for a week to read journals and enjoy the fall foliage viewed from the picture windows of a lovely bed and breakfast. Back in Rochester, I discovered interlibrary loan, which Robert Pierce at the Local History Department of Rochester's Main Library helped me facilitate.

My research assistant and friend, Shanti Parnell, spent weeks helping me access letters digitally that I would never have found without her. She also organized, filed, and transcribed them. Together we selected which photographs to use.

Once we chose them from a vast collection I accumulated over the years, I had the daunting challenge of procuring permission and high quality scans. For these services, I owe special thanks to Wendy Essery at Worcester Historical Museum; Patricia Boulos at the Boston Athenaeum; Karen Kukla and Nichole Calero at Smith College; and Dean Rogers at Vassar College.

Every book relies on its cover to invite the reader inside. Again, I thought back to my inspirations: my students and my friends. I thank my son and graphic artist, Aaron Schnittman, who created the concept and executed the design. He chose Victorian-era wallpaper as a backdrop, a script to match the age, and the photographs that best capture the mother/daughter teams.

No historian writes without inspiration from her colleagues. I thank my dissertation advisor, Stanley Engerman, for inspiring me years ago to pursue an advanced degree, even though I was a mother of two young children, and for cheering on my career. He read the entire manuscript with his keen insight, saluting its premise and story.

I also benefited from the advice of historians who have advised me on individual chapters: Harriet Alonso, Michael Brown, Susan Goodier, Teresa Lehr, Jenny Lloyd, Alison Parker, Karen Pastorello, Elaine Weiss, and four anonymous university press readers.

My writing class has been with me throughout the journey, learning about the lives of the reform mothers and daughters for years. They raised poignant questions, never missed a grammatical error, and always commanded me to make sense. I thank Joanna Hodgman, Dia Lawrence, Cali Lovett, Elaine Miller, Anais Salabian, and Dottie Waldron. I remember two of the women who were part of this group, but have died, in an especially poignant way: Joy Nimick and BJ Yudelson.

People in the publishing business have encouraged me along the way, but I owe special thanks to Deanna McKay, who first accepted the project. Katie Cline from Atlantic Publishing Group has supported me editorially throughout the production.

Without friends and family, this daunting task would have been more difficult. Carol Crossed inspired the idea. My dear friends, Mary Jane Ramsey, Nancy Blanda, Nancy Thomas, and Barbara McMullen, stayed the course, kept me uplifted, and, at the end, helped me express my voice. My sisters, Barbara Mahoney and Betsy Brinkworth, persisted in sending me encouragement, from long distance and as part of live audiences. My sister-in-law, Patti Gehring, read the manuscript during its early stages and never let me give up, always urging me to increase the personal stories. My two sons and their wives, Aaron and Kate, and Jeremy and Nomi, cheered me on. My grandchildren kept me sane and were the first people to call me a writer. Thanks to Talya, Max, Chaim, Ellie, Ceci, Ilan, and Meira.

My husband, Michael Schnittman, lived with the text for more than a decade. He began as a copy editor, red pen in hand, looking for spelling errors. He matured into a valued reader who deeply understood where ideas worked and where they did not, never letting me off the hook with an easy answer. He supported me in countless other ways, and it is to him I dedicate this book.

About the Author

Suzanne Gehring Schnittman, PhD, is a historian, independent scholar, and lecturer. She lives in Rochester, New York, with her husband, Michael, and is the proud mother of two sons and seven grandchildren. Learning between the generations has engaged her work, as has the inspiration of loving family members, each of whom has participated in this project in various ways over the years.